Mental Illness

of related interest

Getting Into the System
Living with Serious Mental Illness
Gwen Howe
ISBN 1 85302 457 0

Mental Health Assessments
Gwen Howe
ISBN 1 85302 458 9

Hospital Treatment and Care
Gwen Howe
ISBN 1 85302 744 8

Working with Schizophrenia
A Needs Based Approach
Gwen Howe
ISBN I 85302 242 X

Rehabilitation Counselling in Physical and Mental Health
Edited by Kim Etherington
ISBN 1 85302 968 8

Managing Manic Depressive Disorders
Edited by Ved Varma
ISBN 1 85302 347 7

Mental Illness

A Handbook for Carers

Edited by

Rosalind Ramsay, Claire Gerada,
Sarah Mars and George Szmukler

Jessica Kingsley Publishers
London and Philadelphia

First published in the United Kingdom in 2001 by
Jessica Kingsley Publishers Ltd
116 Pentonville Road
London N1 9JB, England
and
325 Chestnut Street
Philadelphia, PA 19106, USA

www.jkp.com

Second Impression 2002

Copyright © 2001 Jessica Kingsley Publishers

Library of Congress Cataloging in Publication Data
A CIP catalog record for this book is available from the Library of Congress

British Library Cataloguing in Publication Data
A CIP catalogue record for this book is available from the British Library

ISBN 1 85302 934 3

Printed and Bound in Great Britain by
Athenaeum Press, Gateshead, Tyne and Wear

Contents

Acknowledgements   8

Introduction   9

Section 1: Mental Illnesses

1. Schizophrenia and Related Disorders   15
    *Elizabeth Kuipers, Professor of Clinical Psychology, Institute
    of Psychiatry, King's College London*

2. Bipolar Affective Disorder or Manic Depression   28
    *Rosalind Ramsay, Consultant Psychiatrist, South London
    and Maudsley NHS Trust, and George Szmukler, Consultant
    Psychiatrist, South London and Maudsley NHS Trust*

3. Depression   39
    *Anne Farmer, Professor of Psychiatric Nosology, Institute of Psychiatry,
    King's College London*

4. Anxiety Disorders   49
    *Susan Grey, Consultant Clinical Psychologist, South London and
    Maudsley NHS Trust*

5. Obsessive Compulsive Disorder   60
    *Richard Parkin, Consultant Psychiatrist, Barnet Psychiatric Unit,
    Barnet General Hospital*

6. Post-Traumatic Stress Disorder   69
    *Felicity de Zulueta, Hon. Consultant Psychiatrist in Psychotherapy,
    Institute of Psychiatry, King's College London*

7. Medically Unexplained Physical Symptoms   79
    *Alicia Deale, Lecturer, Institute of Psychiatry, King's College London,
    and Vincent Deary, Therapist, South London and Mudsley NHS Trust*

8. Mental Health Problems alongside Physical Illness   89
    *Andrew Hodgkiss, Consultant Liaison Psychiatrist,
    South London and Maudsley NHS Trust*

9. Eating Disorders   97
    *Gill Todd, Clinical Nurse Leader, Eating Disorders Unit,
    South London and Maudsley NHS Trust,
    Wendy Whitaker, Social Worker, and Kay Gavan, Social Worker*

10. Drinking Problems   108
*E. Jane Marshall, Consultant Psychiatrist, South London
and Maudsley NHS Trust*

11. Drug Misuse and Dependence   121
*Claire Gerada, General Practitioner, Hurley Clinic, London,
and Sarah Welsh, Consultant Psychiatrist, South London
and Maudsley NHS Trust*

12. Personality Disorders   132
*Jane Tiller, Consultant Psychiatrist, South London
and Maudsley NHS Trust*

13. Mental Illness in Older People   141
*Amanda Thompsell, Specialist Registrar in Psychiatry, South London
and Maudsley NHS Trust, and Marisa Silverman, Old Age
Consultant Psychiatrist, South London and Maudsley NHS Trust*

Section 2: Mental Health Services

Introduction   152
*Frank Holloway, Consultant Psychiatrist, South London
and Maudsley NHS Trust*

14. Mental Health Services   159
*Sonia Johnson, Senior Lecturer in Social and Community
Psychiatry, University College, London*

15. Mental Health Professionals   171
*Wendy Maphosa, Carers and Families Nurse Specialist, South
London and Maudsley NHS Trust, and Emma Staples, Senior
Registrar in Psychotherapy, Tavistock Clinic and Royal Free Hospital*

16. Primary Care Services for Mental Health   180
Claire Gerada, General Practitioner, Hurley Clinic, London

17. Social Work Provision   185
Nick Hervey, Head of Mental Health Practice, Southwark Social Services

18. An Appropriate Place to Live   190
*John Wade, Mental Health Service Manager, Bromford Housing
Group, and Claire Henderson, MRC Training Fellow, Institute of
Psychiatry, King's College London*

19. Benefits   197
*Claire Henderson, MRC Training Fellow, Institute of Psychiatry,
King's College London, and Rory O'Kelly, Manager, Welfare Benefits
Advice Service, Mind, Croyden*

20. Employment   203
*David O'Flynn, Specialist Registrar in Psychiatry, South London and
Maudsley NHS Trust*

21. Forensic Psychiatry 209
Alec Buchanan, Clinical Senior Lecturer in Forensic Psychiatry,
Institute of Psychiatry, King's College London

22. Mental Health Legislation 213
Frank Holloway, Consultant Psychiatrist, South London
and Maudsley NHS Trust

23. Driving and Mental Health 220
Anne Cremona, Consultant Psychiatrist, South London
and Maudsley NHS Trust

24. Other Legal Issues and Mental Health 224
Mind Legal Unit

25. Confidentiality and Mental Health 231
George Szmukler, Consultant Psychiatrist, South London
and Maudsley NHS Trust

26. How to Cope with the Stigma of Mental Illness 236
Geoffrey Wolff, Consultant Psychiatrist, Leeds Community
and Mental Health Services NHS Trust

27. Ethnic Minorities and Mental Health 243
Kwame McKenzie, Senior Lectur in Transculteral Psychiatry,
Royal Free and University Hospital College Medical School, London

28. Being a Carer 250
Kate Harvey, Research Fellow, Guy's, King's and St Thomas's
School of Medicine

29. Psychological Treatments 254
Anne Ward, Consultant Psychiatrist in Psychotherapy, South London
and Maudsley NHS Trust, and Stirling Moorey, Consultant Psychiatrist
in Cognitive Behaviour Therapy, South London and Maudsley NHS Trust

30. Suicide and Suicide Attempts 259
Mike Crawford, Senior Lecturer in Psychiatry, Imperial College School
of Medicine, London

31. Violence 263
Mari Anne Harty, Consultant Forensic Psychiatrist, South London
and Maudsley NHS Trust

Glossary 268
Resources 284
The Contributors 294
Index 296

Acknowledgements

We are grateful for the generous support from the Chief Executives of the former Lambeth Healthcare NHS Trust, Erville Millar, and former Bethlem and Maudsley NHS Trust, Eric Byers, and the current Chief Executive of the South London and Maudsley NHS Trust, Stuart Bell, whose grant made this project possible. We would also like to thank all the carers, service users, colleagues and members of voluntary organisations whose help and participation were greatly appreciated.

Sarah Mars carried out all the interviews with the carers.

Introduction

Caring for a family member or friend with a mental illness is not something new, but has been happening for a long time. In some cultures it is still the family who are the key people in supporting a relative with mental illness. Over the last 150 years western countries have seen the development of services to care for people with a mental illness, often away from their home environment. The Victorians built large asylums in which people with a mental illness were segregated away from the rest of society, including their families and friends.

In the second half of the twentieth century we have seen a move towards providing more locally based services. Today mental health professionals increasingly work in the community, and in some cases assess and monitor their clients in the clients' own homes.

Often the role of the family and friends has gone unnoticed.

Indeed at times there have been attempts to exclude family members from discussions about their relative's mental health care. In the 1960s, with the movement towards greater support for the rights of the individual, if someone did not want their family involved, the health professionals were likely to accept without questioning that person's request for confidentiality.

More recently the pendulum has been swinging increasingly in favour of the need of family members to take part in making plans for their relative's health care. Mental health professionals are often grateful for information the family can provide and for the support they offer, sometimes 24 hours a day, 7 days a week. If a patient is refusing to involve family members in discussions about his or her care the mental health professionals may question this stance, and in certain circumstances will consider it their duty to inform the family about key issues.

The government too has been starting to realise the vital role that families and friends can play in supporting people with a mental illness in their homes. The current strategy document for mental health services, The National Service Framework for Mental Health (1999), has as one of its targets a requirement that mental health professionals consider the needs of carers. The NHS Plan (2000) sets out government plans for the health service over the next five years.

It states that by 2004, 700 more staff are to be recruited in order to increase breaks available for carers and to strengthen carer support networks.

What does this mean in practice for carers? Perhaps one of the most important things is the public acknowledgement of the role of carers in enabling people to live at home, and not to be segregated in institutions away from their local community.

Listening to carers is of great importance because one of their biggest needs is information – about their relative's illness, the treatment plans, what to do in an emergency, what mental health professionals can do, and how other agencies such as housing and social services can help. The list is endless. There is a huge need for information. With increasing access to the internet some people are able to get more answers to their questions through different websites, but not everyone has access to this sort of information, and the quality of the information varies from site to site.

This book aims to provide some essential basic information, the sort of information we believe will help family members and friends understand their relative's mental health problems. It should allow you to know what services there are to help your relative, both in terms of health services and over practical issues such as housing, work, benefits and so on.

The first section of the book has chapters on each of the main types of mental illness. Quite often a person may have more than one mental health problem. For example, a woman may have problems with feeling depressed and also have panic attacks and anxiety. She may have tried using alcohol to help cope with these problems. Or a man may have an episode of psychosis and the doctors may talk about it being schizophrenia, but when there is a further episode that seems more like bipolar affective disorder. The situation could be complicated by the fact that this man also has some personality problems, and uses cannabis and occasionally crack cocaine. In these and many other cases, you may find yourself wanting to read about a number of the disorders.

Your relative may meet people on the ward, or at the day hospital or day centre with different problems, and you may be interested to learn more about them. You may also meet other carers and want to understand more about the sorts of problems they face in coping with their relative.

Each of these chapters starts with a real case story. One of our editors, Sarah Mars, met with a carer involved with someone with each of the different types of disorder. She asked them to tell her about their experiences of being a carer. We hope these stories will bring some of the more dry facts about the illnesses to life as you read about how another carer has learnt to cope, what remains difficult and so on.

The second section of the book has short chapters covering lots of practical issues you and your relative or friend may be facing. What are the services available for your relative from the GP practice, and from mental health services and from social services? What do different health professionals do? What about help with housing, benefits and employment? How do services deal with someone who has a mental illness and also gets involved with the criminal justice system? What about legislation to do with people being admitted to hospital against their will, and other legal issues including the regulations on driving after having a mental illness? There are chapters discussing confidentiality, stigma, and cultural issues. The chapter on psychological or talking treatments gives information that may be useful in relation to a number of mental health problems. Finally there are chapters on how to cope with specific worries about risks of self-harm or violence.

The book concludes with a glossary of terms and abbreviations sometimes used by health professionals. There is also resource list of useful organisations, publications and websites you may wish to contact.

Remember that one of the key issues in helping your relative is to get as much information as possible. Many of the carers Sarah Mars interviewed speak about this. We hope that this handbook will help you in that process. You will probably still have a lot of questions, and will then need to pursue these with relevant support groups as well as with the professionals involved in your relative's care. We wish you good luck.

SECTION 1
Mental Illnesses

CHAPTER 1

Schizophrenia and Related Disorders

Elizabeth Kuipers

Jane's grown-up daughter Lisa has had a schizophrenic disorder for many years. Lisa lives separately and Jane looks after Lisa's son and daughter full time.

'For me caring has meant feeding and clothing Lisa, doing her washing, sorting out her finances, getting up in the middle of the night when she's lost her key and coping with her moods. The main issue is that Lisa can't function properly, particularly when she isn't taking her medication. I feel more like a "manager" than a "carer" – it's about managing the situation we are faced with in the best interest of the whole family and not prioritising the ill person beyond what is essential. For me it's these practical problems that are central and are often over-looked by other people.

There are constant interruptions – on some days Lisa has knocked on the front door every quarter of an hour. Several years ago I felt bullied by my daughter's demands but now I've got the situation under control. I've had to set limits: if she's very ill, she gets fed and watered and then sent home; if she is being disruptive or aggressive she is not allowed to stay or visit. In extreme cases I've called the police. I've learnt not to take her behaviour personally and to accept that aggression can be part of the illness, but this doesn't mean that the family should be on the receiving end of aggression. Because the illness presents in terms of behaviour, you think that you can change it, but you have to accept that because the person is unwell, they are not functioning normally. There are some things that you can do nothing about and realising this relieves you of an intolerable burden.

Recently the community team has been excellent because I have drawn a line at what I am prepared to do and pushed hard for help. It is practical and material help that has been the most valuable in this situation. I've had to ask myself, "How can I minimise my role so that the caring I do is beneficial to my relationship with my daughter?" Activities such as sorting out bills can be very stressful between you both and there are professionals who can help with these things. It was many years before I knew of the welfare rights officer who could sort out all Lisa's finances so that she now obtains her full benefit entitlements. Carers need to be told what services exist because there is an assumption that they will take on the burden of care with a disregard for their own needs.

The one thing that would make a big difference is if there was a safe place where Lisa could go to be looked after for a few days when she is very ill. Sectioning is too slow; by the four or five days it takes she'd probably be back on her medication and the crisis would have passed. Suicide is always a worry – what is going on in the ill person's head can be a nightmare for them – the voices in their head seem to be more than can be borne at times.

Relationships with neighbours are much easier when you're accepting of the reality of the situation and not getting into a tiz. When the ill person is behaving strangely, you don't have to "keep up appearances" as if nothing's happening. At the same time, I won't let Lisa spoil other people's special occasions – if she isn't well enough to come to a family or social event, for instance, I don't let her. But worrying about how she is going to behave at these events is always a source of stress – like walking on eggshells.

What I would advise other carers to realise is that there is a limit to what can be done. Caring should not become anyone's total life – it is the mental health team who are responsible for caring for the ill person and the carer's role to provide support. It's about not letting the illness dominate your life – it doesn't have to – and understanding that some people's needs are infinite and can never be satisfied. Don't feel guilty about doing other things – you need to take into account your own personal needs and set limits on what you can and are prepared to do. Finally, developing a sense of humour is important.'

What are these disorders?

The terms 'schizophrenia' and 'psychosis' are diagnostic names for the more serious mental health problems that people can have. 'Psychosis' is a general term; 'schizophrenia' is used for a particular set of problems a person may have.

In this context 'serious mental illness' means that many aspects of a person's life and ability to do things, such as having a job and relationships, are likely to be affected. 'Psychosis' refers to conditions in which people may have particular odd, distressing or unusual experiences. These can include finding that their thinking has been affected (thoughts may become blocked, thoughts may feel as if they are not a person's own), being totally convinced about unlikely or bizarre ideas (delusions), and hearing or seeing things that others do not hear or see, such as voices (hallucinations).

The word 'schizophrenia' does not mean 'split personality' in spite of being used in this way in the media. It actually means being split off from reality so that unusual thoughts, feelings and experiences become a person's reality, and the more humdrum day-to-day concerns become less important.

Quite often diagnoses overlap; people who have delusions and hallucinations that are typical of schizophrenia may also have the mood swings that are more typical of bipolar affective disorder (see Chapter 2). The condition is then called schizoaffective disorder.

For some people symptoms occur very rapidly, and also get dramatically better in a few days. These are called acute or transient psychotic disorders, and are less likely to cause long-term problems. For other people, there is just one main symptom, a fixed unusual belief (or delusion); this is called persistent delusional disorder. Only if the beliefs are unusual, distressing or causing problems for others are those having them likely to need help from mental health services.

Finally, in all the psychoses there may be not just positive symptoms – unusual experiences and behaviours – but what are called negative symptoms – a reduction in the number and variety of activities a person does. In schizophrenia, negative symptoms will typically include reduced interest, poor motivation, and reduced pleasure in day-to-day situations (anhedonia). At their worst, these problems can lead to a person neglecting their personal hygiene, not looking after their personal surroundings and being unwilling to try new activities or to make new relationships. Negative symptoms are not the same as a person's loss of ability or intelligence; the main problems in this area relate to reduced attention, motivation and the ability to concentrate.

It can be seen that these conditions can affect the way people feel about themselves, how they view others and their surroundings, how they behave, and what activities they do. It is these disruptions in the activities of normal day-to-day living that may prove destructive to relationships, employment and personal circumstances. Typically a person will lose friends, find it difficult to keep a job and put a considerable strain on family relationships. Individuals themselves may feel desperate, terrified and isolated, or so full of unusual and special ideas that they put themselves into unhelpful situations.

Finally, society is still very fearful of people with mental health problems and currently associates them with a high level of dangerousness. Although this accounts for little of the violence in our society, a small proportion of people, particularly some of those with command hallucinations (voices telling you to do something) or those who abuse drugs, will be aggressive, and this has fuelled the public assumption. As a result society stigmatises and discriminates against those with mental health problems.

It can be seen that for some people, their problems are severe and worrying. Other people only have one episode of illness and no recurrence. Individuals also vary in how badly they are affected, how they feel, how others react to them and how they learn to cope with their difficulties. Some may never agree that there are any problems; this is called a lack of insight. While we probably all have times when we fail to appreciate the impact of a problem on ourselves or others, in psychosis it is particularly common for an individual not to share the views either of society or of friends and relations about their difficulties. This poor insight is one of the reasons why people with schizophrenia can be so difficult to help.

How common are they?

While research estimates vary, there is a reasonable consensus that around 1 person in 100 will be diagnosed with schizophrenia during their lifetime. In the UK at any one time between 100,000 and half a million people may be experiencing these kinds of problems. There is a tendency for schizophrenia to be found more often and to be more severe in men than women. Typically it is first diagnosed in early adulthood, just when people are trying to make their own way in life.

What are the causes?

Nobody knows the cause of schizophrenia at present. What we do know is that there are various factors that contribute to the likelihood of becoming ill. The first of these is that there are some families in which a number of people have schizophrenia or related problems, so that there seems to be a genetic component. The chance of someone developing schizophrenia if their identical twin has it is around one in two, and if a parent has it around one in ten. (The latter is not an especially high risk.) Other factors that have been identified range from poor nutrition in the mother during pregnancy, the mother having difficulties during childbirth, and living in socially very adverse circumstances. Factors that may help to trigger an episode include stressful life events, trauma, and high levels of drug or alcohol misuse. Psychological factors include how a person reacts to unusual experiences, and whether they have always been socially anxious or become socially isolated.

As can be seen, there will always be people who have none of these problems and still become ill, and other people who experience all of them and remain unaffected. For most people, there seems to be a combination of causes. Our current understanding is that in people who are vulnerable in some way – for example, through their genes or adverse circumstances – the illness may be triggered by current stresses, such as experiencing trauma, drug misuse or social isolation. So far as we know, factors such as diet, particular sorts of parents or parenting, accidents or eccentricity are not related to schizophrenia.

How do we treat these disorders?

'Treatment' is a medical term, and not everyone agrees (not least the people who are affected) that these problems are simply medical. However, most people with schizophrenia get help within the health service from doctors, nurses and other health professionals such as occupational therapists and clinical psychologists.

There are two main ways in which to help people with schizophrenia:

- medication
- psychological and social therapies.

Medication (see Tables 1.1, 1.2 and 1.3)

This is a complex area. The names of drugs may be hard to pronounce, and it is sometimes difficult to understand how they work.

The main group of drugs for treating schizophrenia is the antipsychotic drugs. They have an effect on the nerve cells in the brain. Activity in the brain requires that the nerve cells can influence each other. They do this by releasing tiny quantities of a neurotransmitter or 'chemical messenger' that crosses the tiny gaps between the cells. The drugs used in schizophrenia affect these chemical messengers. They all seem to act on a messenger called dopamine and they also affect other chemical messengers to a varying degree. Antipsychotic drugs reduce the amount of dopamine at the ends of the nerve cells, and this may be how they have their effect in schizophrenia.

Some of these drugs can be given by intramuscular injection every few weeks so a person does not need to remember to take tablets every day.

Table 1.1 Typical antipsychotic medication

Drug	Proprietary name	More common unwanted side effects
Chlorpromazine	Largactil	Blurred vision
Droperidol	Droleptan	Constipation
Flupenthixol	Depixol	Difficulty in passing water
Fluphenazine	Moditen	Dry mouth
Haloperidol	Haldol 'Serenace'	Faintness on suddenly standing up
Loxapine	Nozinan	Increased appetite
Pimozide	Orap	Increased effect of alcohol
Sulpiride	Dolmatil	Loss of facial expression
	Sulparex	Lowering of body temperature
	Sulpitil	Odd movements of body and face
Thioridazine*	Melleril	Restlessness
Trifluperazine	Stelazine	Sensitivity of skin to sunlight
Zuclopenthixol	Clopixol	Stiffness
		Tremor

* discontinued due to concerns about adverse effects

Source: Kuipers, E. and Bebbington, P. (1997) *Living with Mental Illness.* Second edition. London: Souvenir Press.

Alongside their beneficial effects, neuroleptic drugs have unwanted side effects, and these can be a real disadvantage. Some people who experience side effects feel they outweigh the benefits and refuse to take medication at all. Perhaps the worst side effects are the extrapyramidal side effects (EPS). These involve being stiff, having muscle pain, and shaking as in Parkinson's disease. People may develop other unwanted movements over time. All of these side effects are a particular problem with the older 'typical' antipsychotic drugs.

In the last ten years newer drugs, the atypical antipsychotics, have been introduced (see Table 1.3). Many people claim that they are less likely to cause EPS. However, the higher level of unwanted EPS with the older typical antipsychotic drugs may be due in part to the dose of medication used being too high.

The atypical antipsychotics can cause other unwanted side effects. One of the most distressing for people taking the drugs is weight gain.

One atypical antipsychotic drug stands out on its own. Clozapine helps some people who do not respond very well to other drugs. It also does not produce any EPS. Its disadvantage is that in a small number of people it brings on a (potentially fatal) drop in the number of white cells in the blood. This reduces the body's ability to fight infection. For this reason people taking clozapine are closely monitored and have to have regular blood tests.

There are three main issues about medication:

- It may help prevent further episodes of illness, and so a person should continue to take it even when feeling better.

- A person may need to take it for many months or years, or even for the rest of their life. This can be a daunting prospect, and people in this position generally need considerable help and support to feel that medication will be helpful to them over such a long period of time.

- Like other medication, all antipsychotic drugs can have unwanted side effects. This does not mean they are addictive, but simply that they may change the way a person feels in a number of ways, some trivial, some more worrying. Individuals taking medication often feel that the side effects are the most important and unpleasant features of the drug, while health professionals may regard the side effects as relatively trivial, and a worthwhile price to pay given the benefits of fewer episodes of illness in the future. These divergent views can cause difficulties. One of the main reasons people have further episodes of illness is that they have stopped their medication due to the unwanted side effects.

As a carer it can be helpful to find out as much as possible about the medication prescribed for your relative and what the likely problems are going to be. You may be able to get verbal information from the mental health team or pharmacist or an information leaflet.

Psychological and social therapies

This section includes information about some of the therapies that you and your relative are most likely to come across. The availability of particular types of therapy varies around the country. In general your relative's key worker or psychiatrist should be able to offer general support with regular meetings. The frequency of these meetings could be weekly or less often, perhaps every month or three months.

COGNITIVE BEHAVIOURAL THERAPY (CBT)

This is a relatively new therapy offered to people with schizophrenia, although it has been used for some time for other conditions such as anxiety or depression. CBT focuses on how you think about a situation (cognitions) and what you do about it (behaviour). It aims to increase your understanding because how you think and feel affects your actions. By helping a person change how they think and feel, CBT aims to help someone try out new and more productive behaviours. A cognitive behavioural therapist may ask about childhood experiences, but most of the focus is on the 'here and now'; that is, how a person sees and does things in the present. Evidence for its effectiveness for treating psychosis is emerging. Some community psychiatric nurses, clinical psychologists and a few psychiatrists are able to offer CBT.

ADHERENCE OR COMPLIANCE THERAPY (AT OR CT)

This is a new therapy which aims to use 'motivational interviewing' to help a therapist discuss with their client the pros and cons of taking medication. The idea is to help someone understand the risks, the good effect and the difficulties, and to come to an informed choice about the need for medication.

Table 1.2 Typical antipsychotic medication given by injection

Drug	Proprietary name
Clopenthixol decanoate	Clopixol
Flupenthixol decanoate	Depixol
Fluphenazine decanoate	Modecate
Haloperidol decanoate	Haldol decanoate
Pipothiazine palmitate	Piportil depot

Source: Kuipers, E. and Bebbington, P. (1997) *Living with Mental Illness.* Second edition. London: Souvenir Press.

Table 1.3 Atypical antipsychotic medication

Drug	Proprietary name	Unwanted side effects
Clozapine	Clozaril	Does not produce shaking, stiffness or abnormal movements. Sometimes works when other drugs have failed. Needs monitoring with a regular blood test as it may cause a dangerous drop in white blood cells. Other side effects include drowsiness, drooling, weight gain and epileptic fits. May induce diabetes.
Risperidone	Risperdol	Only rarely produces shaking, stiffness or abnormal movements. Can be taken once daily. Makes some people anxious or sleepy. May cause stomach upsets and dizziness. Weight gain less than with other atypicals.
Olanzapine	Zyprexa	Only rarely produces shaking, stiffness or abnormal movements. Can be taken once daily. May cause sleepiness, dry mouth, blurred vision and dizziness. Significan weight gain common. May also induce diabetes.
Quetiapine	Seroquel	Side effects are not very apparent. Only rarely produces tardive dyskinesia (abnormal movements that appear after long treatment and are particularly hard to treat). May cause lowered blood pressure (especially in older people), drowsiness, dizziness, constipation and a dry mouth.
Amisulpiride	Solian	May produce shaking, stiffness or abnormal movements. makes some people anxious or sleepy. Stomach upsets and weight gain occur
Zotepine	Zolephil	Affected appitite, wright change, general malaise, headache, stomache upsets, blurred vision.

Source: Modified from Kuipers, E. and Bebbington, P. (1997) *Living with Mental Illness.* Second edition. London: Souvenir Press.

FAMILY INTERVENTIONS FOR PSYCHOSIS

One kind of family work is psychoeducation. This does not focus on the family as a cause of problems, but sees the family as a resource, which can maximise an individual's potential for recovery. Psychoeducation work often takes place in the home, and may involve visits from two therapists. It focuses on information giving (education) and problem solving, and tries to help all family members, including the person with the psychosis, feel equally valued, and equally able to help improve things. This kind of help can be very effective but is intensive in terms of therapist time and not always available.

OCCUPATIONAL THERAPY (OT)

Occupational therapists (OTs) specialise in helping people to recover their activity levels and their self-esteem. In psychosis, OTs often emphasise helping people recover lost skills and motivation. They may provide specialist centres or services in which people can practise looking after themselves, getting used to structuring their day. There may also be (rehabilitation) opportunities to help people get back to open employment via sheltered work settings.

WELFARE ADVICE AND SOCIAL WORK SUPPORT

Often the most important intervention after an episode of psychosis is welfare advice. A trained welfare worker can help a person sort out their benefits and entitlements. Social workers – in social services departments and in local community mental health teams – can help obtain suitable housing and look at how best to meet other social needs such as getting help with shopping or cleaning.

How do these disorders affect families and friends?

Someone with psychosis can make things very difficult for their families and friends. An individual may deny having a problem, cause disruption and upset, or even blame family members for their difficulties. However, for about half the people who have schizophrenia, over the long term there is a family carer such as a parent (usually a mother) or a partner, and more rarely a sibling or a child carer. As these problems, typically arising in young adulthood, are associated with both reduced social networks and strained relationships, an isolated older mother looking after an adult son with psychosis is still the most common scenario.

When you find out that a close relative, perhaps a son, daughter or partner, has a diagnosis of schizophrenia, you are then by definition a carer, whether or not you choose to do this. Many carers wish to stay involved and find the role rewarding, but there is also a burden. The impact of the caring role can be considerable, involving increased levels of stress and distress, worry, anxiety about the future, possible financial problems, social isolation and stigma and feelings of exhaustion. To start with, you may find yourself bewildered by your relative's behaviour, overwhelmed with questions (but with few answers), and involved with an array of services such as mental health, social services, and sometimes the police, the courts and the prison system.

Once an admission to hospital is over, which may in some cases have involved your relative having been detained under the Mental Health Act (1983), he or she may return to live with you. This may be in spite of still having disturbing symptoms such as delusions, and also negative symptoms such as apathy and poor motivation. The situation may be more complicated if your relative abuses drugs or alcohol.

We know from research evidence that carers need information, advice, emotional support, practical help and respite. However, we also know that they rarely feel that they receive them.

What can families and friends do to help?

Fortunately, there is quite a lot that carers can do to help their relative even under these difficult circumstances. Carers generally react in one of three ways. They may become angry or frustrated with their relative and blame them. Alternatively, a carer may try and look after the person and take over the adult roles and decision making. This may be helpful in an acute situation, but in the recovery phase it can be both exhausting and demoralising, and in the end unhelpful for the individual who needs to begin to take back some of his or her adult responsibilities. Finally, carers may understand some of the problems and be able to be both tolerant and encouraging.

People with schizophrenia seem particularly sensitive to their social environment and to high stress levels. If there is a high level of stress they are more likely to become ill again. As a carer it is worth trying to create an environment in the home that is as helpful as possible to your relative, and in a way that is also rewarding and beneficial to other family members and yourself. Thus helpful family situations need to be productive for everyone, not just set up for the person who has had the problem. To maintain progress you may need to keep this going over many years.

We know that it is possible to help difficult family situations to improve. Carers can move from being demanding, critical, intolerant, intrusive or upset towards being more calm and tolerant (while still able to set limits and have expectations) and encouraging. These changes improve the situation for everyone. Some families do this for themselves, but others need some help to make these changes. This help is not yet readily available from local services, although training and support is increasingly being provided, and should mean that it will be more available in the future.

More practically, it can be helpful to find out if your relative has a key worker from the mental health team. If not, you can ask your GP for a referral to your local mental health service. If you and your relative can get linked in to this, the key worker and other team members should be able to provide information and practical and emotional support at times of crisis. There are also self-help groups who can offer information, helplines and support groups; for example, the National Schizophrenia Fellowship or SANE.

You may feel you need help to understand your relative's condition, to solve problems and to negotiate effective solutions. Emotional support and recognition of the grief, guilt, anger and despair that such problems can cause are also important. Increasingly, services aim to provide this longer-term support and to include carers in making multidisciplinary team decisions. The Community Care Acts (1992; 1995) and, more recently, the National Service Framework (1999) have made it a requirement for health professionals to consult carers and consider their own specific needs. For the first time, the needs of carers separate from the needs of their relative are being taken into account.

Tips for carers

- Stay in touch with services.
- Plan in advance what to do if your relative's illness gets worse.
- Find out as much as you can about both the condition and the treatments offered.
- Look after yourself as well as your relative.

What is the outlook?

Schizophrenia may be seen in a negative light as a permanent condition in which a person's condition gets worse over time. This kind of idea can make it difficult to see a viable future.

In fact the real outlook is more complicated than this and needs some explaining. A person's actual symptoms, that is, for example, their continuing to hear voices or experience unusual thoughts, may get better or worse independently of a person's social abilities. So, some patients may continue to hear voices but hold down a job and have relationships. Others have few remaining symptoms such as hearing voices, but seem unable to get back to their old self.

About a quarter of people with this diagnosis have one episode and recover completely. About one in ten people have a poor outlook associated with considerable disability, and may need long-term care. People in between these two extremes have a variable outcome. They may recover and then have a further episode or relapse of their symptoms. They may continue to be 'vulnerable' to relapse. This may be due to biological reasons, or due to social reasons associated with stress; for example, upsets beyond the carer's control such as significant life events. This 'stress-vulnerability' idea suggests that for some people virtually any stress will make them liable to have new problems, whereas for others, stress will be less likely to have this effect.

Although there may be continuing problems, this is not inevitable, as the type, frequency and duration of new episodes may improve. Unlike many other serious conditions the outlook in the long term can be positive. Even very difficult problems can be overcome and situations that look completely hopeless can get better.

CHAPTER 2

Bipolar Affective Disorder or Manic Depression

Rosalind Ramsay and George Szmukler

Jon Pennington experienced bipolar affective disorder (manic depression) in his late teens but it was not diagnosed until a decade ago. His wife has been caring for him since then. Mr Pennington is usually manic in the spring and summer and depressed in the autumn and winter, although in the last few years the depressed phase has lengthened.

'Knowing that the illness isn't curable can be devastating. If at the beginning I could have talked to somebody who understood about bipolar disorder – a self-help group or a helpline – that would have been a huge help. One of the comforting things is that it can be controlled with medication. When his illness was diagnosed the genetic aspect was a great worry – we have two children. My daughter later turned out to have manic depression. If you are aware of this illness and that one or more of your children may be affected, you *do* treat them differently and you'll get criticism from others for that but you've got to ignore it.

One year my daughter had a severe manic episode and my husband was fantastic (he *is* a fantastic guy – I wouldn't still be there after all these years if he wasn't). Then my own father died and Jon was down. Some of the time I was caring for my daughter and my husband and my son (who was devastated by his grandfather's death and by his sister's illness). I was stuck right in the middle – you can't give up – you have to be there. There is no one to share the caring with. If I had sunk who knows what would have happened.

We have always had a very close relationship. There's never been any question in my mind of finding another bloke, ever. But the illness has made me turn away from him mentally for my own preservation. What you get is somebody who is like a child, who needs your physical affection to feel safe. I get quite resentful about it. I want to say "You're a grown man. I'm not your mother and I don't want another kid" which is awfully cruel. I still *do* hug him and make him feel safe but the fact that you're behaving like a mother means that it's very hard to be like a wife physically. The whole balance of the relationship goes out of kilter and that causes a rift.

The financial mess is mind-blowing. When Jon was first severely ill he spent unbelievable amounts of money that we didn't have. I have my own account and at least I've been able to work. Now I'm looking into arranging an enduring power of attorney, and Jon's agreed, so that'll give me some control to help with the practical side of life if at some point he's incapable of making decisions.

Personally I've become much tougher because I've had to be. I have my own work and my own life. This is vital because otherwise you lose a sense of balance yourself. You've got to get away from it at times and I have close friends whom I go out with. They all know the situation, which is terribly important, and they're very supportive. Honesty is important not just for the carer but for the sufferer and the children. And my friends all know that they can joke about it. Humour – seeing the ridiculous in the situation – helps.

For someone like me who's always busy, quite organised, and quite bossy, the down phase is incredibly difficult to deal with. When you get someone who stays under the duvet for days with everything piling up around you, you feel like hitting them with a mallet. I try to be rational with him and of course it's a waste of time. "Why don't you make lists?" I say. How stupid! When he's like that he's not capable of writing a list about anything.

Someone with bipolar affective disorder doesn't notice that practical things need doing so I am responsible for almost everything to do with running the house and the children's lives. But it's also the emotional side that's difficult: you feel totally trapped. I would be scared to leave him because of the risk of suicide. Even if I wanted to, I couldn't get out of this financially; if I did get out of it he's going to kill himself, and if that happens what happens to the kids? That's where friends come in, your own life, caring agencies if possible, anything at all you can hang on to that'll get you through that bad patch – even the Samaritans.

I'm naturally very independent but Jon's illness has taught me to ask for help. My first port of call is the GP surgery, which is really good. Instant help comes from voluntary organisations who are on the end of a phone. You don't necessarily want answers but you need someone to listen to *you* and GPs don't have the time. I've found that psychiatrists often don't give carers the same kind of consideration as patients and when things go wrong it's the carer who has to pick up the pieces. If you're trying to get help from services, don't appear to be "all-coping" – look like you *are* coping, but admit the need for support. If you have young children, contact the school: you may only need to tell one teacher – anyone whom your child trusts and gets on with. A sympathetic teacher can be a lifeline for your child to talk to.'

What is the disorder?

Bipolar affective disorder, also known as 'manic depression' or 'manic depressive psychosis', is a form of mental illness in which people experience big changes in their mood. At one extreme, people experience *mania*, and feel 'high' or elated. At the other extreme they experience severe *depression* and feel very low or depressed. These mood swings are more extreme than the normal ups and downs most people experience, maybe as a result of some happy or sad event.

Some people experience only one extreme, either mania, or depression, but for other people their mood will change quickly between high and low, sometimes over days, or more slowly with months or years between times of mania and depression. Although people suffering from this illness can have very different experiences, certain things happen to almost everyone during times of mania or depression.

Mania

As well as being 'high' in mood your relative may be much more active, with more energy, and needing little sleep. He or she may become very noisy, irritable, provocative or promiscuous, and may behave irresponsibly and in a way that is out of character; for example, spending a lot of money, or becoming involved in damaging sexual relationships. Running up large bills on a credit card can be a particular problem. Speech may be speeded up or 'pressured' and your relative may jump from one topic to another, making it difficult to follow his or her thoughts. You may notice that your relative lacks concentration and seems distracted, as he or she flits from one thing to another. Some people have unrealistic ideas; for example, that they are especially gifted or talented, or that they are a very important person. They may also believe that others want to upset them. These false ideas may become 'delusions'. It does not help to argue against them as your relative may be unshakeably convinced they are true even though to you and others the thoughts are clearly irrational or fantastical.

Some people also hear 'voices'. These are called hallucinations, and in mania they usually say how important or special the person is.

Depression

Here a person's mood is sad or 'down'. This lowness of mood is persistent and does not change even when good things happen. There may be trouble eating and weight loss, and difficulty in sleeping, often with waking early in the morning. Thinking and movements may be slowed up, with a lack of energy to do the simplest things. Sometimes in severe depression, people become agitated, with distressing thoughts, restless pacing and wringing of their hands. It is common in depression to feel guilty, worthless, useless and to blame oneself. Your relative may feel a burden on you and others. Sometimes there is a feeling of hopelessness about the future, with thoughts that nothing will ever get better and the person may then think about suicide. Some people who are depressed have delusions related to their depression, believing, for example, that they are wicked, poor, in hell, deserving of punishment or even dead. At other times the person may become convinced he or she has a serious physical illness; for example, a cancer.

How common is it?

Bipolar affective disorder is not rare. One in one hundred people will suffer from it during their lifetime. It can affect anyone, both men and women, and may occur at any time from adolescence onwards, but most commonly it starts when people are in their twenties.

What are the causes?

Inheritance or genes play some part in the development of bipolar affective disorder. There is sometimes a history of the illness in the family. However, if bipolar affective disorder appears in one family member, this does not mean that other family members will necessarily develop it. Often no other family members are affected. The chance of the child of a parent with bipolar affective disorder developing the illness is around one in ten.

Besides genes, there are other explanations for how bipolar affective disorder occurs. One idea is that the way we usually understand or interpret things goes wrong. Our basic picture of how the brain works is that our thoughts and moods result from the constant passing of electrical and chemical messages through the complex network of nerve cells that make up the brain. If this process is not working well it may lead to a change in a person's mood or behaviour. The most important and sensitive part of the process is the small gap (synapse) between one nerve cell and the next. This is bridged by chemical messengers, or neurotransmitters (for example, serotonin and noradrenalin). People with bipolar affective disorder may not have enough of these chemical messengers present in the gap between the nerve cells in their brain. This will affect the way the brain deals with information, which in turn will affect how a person feels.

There are some causes of mood changes with which we are all familiar: the feelings of sadness when things go wrong, or when we experience bereavement or physical illness; and contrasting feelings of joy over a good event. Such changes in mood are more understandable, and even predictable, although a lowering in mood can still be very distressing. The changes are usually smaller than those that happen in bipolar affective disorder.

People with bipolar illness may be more likely to react to outside events or issues by becoming unwell again. This is called being vulnerable to relapse. Upsetting events can result in that person being more likely to have another attack of either depression or mania. On the other hand, support from other people can protect someone against the effects of bad experiences.

Other factors that may trigger a mood swing are physical illnesses, some medication, alcohol, illegal drugs including cannabis and big changes in life style such as staying up very late for a period. Sometimes a mood swing occurs without any obvious trigger.

How do we treat it?

Treatment has a number of important components.

- *Medication* usually has an important part to play, both in treating attacks of depression or mania, and also in preventing further episodes.
- *Psychological treatments* are important in helping the sufferer through illness episodes, recovery and in preventing relapse.
- Sometimes *admission to hospital* is necessary during severe bouts of mood disturbance to ensure a safe environment.

Medication

TREATMENT OF DEPRESSION

Doctors use *antidepressant* drugs to treat an attack of severe depression in bipolar illness. These act on the chemical messengers in the brain. It usually takes two weeks before changes occur in how a person is feeling. Some symptoms such as a person's energy level or pattern of sleeping or eating may improve before their depressed mood lifts.

The different antidepressant drugs differ in their unwanted side effects. One of the groups of antidepressants is the new 'selective serotonin reuptake inhibitors' (SSRIs), such as *fluoxetine, sertraline* and *paroxetine*. These drugs may cause fewer side effects than the older antidepressants, and they are fairly safe in overdose. Side effects of the SSRIs include feeling a little sick or agitated when starting the treatment.

An older group of drugs are the *'tricyclic' antidepressants* such as *amitriptyline, imipramine, dothiepin* and *lofepramine.* These can cause a number of unwanted side effects; for example, dry mouth, drowsiness, tiredness, blurred vision, constipation, palpitations and weight gain. Tremor of the hands and dizziness on standing up may also occur. Most of these side effects will disappear or improve after a week or so. The dose of medication is usually built up slowly to minimise any side effects. An overdose with these antidepressants can be lethal and requires immediate medical treatment. Doctors sometimes only prescribe a few days supply of these drugs at a time if there are any worries about overdoses.

The doctor is likely to continue treatment with an antidepressant for at least six months after the person has recovered from the episode of depression. If your relative has repeated episodes of depression the doctor may use antidepressant medication as long-term treatment to reduce the frequency and severity of future episodes.

Very occasionally, in extreme depression, if other treatments have failed and there is an urgent need to achieve results quickly, a doctor may prescribe *electroconvulsive therapy (ECT).* Although it has a bad image with people, as used today, ECT is a simple, painless and safe technique. Nobody knows in detail why this method works, but it can be effective in helping improve very severe depression.

TREATMENT OF MANIA

Lithium is the drug most often used to combat a manic high. It will usually reduce severe manic symptoms in about two weeks, but it may be a month or more before the condition is controlled. We will discuss lithium in more detail below.

In the first few days or weeks of treatment the doctor may give your relative an *antipsychotic* drug to control manic symptoms until the lithium begins to take effect. Examples are *haloperidol* and *chlorpromazine*. These drugs do not cure the illness but are effective in reducing the elation and associated symptoms such as racing thoughts and hyperactivity. They work more quickly than lithium. They are usually stopped when the symptoms have settled.

These drugs also have side effects. Some may be helpful; for example, the sedation in someone who is having trouble sleeping. Unwanted side effects include a dry mouth, blurred vision, drowsiness, and affected movements. The doctor may give another drug such as *procyclidine* to counteract these effects.

Benzodiazepine drugs may also be used for tranquillisation together with an antipsychotic as short-term treatment.

MOOD STABILISING DRUGS

'Mood stabilising' drugs help to stop mood swings, and people need to carry on taking them regularly for a long time after they are feeling better to try and prevent further attacks of mania or depression, and remain well.

A person may have one episode of bipolar illness and never have another, or be free of illness for several years. However, for those who have more than one episode, the doctor may recommend continuing treatment with *lithium*. Some people will respond well to ongoing treatment and have no further episodes, while others may have moderate mood swings that lessen as treatment continues, or episodes that are less severe and less frequent.

If the lithium level in the blood is too low, treatment will not be effective, and if the level is too high, side effects may occur. The difference between an effective dose and a toxic one is fairly small and so regular blood tests are an important part of the treatment. The doctor regularly checks the lithium level at the start of treatment to work out the correct dose for that person. Once a person is on the right dose the doctor will only need to check the level of lithium in the body every three to six months.

The commonest side effects of lithium are a fine tremor of the hands, increased thirst, increased urination and weight gain. Lithium may also affect the thyroid gland, and regular blood tests are needed to check how it is working. If the level of lithium is too high and in the toxic range, drowsiness, nausea, vomiting, slurred speech, shakiness, confusion, and unsteadiness of the legs may occur. You or your relative should contact the doctor about these symptoms immediately.

Not all patients with frequent recurrences of their illness benefit from lithium, and some respond to another type of medication, one of the anticonvulsant drugs used to treat epilepsy. Doctors may prescribe *sodium valproate*. Unwanted effects include nausea and vomiting, and drowsiness. An alternative drug is carbamazepine, especially for people who have very rapid changes in mood. Unwanted effects include drowsiness, unsteadiness, nausea and headache; however these usually improve. A new anticonvulsant drug that is starting to be used more is *lamotrigine*. Sometimes more than one drug will be used together.

For people who have repeated attacks of severe depression, but no mania, the doctor may use an antidepressant in the same way as lithium for long-term prevention.

Psychological treatments

Drug treatments are useful in treating attacks of bipolar illness and preventing future attacks, but they are not the whole story. Your relative or friend may also find a 'talking treatment' helpful. Talking treatments are a special kind of discussion between a patient and a therapist looking at a person's thoughts and feelings. This is important in all stages of treatment. During episodes of illness, psychological support from the doctor or other members of the treatment team is essential. After recovery, therapy may look at aspects of a person's life style that may increase the chance of more mood swings in the future. These may include unrealistic ambitions or demands. A special form of psychological treatment is *cognitive behavioural therapy*. This treatment helps people identify and challenge the way they think, such as 'I'm a bad person' or 'I've always been a failure', which can become self-fulfilling prophecies. This treatment can be very effective, particularly if combined with medication. It is likely to continue for some weeks or months.

The doctor may also recommend other interventions aimed at, for example, improving communication between the sufferer and other family members, dealing with feelings of isolation, difficulties at work or financial problems.

Admission to hospital

In a severe episode of depression or mania, the doctor may advise admission to hospital. Occasionally this may be against the wishes of the person concerned if health professionals are worried about, for example, a significant risk of self-harm. In this case a person may be detained in hospital under the Mental Health Act (1983).

How does it affect families and friends?

Episodes of mania or depression can be very distressing for families or friends. A manic episode is likely to leave the carer feeling exhausted, while with a depressive episode you may feel powerless to help. When your relative is depressed you may also worry about the chance of self-harm. Often one of the most difficult things for carers to cope with when someone has a severe mood swing is their lack of 'insight' into the fact that he or she is ill. While it is obvious to everyone else that there is something seriously wrong, the sufferer may not see this at all. You may also have concerns about your relative's ability to care for themselves or any children. Particularly in mania a person may become irritable and hostile and you may feel frightened by this change in behaviour.

What can families and friends do to help?

It is helpful to know about the illness and treatment, and to ask about aspects of the illness and treatment you or your relative do not understand. You can get information and support from self-help groups and groups for carers. It is worth keeping in contact with the doctor or other members of the treatment team, and getting in touch immediately if there are early warning signs of another attack. You might ask about whom to contact at times of crisis.

If your relative has been in hospital, it is worth finding out if he or she has a *key worker*, a member of the treatment team responsible for co-ordinating his or her care, so you can contact the key worker if you are worried. This would include times when you are concerned about your relative's safety – for example, if he or she is expressing suicidal thoughts – or if your relative may be putting others at risk by their behaviour. It is useful for sufferers to tell trusted relatives or friends about their illness and treatment so others can be alert to early signs of illness and know what steps to take, as much as possible in accordance with the sufferer's wishes. This preplanning of what to do before an attack happens can ease the stress of a crisis at a later date.

There are some specific issues to consider in relation to mania, and to depression.

Mania

RISK OF DEBT

Reduce the chance of your relative getting into serious debt by not keeping a credit card, or agreeing that you look after it when your relative is starting to get high. You may also want to make sure you have a bank account in your name only to which your relative has no access when unwell. In some cases you may want to consider using a power of attorney (see Chapter 24).

UNWANTED PREGNANCY

For a woman with bipolar affective disorder you may want to discuss with her when well issues around contraception to reduce the chance of an unwanted pregnancy when she is high and may be sexually disinhibited.

DRIVING

If you are worried that your relative may want to drive when manic, see if you can get his or her agreement when well to keep the car keys. If you have further concerns about your relative driving when unwell you may wish to consult with the DVLA and discuss the issue with your relative's key worker or doctor.

HOSTILE BEHAVIOUR

If you feel your relative is becoming hostile and suspicious of you do not get into an argument but get professional help immediately. Your first port of call may be your relative's key worker or doctor.

Depression

SELF-NEGLECT

Check that your relative is looking after him or herself. If your relative is not eating or drinking you will need to contact your relative's key worker or doctor.

SELF-HARM

If you have any worries that your relative has plans to harm him or herself you will need to get immediate professional help from your relative's key worker or doctor or the emergency service.

Tips for carers

- Have contact details of your relative's key worker or doctor, and let the key worker know if you notice any early warning signs of mania or depression.

- Make sure your relative does not have access to all your finances.

- Discuss issues around contraception with your relative.

- If you have any worries that your relative has plans to self-harm, try to talk about them together, and talk to your relative's key worker or doctor.

What is the outlook?

Some people may have only one or two episodes while others become ill repeatedly, sometimes at certain times of year. Between episodes of illness, sufferers usually enjoy good health and things may go back to normal. In its most extreme form, depression can lead to suicide. However, the illness is treatable, usually with very good results. Knowing the early warning signs and getting help quickly can prevent and reduce future problems.

CHAPTER 3

Depression

Anne Farmer

Ron met Diane many years ago when she was ill with depression. Diane came to live in his flat and they remain friends today. Diane has also developed several physical health problems and she suffers from both physical and psychological pain. She now uses a wheelchair and Ron cares for Diane full time.

'Right from when Diane first came to stay, I've been everything to her – doctor, friend, companion, and I sort out all her problems. I keep a diary of all her appointments and I see that she has all her medication on time. Since Diane has become a wheelchair patient, I also do the shopping, cooking, washing and ironing, washing up and everything else in the home apart from the cleaning, which she likes to do herself. Caring for somebody is not easy and it's got more difficult over the years because Diane's health problems have got worse and, of course, there's my age – I'm a lot slower than I used to be. My constant worry is what will happen to her if anything happens to me.

When you've treated somebody for many years, you learn to know what you're doing. I understand the medication, how it works and the side effects and if I'm not sure, I look it up in my medical books. In fact, I have to remind the doctors what to give her, like blood checks for her lithium. I have to be on the ball all the time. The patient actually becomes your responsibility, and if anything goes wrong you feel it's your fault.

Sickness doesn't invite friendship; we both lost our friends through becoming ill but we had the friendship of each other. Outside friends just became acquaintances. After all, if you tell the truth, there aren't many people who have more than one or two real friends.

I think that Diane's depression is getting worse year by year. If she could have been cured over all these years she would have been by now. To the present day she has had approximately a quarter of a million pills. Most of the medication doesn't help – tranquillisers and the pain killers are the only pills that give some sort of relief. What has really helped Diane has been help from a therapy point of view.

Over the years we've tried everything: acupuncture, hypnotherapy, osteopathy...I have not found anything yet that cures her depression, only that gives pain relief. But we've come to the conclusion now that all we're interested in is helping make Diane's life a little bit happier so that she's not in so much pain.

There are lots of things that can upset you during the day. Depression is a very selfish illness and the patient can be very awkward at times. You have to remember that you can't lose your temper and of course, every now and again, you are inclined to forget that. You have to put things right immediately. Probably the hardest thing of all is not worrying about your own problems and putting the person you're caring for first, but over the years you get very experienced at it.

I think that Diane looks on me mainly as a father figure because she never really had the parental care that she should have had and I think this is basically what started off the nervousness and the depression. Her mother phones her and asks her how she is but whether it's because she wants to know or just because the neighbours want to know – whether she feels guilty – I don't know.

I've known lots of illnesses and I've seen people dying but I've never seen a pain like depression. It makes you feel so helpless. The most terrible thing I find is when Diane says "I'm in pain" and I just don't know what to do...it's hard. When she's had her pills and she gets pain in between doses, you know that you can't give her any more. You just have to talk. The funny thing is, we always seem to find time to laugh and have a joke. People can't understand that Diane can enjoy a joke. At the time you wouldn't think that there was any problem at all.

I can leave Diane alone if I go down to the post office, or to the garage to buy a pint of milk, but I don't like to leave her for long periods because she keeps on asking me if she can do away with herself. And after trying it once I don't want to leave her alone again.

My advice to carers and the people they're caring for is to make sure that you are both getting the full benefits you're entitled to. I was stupid and didn't claim anything until the Carers National Association told me what we should be getting. At the moment I think that we're getting all the professional, medical help available; the help we need now is financial.

To really give someone the full care that they're entitled to you've got to love and respect them and want to care for them. You've got to realise that it is a full-time job and put the person you're caring for before anyone else. The fact is that when you're looking after somebody, it's like a mother looking after her children. There are certain things that you have to do every day and you cannot afford to be sick so you have to take very good care of yourself. If I didn't have Diane, I don't know what would keep me going.'

What is the disorder?

Depressive illness is characterised by an overwhelming and persistent low mood that may last for several months. It interferes with a person's relationships and their ability to work effectively. The illness is associated with a number of other problems, such as feelings of inadequacy, guilt or self-blame, lack of confidence, and poor self-esteem. There may be tearfulness or the depressed person may be 'beyond tears', wanting to cry but not being able to do so. He or she may find it difficult to enjoy anything, or to anticipate events such as holidays with any pleasure. The depressed person may also feel that they are incapable of loving their family as much as they should. This 'emptiness' of feelings for others can be one of the most distressing aspects of the illness.

As well as these changes in feelings and thoughts, depression causes difficulty in getting off to sleep, and waking throughout the night or too early in the morning. Poor appetite is another feature of the illness. Those with depression often say that their food lacks taste and texture, or that it is like 'eating cardboard'. In more severe forms of depression, poor appetite can lead to dramatic weight loss, with refusal to eat or drink.

The illness can also cause slowed thinking. This can lead to difficulty in making even simple decisions. Poor concentration and memory may be accompanied by feelings of anxiety so that a person feels tense and panicky. Such anxiety problems may be associated with irrational fears (phobias) of meeting people, going shopping or being in other crowded places (see Chapter 4). Depressed people may also be irritable and angry or they may complain of multiple aches and pains.

In severe episodes of depression a person may have false beliefs (delusions) and hear voices which are not there (hallucinations). These beliefs and voices (psychotic experiences) differ from those experienced in schizophrenia (see Chapter 1), in that they seem to issue from, and reflect, the depressed state of mind; they are known as 'mood congruent' psychotic experiences. A depressed person may believe that they are personally responsible for all the evil in the world, are financially ruined or that a part of their body has rotted away. They may also say that they hear the voices accusing or cursing them. Sometimes the voices may tell them to kill themselves. Both these beliefs and voices are very distressing but they generally stop once the person has responded to treatment.

Suicidal thoughts – a wish to be dead or not to wake up in the morning – may occur. In moderately severe illness this may amount to making plans for a suicide attempt; for example, keeping a secret hoard of tablets. Suicide attempts require urgent medical treatment, and generally indicate a severity of illness that requires inpatient care. Further details regarding how to cope with a relative's suicide and attempts at suicide are discussed in Chapter 30.

How common is it?

Depressive illness is a common disorder, affecting at least 1 in 20 people at some point in their lives. Women are twice as likely as men to develop depression, although depressed men are more likely to try and treat themselves through excess alcohol use.

What are the causes?

Depression results from an imbalance in the chemical messengers (*neurotransmitters*) in the brain, which the nerve cells use to communicate with each other. The chemical messengers are released at one end of a nerve cell, travel across a tiny gap (*synapse*) between cells, and attach to the second cell at a *receptor* site. Depression is associated with low levels of two of the chemical messengers, serotonin and noradrenalin. The drugs used in the treatment of depression act at various places around the gap between nerve cells to increase the availability of these chemical messengers.

What is less certain is why an individual develops this lack of serotonin or noradrenalin. Depression tends to run in families, and the close relatives of a depressed person are more likely to develop depression than other people. Research studies examining how common depression is in identical and non-identical twins provide evidence that genes are involved in causing depression. However, the same work also points to the contribution of environmental factors such as negative life events in causing depression.

Depression is not caused by a single gene, but rather by a number of genes acting together to make an individual susceptible to developing depression when bad events happen. These susceptibility genes are inherited from both parents. Even if neither parent has suffered from depression themselves, each may have passed on a sufficient number of susceptibility genes to lead to their child developing the illness.

We have all felt low-spirited when something bad has happened, so it is not surprising that such events can trigger the onset of an episode of depression. It is possible to identify the type of loss events that may lead to a depressive illness. Examples include the death of a close family member, separation or divorce, severe financial difficulties and loss of a job. These events may occur against a background of vulnerability caused by a difficult childhood, sexual or physical abuse or previous episodes of depression.

Seasonal affective disorder

For some people, low mood is a response to shortening day length. In seasonal affective disorder (SAD), depression starts in the autumn and continues until the spring. During the summer the person is usually free of any depressive symptoms. This pattern of depressive episodes is associated with carbohydrate craving and weight gain rather than loss. SAD responds to light treatment (see below) although sometimes drug treatment with an SSRI type of antidepressant (see below) is needed. Even depressed individuals who do not have 'pure' SAD often feel worse during the winter months.

How do we treat it?

It is helpful to think about treatment as a series of steps. Try the first step. This may work. If it does not, then try the second step, and if necessary there is the third step.

First step of treatment

MEDICATION

There is a new range of antidepressant drugs which have revolutionised the treatment of depression and which can be prescribed by GPs. Older drugs are also effective but are more often associated with unwanted side effects and are particularly dangerous if taken in an overdose. The new antidepressants are safer and associated with fewer side effects, making them more acceptable to the user.

Two main groups of drug are regularly prescribed. The first of these, and the one most likely to be chosen initially by the GP, is the selective serotonin reuptake inhibitors (SSRIs). They work by preventing the brain chemical messenger serotonin from being reabsorbed, so increasing the amount of it available to the nerve cells. There are a number of drugs in this group; some of the best known are citalopram, fluoxetine (Prozac), paroxetine, and sertraline. The most common side effects of these drugs are nausea and headaches, although they may also cause restlessness, irritability, anxiety and some difficulty in getting off to sleep. These side effects are generally mild and usually only occur in the first few days of taking the medication. When coming off these tablets, it is important not to stop them suddenly, but to tail off the dose gradually with the advice of a doctor.

The second important group of drugs are the tricyclic antidepressants. These are more sedative than the SSRIs, and may be associated with more troublesome side effects, such as a dry mouth, blurred vision, dizziness, constipation and difficulty passing water, which can rule out their use in the elderly. However, they are effective antidepressants and suit some people well. This group includes amitriptyline, clomipramine, dothiepin and imipramine. If taken as an overdose these drugs can cause heart irregularities, which may be fatal.

Most people with an episode of depression respond to the first drug they try. For all antidepressants it takes about 10 to 14 days before any change in mood is apparent. The improvement in mood will be gradual, and a person may still have 'bad days' even though they are significantly better. It is important that the drug is tried for at least one month, and is taken regularly as prescribed. This allows an adequate level of the drug to build up in the bloodstream so that it can pass into the brain. If tablets are only taken sometimes, a person's mood is less likely to improve. Unlike tranquillisers such as diazepam (Valium), antidepressants are not addictive.

Some depressed people require higher doses of the drug than is first prescribed by the doctor. Gradually increasing the dose under medical supervision usually results in the expected improvement in mood. If this does not occur, or if side effects are intolerable, the doctor will probably change to a different group of antidepressants.

PSYCHOTHERAPY

Another first step intervention is *psychotherapy* (see Chapter 29). The type of psychotherapy that is effective in depressive illness is cognitive behavioural therapy (CBT). This is a technique for looking at the negative thoughts or *cognitions* that lead to low mood. The therapist helps a person to reinterpret these negative thoughts so that they become neutral or even positive thoughts.

As a result a person's mood will improve. CBT is offered by a trained therapist and usually consists of 12 to 20 individual sessions, each lasting one hour. 'Homework' is undertaken between sessions. This may include the person keeping a record of their negative thoughts for discussion at the next session.

LIGHT TREATMENT

This may be used during the winter months for SAD. A person sits in front of a light box, which provides bright artificial daylight. Previously light treatment was time-consuming (up to six hours per day), but a stronger (10,000 lux) appliance is now available, which is needed for just 30 minutes daily. Improvement in mood occurs over four days, but the person will relapse if they do not continue treatment throughout the winter. More information about SAD is available from the SAD Association (see Resources).

Second step of treatment

If first step treatment does not lead to an improvement in a person's mood and ability to function, it is worth considering a different approach. The GP may suggest a change in antidepressant or do a blood test to see whether the medication is at the correct level in the blood to work effectively. Another option is for the GP to refer someone to the local mental health service, either a community mental health team or to a psychiatrist. In both cases a mental health professional will do an assessment and review the treatment plan. If two or three antidepressants have already been tried at a high enough dose for a long enough time, a second drug may be added to increase the effect of the antidepressant. Lithium carbonate or thyroxine (thyroid hormone) may be used in this way. If a depressed person is psychotic, the doctor may prescribe some antipsychotic medication. These drugs include chlorpromazine, haloperidol, olanzepine and risperidone. One of these drugs may also be used in a low dose if the person is experiencing anxiety or irritability.

Third step of treatment

This involves admission to a mental health unit. Such circumstances occur when a person's mood becomes profoundly low, or when failure to eat or drink is life threatening. Clearly significant suicidal thoughts or acts or psychotic symptoms becoming overwhelming also mean a person needs 24-hour nursing care and more intensive treatment.

Electroconvulsive therapy (ECT) may be considered in such circumstances. Patients and their families may be distressed when such a treatment option is discussed. Although a general anaesthetic is needed to give ECT, it is a safe and effective treatment, lifting a person's mood more rapidly than antidepressants. It is usual to give ECT on a twice-weekly basis, for a course of six treatments. As with any general anaesthetic, no food or drink is taken from midnight the night before the treatment. An anaesthetist administers a general anaesthetic with a muscle relaxant. When the person is asleep, electrode pads are placed across both temples and an electrical charge passed across the brain in order to induce a short fit. The general anaesthetic and muscle relaxant ensure that the fit is noticeable only by a slight twitching of the fingers and flickering of the eyelids. The treatment lasts a few seconds, and then the person is moved to the recovery room. On waking, they may have a temporary headache and some memory loss. The latter generally improves over time, and may be less if the electrodes are placed on one side of the head, rather than across both temples.

The improvement in mood following ECT can occur almost immediately with the person feeling substantially better after the first or second treatment. This improvement is somewhat transient at first, but builds up over the course of the six treatments. Sometimes a second or third course of treatment is necessary to give a lasting improvement in mood.

Admission to hospital is often distressing to both patients and their families. The situation may be worse if a person is refusing to go in voluntarily. In such cases, a decision has to be made about using the Mental Health Act (1983) to insist on admission and treatment (see Chapter 22).

How does it affect families and friends?

It is difficult to convey the awfulness of depression in a few brief sentences. The illness has been described as a 'living hell', and the pain of the experience is felt by both carers and sufferers. You may notice the many ways in which your relative is not functioning as usual and struggles to do basic day-to-day tasks or to get to work. You may find yourself taking on responsibilities your relative would normally shoulder, and this may leave you feeling overburdened and tired. Your relative may be reluctant to see friends, and you may feel more isolated.

What can families and friends do to help?

It is important to keep the focus of caring on the fact that depression is an illness, with effective treatment. A depressed person cannot just 'snap out of it', 'stop feeling sorry for themselves' or get better with a good holiday. Such comments or advice are unhelpful and may lead to the sufferer feeling more inadequate, isolated and miserable.

It goes without question that carers need to be supportive, patient, reassuring and encouraging of a co-operative approach to medical advice. Doing something physical can be helpful, so you may want to encourage your relative to get out for a walk, or to do something at home like the cleaning or ironing. Try and find out if there are any people your relative would like to see and talk to about their feelings. Discourage less helpful ways of trying to cope such as drinking more alcohol. Sometimes if a person is having difficulties sleeping it is worth cutting out any caffeine-containing drinks such as coffee and cola.

Do not be afraid to ask the doctor about the medication being prescribed; for example, what it is, what is the dose, how it works and what unwanted side effects to expect. Ask about the availability of psychotherapy treatment. Your relative may not be able to ask for him or herself, or to concentrate on the information given. It is also important to ensure that your relative gets medical advice before stopping treatment. If medication is stopped too soon symptoms will often return. Finally, for those who have not responded initially, it is important not to lose hope of eventual recovery. New antidepressant drugs and new types of psychotherapy are being evaluated all the time so there is nearly always 'something else' that can be tried.

Be aware that people with depression do sometimes have thoughts of harming themselves. It is sensible not to leave medicines out that your relative could take as an overdose. If you have concern about any risks of self-harm try and talk to your relative about it, and if you remain concerned, talk to your relative's doctor.

Tips for carers

- Encourage your relative to talk about how he or she is feeling.
- Encourage your relative to do something physical.
- Get information about your relative's treatment.
- Ask about all the options for treatment including psychotherapy.
- Be aware of the possibility of self-harm.

What is the outlook?

Once an individual has suffered from an episode of depression, there is a higher chance of a recurrence at sometime in the future. Unlike the first time, both sufferers and their families will be more aware of the warning signs and are more likely to seek medical advice sooner rather than later. While there may be a reluctance to go back on medication, if started early in the episode, there can be less deterioration in terms of work and social functioning, the medication acting to nip the episode in the bud.

CHAPTER 4

Anxiety Disorders

Susan Grey

*Rosie suffered panic attacks, agoraphobia and a fear of flying for about eight years.
Miles, her husband, provided support throughout that period, and for much of the time
he himself was suffering from depression. Rosie's GP referred her for CBT organised by
the local clinicl psychology service. This helped her to understand her panic attacks and
get on with everyday life. Both have since recovered.*

'Rosie's panic attacks were pretty severe and frightening for her – for a while
she was having them every day and wouldn't go out. At times I had to come
home from work and be with her because of the state she was in. She lost all her
confidence to the point that she couldn't work, which then made her more
reclusive. Initially, I probably wasn't aware how much she was suffering but
when I went into a serious depression I found that many of my symptoms, especially the physical ones, were similar to my wife's and this really helped us to
support each other – we were in it together. In fact, I think that Rosie was
depressed a lot of the time too without realising it – having panic attacks and
agoraphobia is in itself depressing.

Rosie was always urging me to read the self-help books she'd bought and
although they were all useful – especially the ones by people who'd experienced the same thing – it was still very difficult to relate to what she was going
through. The overriding thing for me was never to try and make a panic attack
end – just ride it out and be as sympathetic as possible. It was almost like *posses-
sion*, as if she was taken over. To be honest, I felt pretty helpless most of the time.

We have a child, and though it's hard to be objective, I don't think we were
ever so ill that we seriously affected her life. Rosie's panic attacks were quite
quiet – she never had really bad hysterics. We don't talk about it with our
daughter and I don't think she was ever aware of it – she was very young when
it all started. We also had help from an *au pair* for much of the time.

We've had to be very careful about alcohol intake – it's something you just can't abuse in that sort of condition. We habitually drank heavily for years and had taken drugs – cocaine and sometimes ecstasy – but not in any dependent way. Stopping drugs completely was not a problem for us, though I don't know whether it actually helped.

None of our friends were very sympathetic about Rosie's anxiety but I haven't got a problem with their attitudes because until you've been through that experience there's no way you can understand it. Because Rosie was in a very sensitive condition a lot of the time, she could be very impatient and quite rude to our friends. It didn't bother me when I saw her overreacting – I only intervened in terms of diplomatically trying to deal with the situation.

All the health professionals my wife and I spoke to were as helpful as they could have been and there was a genuine commitment and sensitivity – the local GPs were very understanding and sympathetic to Rosie's condition. But anxiety is just such a difficult condition for anyone to deal with – partner or doctor. She didn't take the beta blockers she was prescribed [to reduce palpitations] because she didn't like their effects. The psychologist she saw she liked and thought was good. The most useful professional help Rosie got was hypnotherapy and acupuncture – but at that stage she was already recovering. It was then that she dealt with her fear of flying which had been a massive problem. Ultimately patience was the most important thing – realising that it wasn't suddenly going to go away. The most destructive thing you can ever say to someone who is suffering from anxiety is that they should just pull themselves together. It just isn't like that.

Recovery is a very gradual process – it doesn't suddenly start or finish – you're just aware years later that the period has passed. At times looking back it feels like a bad dream. I get the impression that from Rosie's point of view her improvement was about the physical symptoms of the panic attacks not frightening her so much. After all, there's only so many you can have before you start to realise that it isn't going to result in your death.

I think we're still convalescing – it's not completely over. We're both working again now and doing well; I don't get depressed habitually like I used to and Rosie doesn't get panic attacks any more, but we're a bit dazed and waiting to enter the next stage of our lives.'

What are these disorders?

For many people who experience an anxiety problem, it is mild and they manage to cope without professional help. For others the problem is intense, distressing and incapacitating. There are seven different types of anxiety disorder. These are:

- panic disorder, with or without agoraphobia
- agoraphobia without a history of panic attacks
- social phobia
- specific phobia
- generalised anxiety disorder (GAD)
- obsessive compulsive disorder (OCD)
- post-traumatic stress disorder (PTSD).

This chapter will concentrate on panic, phobias and generalised anxiety disorder (GAD) (see Chapters 5 and 6 for OCD and PTSD respectively).

A panic attack is an episode of intense fear of rapid onset, accompanied by physical symptoms such as breathlessness, palpitations, dizziness, trembling, choking sensations, nausea, a sense of unreality in the world around you ('derealisation'), and chest pain. In panic disorder these episodes are recurrent and may come on unexpectedly.

Some people with panic disorder also have agoraphobia. The term 'agoraphobia', which means a fear of public places, is used to describe a fear of places from which escape may be difficult, or in some cases a fear of coming to harm when alone at home. In panic disorder with agoraphobia the experience of panic is followed by a tendency to avoid these places. Typically, the person with agoraphobia tries to avoid public places, public transport, crowded shops, waiting in queues and other situations that feel 'unsafe', because of the fear that a panic attack might occur. Occasionally people develop agoraphobia without having had clear-cut panic attacks, but this is unusual.

If a person describes intense and persistent anxiety in social or performance situations they may be diagnosed as having a social phobia. People with social phobias often fear that they might act in a way that will be embarrassing or humiliating. As a result, they tend to avoid situations involving social interaction or public performance.

Specific phobia is the term used to describe intense, persistent fear of a particular object or situation. Common phobias include fears of spiders, mice or heights. People with phobias often try to avoid the object or place they fear.

Generalised anxiety disorder (GAD) describes persistent, excessive and un-realistic anxiety about possible misfortunes. A person suffering from general-ised anxiety does not have discrete sudden episodes of intense fear which meet the criteria for panic disorder, but instead has frequent or continuous anxiety about issues such as health, work, money or the welfare of their family.

Dividing psychological disorders into the seven categories listed above is not entirely satisfactory because in reality they often do not fit into such neat boxes. This is particularly true of the anxiety disorders, in which it can be difficult to decide whether the symptoms are severe enough to warrant a diagnosis, or if more than one type of anxiety occurs together. However, the seven disorders described above share one feature, namely intense and excessive anxiety. In cases of panic and phobias the anxiety is episodic and includes a feeling of fear, while in generalised anxiety it is more or less continu-ous.

How common is anxiety?

Anxiety is a very common psychological problem. Some surveys suggest that as many as 1 in 20 people develop panic disorder, and many more have specific phobias or generalised anxiety. It is twice as common in women as in men and may occur in adults at any age.

What are the causes?

People with anxiety disorders sometimes worry that they may pass on their problems to other members of the family, especially their children. Anxiety disorders are not directly inherited, although some aspects of personality may have a small genetic component, making some people more likely to be upset by difficulties than others. However, because children learn a lot from observing their parents' behaviour and emotional reactions, they may learn to be afraid of the same things as their parents. (It is less likely that an adult will pick up fears in this way, although it can happen.) Other relatives, teachers and friends, who may provide useful models of more confident behaviour, will also influence children.

How do we treat anxiety?

We know from research that medication is not the best treatment for anxiety. Tranquillisers such as diazepam (valium), which were once thought to be useful, can result in physical and psychological dependence and are no longer recommended. They are sometimes used on a short-term basis, for example, to allow someone with dental phobia to have urgent treatment, or to help someone sleep after a major trauma. However, they may interfere with psychological treatment processes so they should not be prescribed for longer than two weeks. Antidepressants are sometimes useful, but this is mainly if a person has depression as well as anxiety. The overwhelming evidence is that psychological treatment, using cognitive behavioural therapy (CBT), is the most effective way of dealing with anxiety.

Panic attacks, agoraphobia and other phobias

In order to overcome panic and agoraphobia it is important to understand the underlying psychological mechanisms. Feelings of anxiety affect both the body and the mind, as shown in Figure 4.1. The initial sense of fear or apprehension may be triggered by a variety of situations, such as a bus journey or a noisy party. Sometimes the trigger may be just an unpleasant thought or memory and may be difficult to identify. Whatever the cause, that initial fear or apprehension leads to the characteristic bodily symptoms. Everybody experiences these bodily symptoms at some time. Anyone who has lost sight of their child in a busy shop, or attended a formal job interview, will be familiar with the racing heart or 'butterflies' in the stomach anxiety may cause.

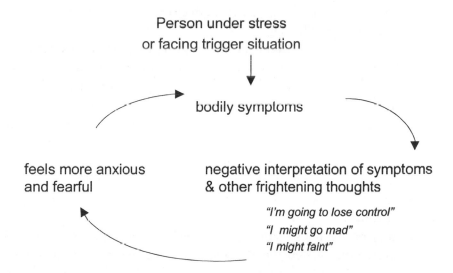

Figure 4.1 The vicious circle of panic

Often these symptoms are understandable and people accept them, but in anxiety disorder the symptoms are worse and seem to make less sense. The anxious person may think that something terrible is going to happen, such as a heart attack, fainting, insanity or loss of control. These thoughts lead to an escalation of the feelings of fear, leading in turn to further bodily symptoms. This sequence of events is often described as the 'vicious circle' of panic.

Over time people who have panic attacks may become especially sensitive to the mildest bodily sensations, which they interpret as a sign that another attack is about to occur. They may be constantly on the alert and mentally checking for any twitches or twinges, which might be a sign of impending panic. Many people talk about having a 'fear of fear', because they realise that they are more frightened of the panic attack than anything else. Unfortunately, if someone is thinking about panic and interpreting bodily sensations as signs of trouble, this is likely to produce fear and cause a panic attack, as can be seen in the diagram (Figure 4.1).

Another important consequence of repeated experiences of panic is the tendency to avoid things. This varies in different people. Some people with agoraphobia feel comfortable travelling on trains or buses with a friend, but avoid travelling alone. Other factors can also affect the decision to go out or not go out; for example, the weather, the traffic, the time of day, the number of people on the street, or simply what mood the person is in. By avoiding feared situations the person with the phobia avoids experiencing too much anxiety. This encourages them to avoid the situation again, leading to habitual avoidance. Occasionally the avoidance of activities develops to the point at which the person becomes housebound.

Treatment of panic and phobias involves breaking the vicious circle. It is particularly important to help a person alter their anxiety-related thoughts and to stop avoiding situations that they believe will make them anxious.

The first step is to identify the triggers that provoke the anxiety. For people with phobias this is fairly straightforward. Most people can make a list of the situations or activities they fear, including the factors, such as time of day, that affect their anxiety. Then put the list in order, with the easiest situations first, to form a programme of graded exercises to practise each day. This approach is known as graded exposure. An example of exercises for someone with agoraphobia is shown in Figure 4.2.

For someone with a social phobia or specific phobia, the list of exercises might look a little different, but the principle is the same as for someone with agoraphobia. Treatment involves practising these exercises, one at a time,

1. Walk to the corner shop and buy a newspaper, with husband

2. Walk down the High Street to grocer's shop and back, with husband, on a weekday

3. Walk down the High Street to grocer's shop and back, with husband, on Saturday morning

4. Take 68 bus two stops from Camberwell Green to Denmark Hill and back, with husband, on a weekday

5. Take 68 bus five stops from Camberwell Green to Herne Hill and return, with husband, on a weekday

6. Walk to corner shop and buy a newspaper, alone

7. Walk down High Street to grocer's shop and back alone, on a weekday

8. Go shopping in supermarket alone, on a weekday

9. Take bus from Camberwell Green to Elephant and Castle alone in the rush hour

Figure 4.2 Graded programme of exercises for a person with agoraphobia

repeating each one until it can be completed without anxiety. Only then should the next exercise be attempted. It takes time to rebuild confidence and there will be days when, after making some progress, an exercise may suddenly seem more difficult than before. This could be because the circumstances have changed in some way, such as heavier traffic than usual, unusually bad weather, or simply that the person has a headache or is feeling worried about some other events in their life. These setbacks are common and should be seen as an opportunity to learn.

The behavioural exercises should be combined with cognitive strategies to change the thoughts a person may have that can feed into the vicious circle and make anxiety worse. As already described, anxious people often fear that something terrible will happen if they do not escape from panic-inducing situations. These thoughts need identifying so that they can be re-evaluated and replaced with more accurate ones. In acute anxiety it is difficult to think clearly, and it is worth practising the alternative thoughts beforehand and writing them down, making them easier to remember when the anxiety starts. Each exercise should then be thought of as an experiment to help a person find out that their catastrophic thoughts are not correct, as they rarely are.

In addition to looking for alternative, more positive, thoughts many people with panic attacks find it helpful to shift the focus of their attention away from themselves and towards the outside world. Looking at the scenery, listening to other people's conversations, or reading street signs can be useful strategies to stop the intense vigilance which is characteristic of people with panics and phobias.

Finally, relaxation training can reduce some of the physical symptoms of anxiety, particularly muscular tension. Relaxation training involves practising tensing then relaxing different groups of muscles in turn, until the whole body is relaxed. This helps a person to learn the difference between tension and re-laxation, so that they can identify bodily tension building up more easily. Daily practice allows natural relaxation to occur. There are many cassettes of relax-ation exercises available in the shops and it is a matter of personal preference choosing which is best.

Generalised anxiety disorder

---

1. Clarify the nature of the problem in detail.

2. Think of as many solutions as possible and write them down – do not exclude any ideas at this stage.

3. Choose the most suitable solution, by weighing up the arguments for and against each one - making this choice is often the most difficult step and only time will tell whether the chosen solution is a good one, but sometimes it is necessary to make a 'best guess'.

4. Put the decision into practice.

5. Evaluate the results - if you decide later that your chosen solution did not work out, you can either try another solution from your list or have a fresh look at the original problem, perhaps defining it differently in the light of your experience, then continue through the same steps again.

Figure 4.3 A guide to problem-solving

The treatment of GAD is less well developed than that of panic and phobias. People with GAD are anxious most of the time and tend to worry excessively. Because the trigger for the anxiety is not obvious and people with GAD do not avoid specific things or situations, the graded exposure technique is unlikely to be helpful. 'Normal worry' may serve to help people plan solutions to anticipated difficulties. However, in GAD, worry is persistent, repetitive and uncontrollable and does not progress towards a solution. It can be helpful to teach people better problem-solving techniques, as described in Figure 4.3.

Problem-solving techniques can be combined with 'worry postponement' exercises, designed to help the person 'let go' of their worries. Some psychologists also believe that people with GAD have a tendency to pay close attention to the way their minds work and that this is counter-productive. According to this theory, these 'worries about worry' need reducing in order for treatment to be effective. Other strategies include time-management, establishing regular sleeping patterns and relaxation training.

How does anxiety affect carers and families?

If someone in your family or a friend is suffering from anxiety they may seem very emotionally fragile, becoming distressed in situations that seem harmless to other people. If the problem persists they may worry about the effect it is having on others and blame themselves for not coping. If they are avoiding certain activities they may become dependent on you to do errands for them or to keep them company. Most people with agoraphobia live with their families and find themselves asking for company on outings or even give up going out altogether. A partner may have to do the shopping, take the children to school and so on. If someone finds staying at home difficult they may keep their children at home with them, or their partner may need to miss work. These restrictions on a family's life will affect everyone and can lead to arguments.

Specific phobias, such as fears of spiders, heights or snakes, may be easier for a family to cope with as they are more limited in their effects on someone's life.

People with GAD may repeatedly ask for reassurance about their worries or turn to alcohol or tranquillisers to get quick relief from their symptoms. Avoidance, seeking reassurance and using alcohol and tranquillisers are all ineffective in the long term, and are likely to lead to the problem becoming more entrenched and even greater friction with those close to them.

What can carers and families do to help?

An understanding of the psychological mechanisms underlying anxiety is as helpful for the carer as it is for the person with the problem. A collaborative approach can help, with family members encouraging a person to use the cognitive and behavioural strategies described above. If a programme of graded exposure is being followed, relatives or friends can provide company in the early stages while the person gains confidence in entering difficult situations.

Psychological treatments are only effective when a person is working towards targets that make sense to them and that they genuinely want to achieve. For some people, it is easier to start therapy with someone who is not emotionally involved, so you can encourage your relative to ask the GP for a referral to a clinical psychologist or other therapist trained in cognitive behavioural methods. You can then offer help later, by encouraging your relative to use the advice given in therapy, giving praise for achievements and helping them to cope with the setbacks that always occur from time to time.

If a person worries excessively about particular issues such as their health, they may ask their family for repeated reassurance. With the help of a therapist relatives can develop a strategy in this situation to remind them that the therapist advises them not to offer constant reassurance, and not to answer such questions.

Tips for carers

- Do not be over-critical of your friend or relative's anxiety symptoms.
- Provide support to your relative in dealing with their problems.
- Encourage your relative not to use alcohol or other substances as a way of trying to deal with their difficulties.
- You may be able to help with some of the treatment; for example, accompanying your relative when trying out some of the new stages in their treatment plan.
- If this is part of the treatment plan, do not offer constant reassurance.
- Encouragement will help your relative to make progress but should not put them under so much pressure that they become distressed or resentful or try to tackle situations that are still too difficult to face.

What is the outlook?

Although many people with anxiety problems do have a general disposition to be fearful or worried, psychological treatments can help them to cope well enough to live normal lives. Because there are wide differences between people in the severity of their problems, there will be differences in the amount of treatment needed. Some people find that learning about psychological strategies and putting them into practice is enough to overcome their anxieties completely. Others, with more severe or long-standing difficulties, will need help from a trained therapist.

After treatment, there may be a recurrence of symptoms at times of stress, such as after a bereavement or during financial or relationship difficulties. At such times it is helpful to make a systematic effort to use the strategies which have worked in the past, or it may be useful to have some 'top-up' treatment from a therapist. The beauty of psychological treatment is that it involves learning skills which can be used again and again and which give people confidence in their own abilities.

CHAPTER 5

Obsessive Compulsive Disorder

Richard Parkin

Mr and Mrs Hughes have been married for 33 years. Patrick Hughes has suffered from obsessive compulsive disorder (OCD) since childhood. The illness has become more severe as he has got older.

'When I first knew Patrick he used to stay at work after hours checking invoices he was sending out, so that's when I first started helping him. As I got to know him better all sorts of different things crept in and it got worse. Forty years ago nobody had ever heard of OCD – it wasn't labelled. I just accepted it – that he needed help with the invoices to make sure they were all right and that's it. I never really asked why – strange, isn't it?

He managed to work full time and have a good social and sporting life for 24 years, but with increasing difficulty. This was only possible with considerable help from me and eventually he had to give up everything because of the OCD. He withdrew to his bedroom for over 15 years including stays in various hospitals. Reading, occasionally watching television, listening to the radio and eating meals were all he did the whole day. Whatever interests Patrick had he became very obsessional about and it all involved checking.

Nowadays Patrick has difficulty with everything he does – even just being. I have to be on the alert, anticipating situations that may give him discomfort and difficulties. Inevitably if you read the newspaper you get print on your hands and he worries all the time whether his hands are clean, what he has touched and whether he has made anything else dirty. Going out is a major undertaking.

For everything I do I have to think, "How would it affect Patrick?" I always feel that I've got to be on time. Not that he's ever jealous or worried about what I get up to, but I worry whether he's going to be all right. If I get home late he can get excessively anxious. If, say, I went to a meeting and afterwards someone said "Let's go for a drink" I'll realise that I haven't told Patrick I might go and we haven't prepared for that situation. He won't answer the phone unless he knows who it's going to be so I can't call him to let him know.

When he's in hospital I lead a completely different life. I do things without thinking and without having to consult anyone. I can sort out the bedroom without thinking he'll still be in bed, and I don't have to plan.

The most difficult thing has been not being able to see as much of my family as I'd have liked when they were alive – to have my mother popping in or me going over to see her. We could have been more spontaneous without having to plan visits.

I have very good friends in the village whom I can turn to at any time and just be with without any questions being asked. I think I would have found it more difficult if I'd been in a town where you don't have the same sort of relationships with neighbours.

Patrick has made some progress with his course of treatment and that's difficult for me because I've got to learn to live again, the same as he has. Sometimes I don't know what to do and I get stuck. Do I now just carry on and ignore it completely? How do I fit in now? I haven't seen the current therapist yet but I've been told that I mustn't help Patrick. When he comes back from hospital he has to do certain things – instead of me making tea, he has to make me a cup and I'm not used to it. I have to hold back and let him get used to doing things for himself and little things for me. I suppose in a lot of ways it's like children leaving home – you've got to let go.

On the whole we've had a lot of help from mental health services and our GP, but what you want and what you need aren't always the same thing. Sometimes Patrick has wanted to go into hospital because it's an escape – in some ways it's easier than being at home because he doesn't have to worry about things so much but it's not necessarily best for him because he's got to face up to ordinary living. In the first instance it took a long time to get help because the patient has got to want it – you've got to get them in the right frame of mind.

In the hospital, though, I found the ward rounds and case conferences really appalling. I know that many psychiatric patients are absolutely terrified of them. You go in a room and there's this ring of people sitting looking at you and it's very intimidating. You probably don't even know all of them either. Every hospital you go to has them but I don't know why they have this format. Several nurses, a social worker and doctors all sit there and they chuck a question at you and you don't know what to say. You've got to say something, you've got to make something up, truth or not. Whether they get a good picture from that I don't know.

In terms of money we could do with more help. We now get disability living allowance, something we never had before. There are a lot of expenses – using up a bar of soap per bath, or replacing perfectly good things which have to be thrown away because they are "soiled".

Knowing what I know now, perhaps I should have been firmer or harder and not accepted it so much but I didn't know anything about OCD. Someone needed help and I didn't realise it was an illness. Perhaps that might not happen quite so much now, but if it's somebody you're fond of, you go along with it and try to make things easier for them, not realising that you're actually making it more difficult.'

What is the disorder?

Do you remember as a child avoiding the cracks in the pavement to ward off harm? You may be aware as an adult that sometimes very unpleasant thoughts pop into your mind that you feel guilty about but are able to dismiss quite easily, or you might have a particular ritual that you carry out to make certain events go well. Most people experience these things. Imagine, however, a life dominated by such thoughts, when not carrying out a certain action or ritual results in terrible anxiety and a fear that something awful will happen. That is what it is like to suffer from obsessive compulsive disorder or OCD.

The main symptoms of OCD can be divided into two main groups: obsessions and compulsions.

Obsessions are repetitive, unwanted, intrusive thoughts, ideas, images or impulses often about threat of harm, violence, sex, or blasphemy. Sometimes people fear that they may have said something out loud that could be offensive. Fear of contamination is the most common obsession and occurs in 50 per cent of sufferers. Obsessions can create feelings of intense anxiety. Sometimes these symptoms exist on their own but more commonly they are associated with compulsions.

Compulsions are usually the sufferer's way of trying to reduce or negate the anxiety created by their obsessions. They take the form of either mental or physical rituals. The most common rituals involve: *checking,* e.g. that switches and taps are turned off or doors and windows are locked; *washing* of hands, body, clothes and surfaces often to avoid fear of contamination; *ordering*; *hoarding,* e.g. never throwing any rubbish away; and *counting.* Counting can take the form of doing other rituals a certain number of times or mentally counting things over and over again. People commonly have other mental rituals such as saying a particular phrase in their head to counteract an obsessional thought. Physical rituals can take many hours to complete and they frequently involve close family and friends.

People with OCD vary in their ability to resist carrying out rituals but if they do try to resist their anxiety tends to increase until they give in, which provides temporary relief. Occasionally people are only troubled with compulsive rituals and they are unable to identify any obsessions. The rituals are not carried out with any pleasure at all and usually with great anxiety until they have been done 'right'. Other 'compulsive' activity such as drinking, eating, shopping, and gambling are not part of OCD because they do give some pleasure even if there is also regret and guilt. People with OCD recognise the senselessness of their thoughts and actions and desperately want to regain control over them.

How common is it?

OCD affects at least 2 to 3 people in 100. The number may be higher, because some people keep their symptoms hidden and do not seek help. It occurs in both men and women. It tends to begin in adolescence but can occur at any age. It may be brought on by stressful events; both happy ones, such as childbirth, and sad ones, such as bereavement.

What are the causes?

We know little about why people get it, although there may be a genetic component. Some research has shown a higher proportion of sufferers to have affected parents than in the general population, but this may be because they have learnt this behaviour from their parents or lived in the same conditions. Behaviour therapists believe that rituals are carried out as a way of avoiding anxiety. For example, a person with agoraphobia avoids going into a supermarket. However, this avoidance actually perpetuates the problem because the person never learns that their anxiety will naturally reduce and that the feared consequence, e.g. contamination, does not occur.

How do we treat it?

There is effective treatment for OCD. Frequently the biggest hurdles are getting someone to acknowledge their symptoms represent a psychological problem and that they need to look for help. Carers are often the ones to seek medical help for the sufferer because they can no longer tolerate the problem. They may feel as if their own life has also been taken over. Sometimes domestic changes such as moving house or a loss such as a bereavement can lead to some improvement, as the suffere may have to confront their problem and so try to seek help. Up to two thirds of people with OCD are also depressed and it may be this condition which prompts them to seek treatment.

The two main treatments that we know are effective are medication and cognitive behavioural therapy (CBT). Antidepressant drugs such as clomipramine, fluoxetine, paroxetine and citalopram can be useful for treating both the OCD and any depressive illness that is also present. Unfortunately these drugs need to be used in a high dose to be effective in OCD so unwanted side effects may be a problem. Although medication on its own can reduce symptoms, when the drug is stopped relapse is common. CBT on the other hand can help to reduce symptoms for good. Often the optimum treatment is a combination of the two, but many people do not like taking medication and therefore prefer CBT alone.

What is cognitive behavioural therapy (CBT)?

This is an effective treatment for a variety of psychological problems such as anxiety, panic, phobias and OCD. In very basic terms the 'cognitive' part looks at thoughts and the 'behavioural' part looks at actions. There is debate about the relative merits of the two parts. Many therapists concentrate more on behaviour because so much of OCD is about trying to avoid anxiety. Behaviour therapy (BT) helps people to identify triggers that set off thoughts and compulsive acts and encourages a person to face these triggers (exposure) without carrying out their rituals (response prevention). At first this increases the anxiety associated with the fear that something bad will happen, but after a short while this anxiety decreases. After repeated exposure and response prevention the sufferer learns that nothing untoward has happened and their anxiety reduces further. As more and more triggers are tackled so the OCD loses its hold and the person is able to lead a normal life.

It is important to remember that behaviour therapy is not an instant cure. To overcome OCD takes time and effort. People cannot on a given day simply decide to stop doing their rituals as some people can, for example, give up smoking so considerable patience and perseverance is needed.

How does it affect families and friends?

It is very likely that you are already involved to some extent. It is possible to hide some obsessions but rituals almost inevitably have an impact on those around. You may have only just become aware of the problem and be unsure how to proceed or you may have been involved so long that you think you're at the end of your tether. OCD can make you feel like that, but try and remember that your relative or friend is not doing their rituals out of spite, or to get at you, or because they're lazy and useless. Also remember that someone suffering from OCD is not 'mad'. Unwell, but not 'crazy', even though you both may sometimes think this is the case. Your relative needs support and encouragement not criticism or mockery.

You are probably thinking, 'That's easier said than done.' There will be times when your patience runs out. It may be best to try and walk away, to get out for a little while, and let the anger subside. Arguments do nobody any good. People who suffer from OCD can become very miserable, sometimes depressed; hurtful comments will only make things worse and soon you're in a vicious circle. Instead, if the sufferer feels supported then progress is more likely.

What can families and friends do to help?

Identifying triggers

The main aim is to identify what things trigger thoughts and/or rituals. It is possible that your friend or relative may be so caught up with their OCD that they have lost sight of what is reasonable behaviour and therefore need some guidance on what is a trigger. For example, someone might be so used to washing that they think it is reasonable to wash their clothes after walking past a pile of rubbish on the ground. You can offer to go through their daily routine with them and tactfully guide them towards all the things that seem to trigger unreasonable behaviour or rituals.

What is reasonable behaviour?

You may soon find that you are being asked repeatedly what is reasonable and what is not; for example, 'Is it OK for me to put the shopping away without washing it?' or, 'Is it reasonable for me to eat this sandwich without washing my hands?' These questions become rituals in themselves and it is vital that you deal with them in the right way. If you are asked such a question you should give a polite and honest answer, but only once. Because of the nature of OCD, your relative may ask you again, at which point you must reply in a deadpan voice, 'You already know the answer' or, 'I've answered that already.' Be prepared to repeat this several times, keeping your patience. By doing so you are helping your friend to carry out an exposure task. A similar problem you may have encountered is the seeking of reassurance.

Reassurance

This is a common occurrence in OCD and one that can put considerable strain on a relationship. The OCD sufferer will repeatedly ask questions such as, 'Did you see me touch the door frame?' or, 'Did you hear me say anything out loud just then?' Asking for reassurance in this way is a ritual and needs to be identified and tackled like any other ritual. If you are asked for reassurance you must reply, 'Your treatment programme says no answer.' This will take practice, perseverance and patience. Unfortunately it is very easy for things to break down into an argument with both of you wanting to vent your frustration and anger on each other. It is vital that you remain calm and deadpan when responding. You may find it helpful to repeat the phrase 'Your treatment programme says no answer' out loud, over and over again on your own so you are ready to respond when the need arises.

What is the difference between reassurance and encouragement?

A common concern expressed by family members or friends is, 'How do I know that I'm not giving reassurance when I'm trying to offer encouragement?' If you are asked 'I did really well there, didn't I?' after an exposure and response prevention (ERP) has been completed you are likely to want to give praise. You could say, 'Well done, that was really good.' This could be thought of by your friend as 'It's OK to have done that, nothing unpleasant will happen', and is therefore reassurance. If you are asked again in a few minutes 'You think I did well there, don't you?' then you will know that asking for praise and encouragement has become a request for reassurance. You then have to deal with it in the same way as above. Be prepared for, 'But you're supposed to praise me, what's the point in doing anything if you're not going to help me?' Explain that you have already said 'Well done' and that you are not going to respond to the ritual of reassurance.

How and when do I give encouragement?

People with OCD frequently complain, 'I never get any encouragement.' This arises because what seems like a small or insignificant gain to you might have taken great effort by your relative or friend. You might think that they should always have washed their hands only once after going to the toilet and that it does not warrant a comment. For the OCD sufferer it is a big step and needs to be recognised as such. Any goal that is completed successfully should be praised, bearing in mind the above conditions. If your relative achieves the goal 'I will not wash my hands for at least an hour after touching the rubbish bin' then congratulations are in order, even if your friend then washes their hands ten times when the hour is up. The important thing is that they completed the specified goal and you can encourage them to carry it out again. If a goal is not completed do not be critical, but try to be constructive, 'OK, so you didn't manage it this time but you can try again tomorrow.'

Behavioural therapy will require your relative to tackle a lot of goals and to record them in their homework diary. You can help them to create suitable, specific goals, and encourage them to carry them out and make the necessary recordings in their diary. Be firm but do not get too pushy. If someone is feeling really low they may find it hard to carry out homework tasks, so try and be sensitive to this. Be supportive and do not give them a hard time when they are struggling.

Do not be too helpful

It is very easy to slip into habits that will get in the way of any improvement being made. You might be unaware of just how much you do as a result of your relative's OCD. You could try doing a mental tour of your day thinking about all the things you do or do not do because of their OCD. Also imagine all you would or would not do if your relative did not suffer from OCD. Typical examples are: washing or checking for them; not having people visit; not using certain household appliances; doing all the cooking; switching things off; the list could go on and on.

Once you have built up a list get together with your friend or relative, create a series of mutually acceptable goals for you to achieve; for example, 'I will not take my shoes off before coming into the house', or, if they have a fear of leaving their bedroom, 'I will not bring your breakfast to you in bed.' It is as important that you stick to these goals as it is for your relative to achieve theirs.

Tips for carers

- Although an OCD sufferer's behaviour can be very frustrating, he or she is probably suffering more than you.
- Unite to fight the common enemy of OCD, and do not fight each other.
- The earlier treatment is sought, the less ingrained the problem will be.
- Do not shy away from talking through your worries with friends or professionals.
- If you do not look after yourself you cannot expect to look after anyone else.

What is the outlook?

Cognitive bahavioural therapy does work. If it is done properly 90 per cent of sufferers make worthwhile gains. However, it is important to seek help early because as time goes on the behaviour tends to become more ingrained and harder to change. The average time from the condition's onset to asking for help is around seven years.

Carers can unwittingly help to maintain someone's OCD by falling in with their behaviour because it's easier to do that than it is to confront it and cause trouble. An important message therefore is to try not to put up with major disruption in order to maintain some kind of harmony. OCD can be a horrible illness for both the sufferer and those close by. It can drive people towards behaviour they never thought possible in themselves. Sufferers and their families and friends need to support each other.

CHAPTER 6

Post-Traumatic Stress Disorder

Felicity de Zulueta

William and Eva Marlowe brought up their grandson Gary from childhood when his mother couldn't look after him. Ten years ago, when Gary was 16, he was violently attacked. He subsequently developed post-traumatic stress disorder.

Mr Marlowe: When Gary was a child we found out that his mother was being cruel to him and he had to fend for himself. He didn't have too good a start but then his life became very stable when he came to us. At first he did well at school but later he started getting into trouble, and eventually got expelled. He never had proper schooling after that – the local authority let him down.

Mrs Marlowe: He was attacked by these five men and badly beaten up. The first thing we heard was when the police called and he was in hospital. We don't know the full facts but afterwards Gary changed. You didn't notice it straight away   it was little things. We would ask him to do something and every time he'd say 'I'll do it later'.

Mr Marlowe: He'd hardly go out at all. He wouldn't leave the house until 7pm and he'd be back an hour later. Then he'd go to his room and play music; he gradually became a recluse.
The hardest thing for us has been understanding – it's been inexplicable to us for someone to go from being an outgoing person to withdrawing within himself.

Mrs Marlowe: Things gradually got worse and worse and we just thought it was laziness. It was very difficult for us to notice the symptoms when we didn't know what they were. I had a rough childhood and I just had to get on with it or I got a clip round the ear, so I wasn't very sympathetic. I couldn't understand why he'd changed. At one time he'd sit and talk to you but then he became morose and said he just didn't know why; he couldn't

69

explain. When I first heard about the diagnosis I thought he was just putting it on — I put it down to him just being awkward.

Mr Marlowe: At its worst he was very withdrawn and always expecting someone to attack him if he went out. Once he went to a club with some boys and ran four miles all the way home, saying they were ganging up on him. They weren't. And he became very aggressive — people only had to look at him and he was immediately asking, 'What are you looking at?' He's a lot better than he was, especially since he's been seeing Alison, the psychologist.

Mrs Marlowe: She's brought him on a treat. Because she's young too he looks on her just like he's talking to a friend. He can be very hard to talk to at times and Alison seems to have hit the button. It's easier for us now that he isn't living here any more because we don't see it all the time. We only get it on the phone now if he's really down. If he's crying on the phone, whatever time of the day or night I go to him. We sit down with a cup of tea and he gradually calms down. He wants our reassurance, that's all. He has some tablets that help. It tears your heart out if you hear him crying.

Mr Marlowe: He's beginning to talk to someone up the street where he lives; up to three or four months ago he wouldn't even do that. He does his own washing and he's clean in his own home for a young man. He's improving quite a bit now.

Mrs Marlowe: I think without the psychologist, we wouldn't be in the position we are now. You need an outsider to see what you can't see and Alison's done that. She's made him a bit more sure of himself. He's always confident the day after seeing her. I think she's pushed him a lot further than if we'd just carried on the way we were.

Mr Marlowe: The psychiatrist, Dr Evans, told me to back off and let him get on with things and it's working. We went abroad and she said he'd done marvels on his own while we were away. We came back to make sure he was all right and then we went away again. He does his own shopping now. We used to have to go to the shops for him — he wouldn't go there.

Mrs Marlowe: He was relying on us too much. He had to get away from that and start to think for himself. We have to help him only when he needs help.

Mr Marlowe: It's difficult for me not to ring him up.

Mrs Marlowe: You're a bit too much of a mother hen, you are! You're worse than I am. You've got to learn to let go.

Mr Marlowe: The only problem for us is financial – sometimes we spend a fortune on petrol travelling to see him and it's time-consuming – having to drop everything to go. He's taken five years off my life – I've had strokes and heart attacks.

Mrs Marlowe: But it's kept you going too.

What is it?

Post-traumatic stress disorder or PTSD is a person's intense, lengthy and sometimes delayed reaction to a stressful event. The immediate response to the event usually involves the individual feeling intense fear, helplessness or horror. Sometimes there may be little or no response at the time, but the reaction develops later.

Two of the most common feelings to develop over time are fear and anxiety. Sometimes these feelings occur as a result of being reminded of the trauma, while at other times they appear to come out of the blue. We can understand the fear and anxiety as a reaction to being in a dangerous, life-threatening situation in which people change their view of the world. A trauma survivor may be more aware of risks or may overestimate how dangerous life is. People normally experience fear and anxiety in two main ways: by continuing to re-experience memories of the trauma and by feeling physically aroused.

Re-experiencing the traumatic event

A person may find visual images of what happened suddenly popping into their mind. These 'flashbacks' can be so vivid that it feels as if the event is actually happening all over again. Trauma survivors may also re-experience the trauma in the form of terrifying nightmares and through intrusive thoughts that leave them feeling out of control. Reminders that are in some way linked to the traumatic experience – for example, a smell, a sound or the anniversary of the event – may trigger these responses.

Avoidance

In order to try to relieve their distress people avoid situations that remind them of the trauma, such as objects, television programmes, places or people connected to the event. They sometimes avoid thoughts and memories of the trauma, which can lead them to forget important aspects of what happened, or they may 'blank out' or 'switch off' when reminders of what happened occur. Emotional numbness – a loss of the ability to feel anything very much, including distress or pleasure – is another common way of trying to avoid painful feelings and thoughts about the trauma. It may result in feelings of alienation as the person feels that no one understands what they are going through. This reaction can have a devastating effect on families who feel that their relative has changed and is no longer the same person they once knew.

Avoidance may seem a good way of reducing distress in the short term, but it is not the best strategy for getting over the trauma. First, attempting to avoid one's feelings and thoughts only makes them more frequent and persistent and increases the sense of being out of control. Second, avoidance is usually a result of predictions based on the assumption that if one faces what one fears, disaster will occur. It therefore stops a person from discovering that these fears may be exaggerated, and that the world is not as dangerous as it seems. As a result of avoidance, a person's life may become increasingly restricted.

Physical arousal

Another common reaction to trauma is for a person to feel that their body is in a state of physical arousal, so that they feel jittery and trembling, and may be easily startled and have trouble sleeping. Sleep disturbance can be one of the most distressing symptoms of PTSD. People may have difficulty getting to sleep or wake frequently throughout the night and they may have distressing dreams and nightmares. At the same time they may feel their heart racing, they may sweat (particularly at night when the sheets can be soaked) and they over-breathe leading to pins and needles in their hands and feet. If a person is feeling tense and jumpy for much of the time they may also feel irritable and snappy and lose their temper with families and friends.

Other problems that may develop in sufferers of PTSD

DEPRESSION

People with PTSD may feel low and tearful. The loss of interest in people and activities that often follows the trauma may lead to a feeling that life is not worth living and that plans for the future are no longer important or meaningful. Sometimes people have thoughts of suicide and try to harm themselves.

Trauma survivors often have trouble concentrating that relates to being both depressed and also aroused most of the time. It is frustrating and upsetting to feel unable to pay attention to things or to remember what is going on. As a result a person may feel as if they are no longer in control of their mind and are going crazy.

GUILT AND SHAME

These feelings may be related to something a person did or did not do, in order to survive. Survivors may blame themselves for not having done the right thing, or for not having been able to put the trauma behind them and get back to normal. This can seem a sign of personal weakness or inadequacy.

Families and friends may blame survivors because we tend to place responsibility on those who have been hurt or victimised, rather than on those who have done the hurting. Equally, others may not understand the nature of PTSD, and give the sufferer the message that they should pull themselves together and get on with life. Self-blaming thoughts are a real problem because they can lead people to feel helpless, depressed and bad about themselves.

ANGER

This is a common reaction to trauma. The anger is often directed at the person responsible for causing the physical injury, or abuse and disruption in the sufferer's life. People or circumstances that simply remind a person of the trauma may also stir up feelings of anger even if these people had nothing to do with it. Sometimes PTSD sufferers feel so angry that they want to hit someone or swear. If people direct feelings of anger against themselves this may intensify self-blame, guilt, helplessness and depression.

USING DRUGS AND ALCOHOL

Although using drugs or alcohol can give some relief from the problems of PTSD, it may lead to problems of dependence and will not help with recovery.

Past trauma

A recent traumatic experience may remind a person of similar experiences in the past which they had previously forgotten or ignored. These additional memories and accompanying flashbacks and nightmares may make the sufferer feel overwhelmed and out of control. This is a particular problem in complex PTSD for people who have gone through long-term trauma either as a child or adult.

Making a diagnosis

Most people find that within six to eight weeks of the trauma all these problems have started to reduce and they feel better and do not need to seek help. But in others, who have developed PTSD, these problems carry on and the person will need help to get over them. In this case the sooner they can get specialised help the better.

How common is it?

This varies depending on how common different traumatic experiences are. In any particular situation the number of people who go on to develop PTSD varies according to the nature and severity of the event.

What are the causes?

PTSD develops in response to stressful events. These might include a serious threat or harm to someone's life, or witnessing this threat; for example, as a result of a car accident, physical or sexual assault, disaster, torture or warfare.

Our bodies respond in a primitive way to traumatic events. Feelings of being in danger trigger a protective mechanism, 'the fight or flight' response. Chemical messengers in our body cause an increase in our heart rate, blood pressure and breathing rate as well as feelings of alertness and vigilance. When this response occurs in relation to real danger and is time-limited, it can be life-saving and very useful. Problems arise when the response continues or occurs in the absence of any threat, as in PTSD. In this case, the repeated memory of the traumatic event keeps setting off the fight or flight mechanism and the person feels permanently aroused and in danger.

How do we treat it?

Often the first port of call is the GP. If a person is aware that he or she is suffering from PTSD, the GP is likely to refer the patient to a psychologist specifically trained in the treatment of PTSD, or to a specialist trauma service offering assessment and treatment. However, not all GPs are aware of PTSD and the treatments available. A referral for treatment may also take place through the police or through solicitors if they are involved.

Types of treatment

The treatment options described below can be offered alone or sometimes in combination with other treatments. Most people have treatment as an outpatient but a few will need admission to hospital. Any of the different types of treatment described below may help but not all are available throughout the country. It is worth discussing with the GP what treatments there are locally.

- *Debriefing.* The value of a specialised intervention right after the trauma is controversial. However, an educational approach that explains what reactions a trauma survivor may experience, and medication to improve the immediate sleep difficulties, can be helpful. Involving the family at this stage helps them to be more understanding and supportive. Often people will need no further intervention.

- *Medication.* An antidepressant such as one of the selective serotonin reuptake inhibitors (SSRIs) – for example, sertraline – can significantly reduce many of the symptoms. However, these antidepressants can have unwanted effects that the doctor should discuss and monitor.

- *Specialist assessment.* Establishing what form of treatment would be most suitable for a PTSD sufferer takes place over one to three sessions depending on the complexity of the person's reaction and any past history of trauma. The therapist will agree a treatment programme with the sufferer that may involve one or more therapeutic approaches.

- *Cognitive behavioural therapy.* This intervention normally involves a person attending between 12 and 24 treatment sessions. It seems to work best for those who have experienced a single traumatic event and who were previously emotionally healthy.

- *Eye movement desensitisation and reprocessing (EMDR).* EMDR is an effective new form of treatment using rapid rhythmic eye movements or lateral sound effects.

- *Dynamic psychotherapy.* Some people, particularly those who have experienced multiple traumas or have had other psychological problems may, require longer-term therapy. Treatment of this type usually involves weekly therapy sessions and can take a year or more.

- *Family or systemic therapy.* PTSD sufferers may become irritable and threatening to their partners and children, especially if they are also drinking heavily to try to relieve their symptoms. The family is at risk of disruption or domestic violence and a family intervention can be very helpful in enabling the whole family – including the trauma survivor – to recover.

How does it affect families and friends?

We can think of PTSD as a social disease because it disrupts our inborn capacity to trust and even to love others. Its effects spread across and down the generations. Many carers feel that their afflicted relative or friend is no longer the same person. He or she may have become cold and detached, irritable and aggressive, or may be oversensitive, tearful and sometimes childlike or helpless. Previously capable men and women may no longer be able to manage their jobs, enjoy sport or even watch a programme on television, particularly if it is violent. A mother may no longer be able to concentrate on her housework or respond as sensitively to her children as she did before. PTSD sufferers can become terribly worried about the safety of those they love and will bully them into staying at home. Sexual partners may feel rejected and unloved. Children may feel neglected and terrified by their father or mother's violent outbursts. Sufferers may start drinking or taking drugs in increasing amounts to reduce their arousal and improve their sleep. In the long term, these behaviour patterns can destroy partnerships and families and even damage the children's emotional development.

What can families and friends do to help?

For all the reasons mentioned above, it is very important for families and friends to know and understand what is going on in the mind and body of someone with PTSD. Families can then realise that the sufferer is not 'putting it on', and sufferers can realise that they are not ill because they have failed in some way. PTSD is a serious and potentially devastating condition. Without such an understanding it will be difficult to help a person with PTSD.

Once both the sufferer and family know what is going on and why life is so frightening, different measures can be taken to help:

- The family should show understanding and loving support and listen without criticism to the sufferer's account of the trauma and its after effects.

- The family and sufferer should seek more information about the condition and ask for treatment. This is particularly important if PTSD leads to domestic violence. If the partner or children's health and safety are at risk, urgent and effective help is vital and legal advice may be necessary to protect the family. Too many women put up with violence in order to protect their partner's reputation. Since anger and violence may be a part of PTSD, it is in the interest of all parties that therapeutic help is provided as soon as possible, or that safety measures are put in place if the sufferer refuses to go into treatment.

- The family should remember that the terror of a person suffering from PTSD lies in their feeling helpless and out of control. The family may be able to offer more support once their relative is in treatment; for example, helping them to tackle the natural tendency to avoid frightening reminders of the trauma. In this way a person can ask for help from their family in conquering their fears and regaining old skills. However, this approach only works if the sufferer asks for it. If others try and force someone to talk about the trauma or face their fears, this will simply lead to more trauma and a worsening of the symptoms.

Tips for carers

- Show understanding and loving support to your relative.
- Avoid telling your relative to pull him or herself together.
- Avoid blaming your relative for their problems.
- Encourage your relative to seek information and treatment for PTSD and discuss the options together.
- If your relative is snappy or losing their temper very easily remember this is part of the PTSD.
- Discourage your relative from using alcohol or drugs as a way of dealing with their problems.

What is the outlook?

The outlook for someone who suffers from PTSD, especially simple PTSD resulting from a single stressful event, is excellent if he or she has access to the right sort of treatment and if the family and friends are supportive and involved. Unfortunately, the condition is often not identified and specialised treatment is not available in many areas. GPs need to be made aware of these people and their needs. Sufferers of complex PTSD resulting from chronic or multiple traumatic experiences such as childhood physical or sexual abuse, domestic violence or torture, usually require long-term specialised therapy. The prognosis in these cases varies depending on the length of exposure to the trauma, its severity and the person's age at the time of the earlier trauma.

The prevention of PTSD involves preventing trauma if it is avoidable. This is particularly relevant to families in which victims of domestic violence may also suffer PTSD and physical damage. People who work in potentially dangerous or violent jobs can be prepared to deal with traumatic events and their potential aftermath. And finally, support and understanding on the part of those who care for sufferers of PTSD can reduce the extent of the psychological damage they experience.

CHAPTER 7

Medically Unexplained Physical Symptoms

Alicia Deale and Vincent Deary

Andrew and Yvonne Banks cared for their daughter Fiona for two years while she was suffering and recovering from chronic fatigue syndrome (CFS). She is now well.

Yvonne: To start with, our GP said to Fiona, 'Well, you'll just have to pull yourself together and get back to school.' At that point she couldn't keep her eyes open for more than about 2 hours out of 24. There was no sympathy, nothing, and the poor kid was in a real state.

Andrew: Once we'd been told she had CFS I rang a lady I knew of who had it, to ask her what it was and what we should do. The thing that sticks in my mind is when she said, 'I've had it for 14 years,' and I'm thinking, 'Christ Almighty! Another 14 years of that, she's going to be a young woman, not a child anymore, and all her life's going to have gone.' That was very frightening.

Yvonne: Then later she wasn't sleeping as much and when she wasn't sleeping at nights at all I was awake. It was at night that the pain came and there was nothing you could give her to take it away. We cried together, we laughed, talked about anything and everything, just to try and take her mind off it, and by about 5am she was so exhausted that she would just drop off to sleep. A lot of the time I'm sure I was on a different planet, I was so tired from it all. But I think you keep going because you've got to for the person that's ill. Fiona was extremely frightened of the state that she was in, and she needed that comfort and strength from her family to help her cope with it. If I'd gone into a massive depressive state that would have made Fiona worse.

Andrew: I would say that the most difficult thing was coping with her when she was in all that pain. That is the most devastating thing for any parent.

Yvonne: We managed not to give up our jobs but it was very difficult – not so much physically, it was more the mental stress. It was a very emotional time, but I needed work to keep me sane and to see somebody else outside this situation because it doesn't just affect the person who is poorly, it affects everybody.
An important breakthrough was when we got a dog. We didn't want one but Fiona was alone in the house most of the day and she asked for a puppy. We fought it for six months and then gave in on the understanding that she looked after it, house-trained it and walked it even though she was ill. It gave her an incentive to work towards. At that point she could just walk to the front door and it was a struggle. She went from going to the front door, to the gate, from the gate to the end of the garden, from the garden to the farm gate over several weeks. I'm sure it did help her to start her recovery.

Andrew: The second turning point was going to the specialist unit. It was a lifeline, not just for Fiona, but for the whole family. It was so good to have somebody else who understood. When CFS was first diagnosed, we didn't know anything about the specialist unit. We'd tried to move her forwards but of course they don't take as much notice of parents as they do of an outsider. We were moving in the right direction but it was very slow. But at the unit because it was somebody else it came together. She got about six months into the treatment and just said one day, 'That's it. I've had enough of this. It's not going to rule me any more.' Once her attitude changed and she started to fight, the recovery process started and gathered momentum very quickly. But it was a long, long time starting.

Yvonne: We found out about the specialist unit through a friend of a friend. It wasn't through our own GP – he didn't have a clue about what to do. After the referral letter it was weeks before we actually heard from the specialist unit and even then there was a six months' waiting list, but that was the beginning of a little bit of light at the end of the tunnel.

Andrew: Fiona and Tony [the Banks' other child] are very sporty kids and before she was ill they played a lot together. Although Fiona was the one who was ill, Tony was like a lost sheep because this other half had just stopped. He felt guilty about going to school and enjoying sports or going out with his friends. He didn't dare speak about it when he got home because it upset her because she couldn't do any of these things. It made him very quiet and moody for a long time. I wouldn't have believed that a brother and sister relationship could have been so affected by one of them being unwell. It proved how close they actually were.

Yvonne: We were worried when she went back to college but two or three months down the line she was really a lot better. Then, one morning going to work I had a panic attack and I couldn't understand why. The psychologist at the specialist unit explained it was the fact that Fiona was getting better and she no longer needed me. Things were getting back to normal and it was very difficult to adapt to that change. All of a sudden she was going out and more so than any other teenager because she'd missed out and wanted to catch up. Even now after she's been well so long, I worry she'll go backwards if she's not careful, but she doesn't see it at all – maybe that's a good thing.

What are medically unexplained physical symptoms?

This term (and the alternative terms 'somatoform disorders' and 'functional somatic syndromes') refer to physical symptoms that cannot be explained by a physical cause. In many cases, investigations show no abnormalities and no identifiable disease process. In other cases, a physical disorder or injury is present, but it does not really account for all the person's problems. For example, some people with angina have more chest pain than their angina can account for; or in chronic back pain, a person's disability may be out of proportion to the actual injury.

Medically unexplained physical symptoms are distressing, often disabling and seldom short-lived. They are *not* imaginary, 'put on', exaggerated or 'all in the mind'. Patients are often very worried by their symptoms, and are not necessarily reassured by being told that nothing is wrong. Many will go on looking for an explanation, seeking referrals to new specialists and undergoing yet more tests and investigations which can be unnecessary and even harmful.

Different types of medically unexplained symptoms

People with 'medically unexplained' disorders suffer real physical symptoms. For example, in chronic fatigue syndrome, they may feel physically and mentally exhausted, have a lot of muscle and joint pain, be sensitive to noise and light, and often have many other disabling and unpleasant symptoms. In irritable bowel syndrome, people suffer from constipation, diarrhoea, stomach bloating and nausea. What is 'unexplained' about these conditions is that while some physiological changes are present (for example, changes in the immune system in chronic fatigue syndrome, or increased bowel sensitivity in irritable bowel syndrome), they do not fully explain all of the symptoms or disability. So, although there are clear physical symptoms, there is not a single physical cause.

Some medically unexplained conditions look like other disorders that have a known physical cause. For example, people diagnosed with 'non-epileptic' seizures have fits that can look very like epileptic fits. However, investigations show that the brain is not behaving as it does in epilepsy. In non-cardiac chest pain, people have symptoms that look very like angina, or seem to herald a heart attack, but, again, on investigation there are no abnormalities found.

In another related condition – often referred to as *health anxiety* or *hypochondriasis* (hypochondria) – the problem is the person's preoccupation with particular symptoms and what they might mean. For example, someone may interpret an ache in the side as a sign of cancer. This fear of having cancer leads the person to monitor the feeling constantly, seek reassurance about it from others, and repeatedly go to the doctor and ask about the diagnosis and about further investigations and seeing a specialist. Often giving a person plenty of reassurance and saying there is no diagnosis to be made does not take away the fear but, if anything, the fears get worse.

Very occasionally, some people may suffer a loss or alteration in their functioning that suggests a physical disorder (for example, paralysis of a limb for which no physical cause can be found): this is called 'conversion disorder'. 'Somatisation disorder' is the condition diagnosed when people have a lifelong history of numerous and very varied medically unexplained symptoms.

How common are they?

These problems are very common. At least one in five patients seeing their GP and half of those referred to hospital medical clinics suffer from medically unexplained physical symptoms.

What are the causes?

Physical symptoms that do not seem to be due to a physical cause are often viewed as 'psychological'. A minority of patients who seek help for medically unexplained symptoms also have a mental illness – generally depression or anxiety – which, if treated, alleviates the other symptoms. However, many patients have no mental illness.

We know that medically unexplained physical symptoms are caused by a combination of physical and psychological factors. A person may be more likely to develop such symptoms as a result of their genes, or because of personal or family experiences of illness or adversity, especially in childhood. A variety of factors can trigger the actual onset of symptoms; for example, physical illness or injury, stressful life events, long-term difficulties, depression or anxiety.

Although we do not understand the entire story of why these symptoms occur in the first place, we do know some of the mechanisms that keep them going and can even make them worse.

Symptom focusing

If you had a toothache and people asked you every five minutes 'How's your tooth?' you would eventually tell them to stop asking, as all they were doing was reminding you of it. This is true of any bodily sensation; the more you focus on it the more intense it becomes. On the other hand, distraction – 'taking your mind off it' – is a common and helpful strategy that many of us employ when we are feeling unpleasant sensations. However, it only works if you are not *too* worried about what the symptom might mean.

Symptom misinterpretation

Imagine you have a pain in your chest and you are half-convinced it is a sign of a heart attack. You focus on it more and it becomes more intense. You become fully convinced and understandably anxious. The anxiety leads to *physiological arousal*, the so called 'fight or flight' reaction in which adrenaline pumps around your body, your chest muscles tighten, you sweat and tremble, your breathing is more shallow and rapid and you become light-headed. All of these symptoms are taken as proof of the impending catastrophe so you become even more anxious.

This combination of symptom focusing, symptom misinterpretation and physiological arousal can very easily make a symptomatic mountain out of a molehill. Although this is an extreme example, a more subtle interplay of these factors seems to be at work in many medically unexplained conditions. In chronic pain, preoccupation with and worry about the pain often only serve to amplify it. In irritable bowel syndrome, anxiety about diarrhoea leads to physiological arousal, which can cause more gut-churning and increase the chance of diarrhoea. In non-epileptic seizures, physical stress and tension can trigger a fit, and has often been brought on by worry about having one.

Avoidance

It is common knowledge that the more one avoids a problem or difficult situation, the worse it can become. A similar mechanism can be seen at work in medically unexplained disorders. For example, if someone with non-epileptic seizures is particularly worried about having a fit in a supermarket, they will tend to avoid going there. The more they avoid it, the more they confirm to themselves that it is a place to fear; if they *have* to go there, they go loaded with tension and anxiety, which makes the fit more likely, and so they will avoid the supermarket even more in future.

Similar mechanisms seem to be at work in chronic pain and chronic fatigue syndrome. Naturally if an activity is painful or exhausting we tend to avoid it. However, the more we get out of the habit of performing an activity – for example, walking to the local shop – the more painful and exhausting it will be the next time we do it. So we avoid it all the more. Slowly our threshold for pain and exhaustion becomes lower and lower, until walking to the front door can be difficult.

Reassurance seeking

This is perhaps the most subtle trap of medically unexplained symptoms, and it is particularly marked in hypochondriasis. If we fear that a headache is a symptom of a brain tumour, it is natural to feel anxious. Often, to reduce that anxiety, we will seek reassurance from others that it is not a brain tumour. This provides some momentary relief, until we feel the twinge again, and the anxiety is rekindled. Again we ask for reassurance, and so on.

Effectively, reassurance is a bottomless pit; the more one asks for it, the more one needs. Although it takes away anxiety *in the short term*, in the long term it is convincing us that *there is a problem we need reassurance about*. In many ways it is like an addiction; although having a cigarette relieves the present craving for nicotine, the very act of smoking keeps the craving alive. Thus many people with hypochondriasis will seek reassurance from their family, friends, colleagues and professionals in ever increasing 'doses', achieving immediate but temporary relief. However, at the same time their underlying anxiety is increasing.

How do we treat them?

Many people, especially if seen soon after the onset of symptoms, can be treated by their GP. Those with long-standing symptoms or disability will probably need to be referred for specialist outpatient treatment, and the most severely disabled may require inpatient management. Before beginning any treatment, it is important that a person receives a detailed medical and psychiatric assessment, in order to exclude previously unrecognised disorders. If severe depression is present it is generally helpful to treat it first, before addressing the rest of the problems. If there is a co-existing physical disease, the therapist needs to be familiar with the illness and its management.

Effective management of medically unexplained physical symptoms depends on developing a therapeutic relationship between the patient and their therapist. The patient must feel that the therapist believes in their condition and takes it seriously. It is important for the therapist to give the patient a valid explanation for their symptoms. Often pointing out the place of some of the mechanisms described above, such as symptom focusing, can help.

The therapist will generally call a halt to further investigations or referrals (unless indicated by a marked change in symptoms) to break the vicious circle of preoccupation and reassurance. Regular contact with the therapist is important in order to contain the patient's anxiety, and to monitor progress. General advice about life style, diet, exercise and stress management can all be helpful.

Graded increases in activity and exercise are important for many people with medically unexplained physical symptoms, particularly fatigue and pain. This helps gradually to break the cycle of avoidance described above. One kind of reassurance *is* important here: patients should be told that gradually increasing activity, although painful, *is not harmful*. Indeed, quite the reverse. For other patients, gradually re-entering situations that they have been avoiding due to anxiety will eventually remove the fear these situations currently evoke.

Relaxation techniques can be used to manage sleep difficulties, pain and muscle tension. Antidepressant medication can be helpful, not only in treating co-existing depression or anxiety, but in improving symptoms such as pain and fatigue in non-depressed patients.

'Reattribution' is a technique for overcoming misinterpretation of medically unexplained physical symptoms. Designed for use by GPs, this is a method of helping people to make the link between their physical symptoms and the psychological and social stresses that can trigger or amplify them. More recently, reattribution has been combined with teaching patients problem-solving techniques, in order to help them cope with the stresses that trigger their symptoms.

Increasingly, cognitive behavioural therapy (CBT) has been shown to be effective in the management of medically unexplained physical symptoms. CBT is generally given as an individual therapy over 5 to 20 sessions. The main focus of treatment is to identify and modify the factors contributing to symptoms, chiefly those already mentioned. The aim is to help people manage their symptoms so that they have less impact on their lives.

How do they affect families and friends?

Medically unexplained physical symptoms can be devastating for sufferers, their families and friends. Many people find their lives turned upside down by the physical and emotional impact of their illness. Everyday activities are often restricted and family life impaired. Some people are unable to work, and become dependent on disability benefits.

Having a 'medically unexplained disorder' can be extremely frustrating. If one has a 'definite' illness – a broken arm, a heart condition or epilepsy – there is generally a clear medical understanding of what this means, and how it should be managed. People with physical symptoms but no clear physical cause are often not believed or written off as neurotic or malingering. Frequently, little information is available about how to manage the condition. As a result, those closest to the sufferer often get caught up in the anxiety and confusion that their relative feels. This can lead to many mixed emotions: guilt about not being able to help; helplessness at the spectacle of another's suffering; confusion; even anger that someone who has 'nothing really wrong with them' appears so disabled.

These conditions can be particularly difficult to manage when it is one's child who is suffering. Lack of a clear diagnosis and management plan can leave parents feeling frustrated and anxious about what to do for the best. Naturally they will become more and more protective of the child, often encouraging them to avoid activities that leave them obviously in pain; or frequently asking about the symptoms that the child is suffering.

What can families and friends do to help?

The first step is to get involved with your relative or friend's care. Go along with them to the doctor or the specialist and get a clear idea of the management plan, and sort out what you can do to help. This is particularly important with the kind of strategies we have described, as they are often the exact opposite of what we instinctively feel is right, so both you and your relative should have a clear idea of why you are doing what you are doing. Here are a few examples.

Overcoming avoidance

It is common for those around a sufferer to take up some of the tasks they are finding difficult, such as shopping, cooking, housework, and so on. In treatment, your relative may be asked gradually to take some of these activities up again. It can be difficult to watch if someone is struggling, and our natural inclination is to 'take over'. This is why it is extremely important to agree with your relative in advance exactly what they will work on (for example, walking to the local shop every day for a fortnight) and to be reassured yourself that although this is difficult, it is not doing them any harm. Instead of 'taking over', it is more helpful if carers offer to do some of the tasks *with* their relative at first, just to get them started.

Stopping reassurance and symptom focusing

Asking your relative how they are feeling is natural and understandable, particularly when there is nothing else you feel you can do. But if it is done too often, it can be making matters worse, by focusing everyone's attention on the problems. It is often better to stop asking, or to limit questions to once a day. Again it is very important that you and your relative are clear that this strategy is used not because you do not care, but in order to reduce the impact of the symptoms on both your lives.

Reassurance seeking can be even more difficult to break, because our natural impulse is to alleviate anxiety in those we know and love. It is recommended that you discuss this with your relative or friend's therapist. At first, stopping reassurance can be anxiety-provoking for you both. Requests for reassurance may get worse before they get better. This can be very difficult to manage, and it is often best initially to 'contain it' to an agreed amount, say asking twice a day. You must both be clear that the long-term effect of stopping reassurance will be a *reduction* in anxiety.

Tips for carers

- Get involved with your relative or friend's care, but do not 'take over'.

- Show your relative that you accept that their symptoms are real and distressing.

- Remind your relative that hurt does not mean harm (symptoms may be unpleasant and painful, but this does not mean that they are doing any damage).

- Avoid focusing on symptoms too much.

- Encourage your relative to resume normal activities gradually.

- Give praise and encouragement for achievements made.

What is the outlook?

Untreated, these problems can persist for years, and often become entrenched and disabling. However, if properly managed, the outlook is very good. It is misleading to talk about a 'cure', as some people will continue to experience physical symptoms in certain circumstances. However, most people can generally expect to see a significant improvement in the impact of symptoms on their daily life, in the intensity and frequency of symptoms and in the distress and anxiety caused by them. We know that patients respond well to the treatment options outlined above, delivered within a framework of good clinical care and a pragmatic approach to dealing with specific problems.

CHAPTER 8

Mental Health Problems alongside Physical Illness

Andrew Hodgkiss

Francis and Jeanette have been married for eight years. Francis is HIV positive and since he developed AIDS five years ago, Jeanette has been his full-time carer. Three years ago he had his first manic episode and was diagnosed with bipolar affective disorder.

'I usually get up around 7am and try to get myself ready before Francis needs anything. I don't get much sleep because he wakes up a lot. When he's mentally ill he refuses to wash and it can take two hours of discussion to get him to take a shower. When he's too physically ill to have a shower I wash him. I give him breakfast but, like with a kid, I have to find ways of getting him to eat. Then he sleeps which is especially important when he's manic. When he's asleep I cook his lunch. It's helpful to distract him from thinking about being ill so in the afternoon we go to the park and feed the ducks, or we visit some friends if he's up to it – we have a lot of fun.

Francis was in denial for so many years about the HIV but because he nearly died in 1995, he saw death face-to-face and it changed his life completely. He admitted to himself he was HIV positive. Because he had been so ill he didn't look the same physically and he was really depressed and crying every day – it was like living with a stranger – but that passed and now he really appreciates every day he lives. He's a very joyful person.

The first time Francis was mentally ill it was frightening. I didn't know what manic depression was and for two or three months he was talking rubbish but I thought it was me who was going mad. Then one night he locked me in the flat, beat me up, and threatened me with a knife. I was so scared. God heard my prayer and someone called the police. Even though now I can recognise the signs and know what to do when he's becoming manic, I'm still scared. I take my marriage vows very seriously but I've told him that he must continue taking his medicine because if it happens again I may leave because I'd fear for my life.

My husband's low immune system and the infections he gets make him more vulnerable to the mental illness and *vice versa*. When he was well for a while, he started to do too much, which triggered the manic depression and when he's manic he doesn't get any rest, which can make him worse physically.

I had to give up work when Francis developed AIDS, because when he's ill it is a 24-hour job. People don't always understand that. I rely on the government for everything, but I'd really like to go back to work – it would probably be more relaxing. Money is a real problem and food is the priority because Francis needs to eat well which costs a lot. If I go out by myself I feel guilty for Francis – I shouldn't but I can't help it – and I have to make special arrangements for a carer to come. Because Francis spends so much money when he is manic, we agreed that I should have legal control of the finances. I feel bad because it's his money as much as mine.

I think Francis sees me like a mother rather than a carer – it's not like a husband and wife relationship. As a wife you sometimes want to be looked after too, to be able to say "my husband will take care of that". I can't and that can be very frustrating. Some men try to take advantage of me and you are so vulnerable you have to be careful not to jump into the arms of strangers.

We are both Christians and I know that without my faith I would have left Francis by now. I wouldn't have been able to carry on mentally or physically. To care for somebody close to you you have to give so much, especially when it's someone destined to die according to the doctors. Our pastor visits my husband to chat and see how he is and sometimes I go on trips with the church and they take care of Francis.

We have a wonderful psychiatric nurse, but our GP has been dreadful. The psychiatric nurse had to plead with him to visit Francis when he was ill with manic depression and when he did come he was tactless and upset Francis hugely. The psychiatric nurse talks to both of us and gives us the opportunity to share things with him. He'll notice if Francis is not well and if he's having a manic episode I call him straight away if it's not the weekend. Although he doesn't actually look after Francis, he relieves the burden a lot.

At first I made the mistake of helping my husband with everything and he became so dependent on me that I couldn't even go around the corner to buy some milk because he would panic and cry. In the end I had a breakdown and had to take a week's holiday, which my mother paid for. With no sleep and no help I was going mad. After that I got a carer from an agency for a few hours a week. Then I could at least go to the hairdressers. If you don't take time for yourself, you start to hate yourself. It's good to be loving and compassionate, but it isn't love to forget about yourself. Carers need to think of themselves as well as the person they're looking after. Also, find someone you can talk to because if you keep everything inside it's a pretty lonely world.'

What are these disorders?

Many different sorts of mental health problems occur in people with physical illness. Psychological distress often depends on the stage of the physical disease or illness. After learning their diagnosis a person may feel numb as they adjust to the bad news, and also uncertain about the future. Over the following months people may have feelings of denial, anxiety, despair and rage. These may disrupt everyday life and be called an 'adjustment disorder'. If a change in mood persists for weeks at a time the doctor may make a diagnosis of an anxiety disorder or depressive illness.

As the physical illness develops, this in itself may cause mental health problems. For example, in cancer if this has spread to involve the brain, it may lead to a person being confused, unsure of their whereabouts and drifting in and out of full alertness. Remember that this may happen in someone who never had any psychological problems until they developed cancer. Another scenario is when a person develops post-traumatic stress disorder after experiencing a life-threatening incident such as a vehicle accident, violent crime or industrial injury. As HIV illness develops into AIDS, complications can include dementia and confusion.

How common are these disorders?

Mental health problems are more common in people with a physical illness than among the physically healthy. If you walked into any general hospital in the UK today you would find many people with a mental illness alongside their medical and surgical problems.

- One in 10 of all inpatients are confused, either in the short term, when this is known as 'delirium', or in the long term, when this is known as 'dementia'. The elderly are particularly prone to both delirium and dementia.

- One in 14 of all medical outpatients suffer from depression.

- In one in 10 admissions to a general hospital for a physical illness, alcohol misuse is the underlying cause.

What are the causes?

People who have enjoyed excellent mental health all their life can develop a mental illness alongside their physical illness for many different reasons. Sometimes just being told a dreaded diagnosis, such as cancer or multiple sclerosis, can provoke psychological distress sufficient to need professional help. Or the physical disease may directly cause a mental illness; for example, a confusional state may develop after a stroke. Any painful, long-term medical condition increases the risk of depressed mood. Even treatment for a physical illness can lead to a mental illness. For example, intensive care units and isolation rooms are notorious for provoking abnormal suspicions and paranoid misunderstandings in those with previously excellent mental health. Or another example, steroid treatment can have a big effect on someone's mood.

If your relative has previously suffered a mental illness then he or she may be at risk of a further bout of that same illness when a physical illness strikes. If other members of the family have had a mental health problem this too can increase your relative's risk of developing a mental illness alongside the physical illness. The scale of these risks varies from condition to condition so it is worth asking for specific information.

How do we treat these disorders?

All the mental illnesses mentioned above are common among both inpatients and outpatients in a general hospital. However, awareness of them among health professionals, and of the services available to treat them, vary from hospital to hospital.

Some large teaching hospitals and cancer centres have 'liaison psychiatry' teams, so called because they liaise or act as a bridge between professionals managing the physical illness and mental health services. Other general hospitals can only direct patients to the local community mental health service. These community teams have responsibility for people with enduring mental health problems, such as schizophrenia, who live in the locality; they may not have the resources to offer appropriate psychological support to, say, an outpatient with cancer.

A wide range of treatments may be relevant to people with a physical illness who also have a mental health problem.

First-rate information and support from the general hospital unit itself can prevent much unnecessary worry and distress. This includes the way bad news is broken and all medical students are now trained in this.

Those struggling with an adjustment disorder may benefit from sessions with a trained counsellor who is not medically qualified but has special experience of a particular physical condition. For example, they may have been working with patients in a renal transplant centre for several years. They might see the patients individually or lead a support group. Meeting others with the same physical problems, who have therefore worked through similar psychological challenges, can be very valuable.

When this level of support seems insufficient and a person is suffering from a more severe depressive illness or disabling panic attacks then specialist mental health professionals need to be involved. Psychological or 'talking' treatments include a form of brief psychotherapy called 'cognitive behavioural therapy'. Over a series of perhaps 8 to 12 weekly sessions the therapist, usually a clinical psychologist, will help someone identify unhelpful thoughts and behaviour patterns and look at alternative ways of dealing with a problem. A psychiatrist may also suggest having medication either instead of or in addition to a talking treatment.

Treatment in the wider sense may include:

- use of a single room on a general ward for a person who is confused
- a psychiatric nurse being present 24 hours for a person who is suicidal or psychotic on a general ward
- application of the Mental Health Act (1983) to detain and treat someone on a general ward.

How do they affect families and friends?

Finding your way through the system

The presence of a mental health problem alongside a physical illness complicates an already challenging situation for patients and carers. There are more issues to find out about, more professionals to relate to, more treatments being offered, maybe a longer hospital stay or one more set of outpatient appointments to fit in. The stigma of having a mental health problem is added to the suffering associated with the physical condition. There may be two different NHS trusts involved in the care of the patient – one providing the physical care, and the other the mental health care.

Impact on your relationship

Seeing a person you care about suffer the double burden of a mental and physical illness can be very hard. There may be particular difficulties with a partner, with a sort of incompatibility between caring for someone who is ill (which can be a bit like parenting) and caring about them as a partner or lover. Over time this can lead to tensions in even the best relationships. The diagnosis and treatment of a physical disease often disrupt sexual relationships. When depression is added to this most couples find sexual relations stop altogether, often for many months. And some relationships do not survive without the closeness of sexual activity to sustain them. In these circumstances it is worth seeking out professional help. People with a long-term medical condition together with a mental health problem can be helped towards an improved quality of life, and that includes a sex life.

What can families and friends do to help?

The first thing you can do is to bring the change in mood, the abnormal beliefs, or confusion to the attention of the doctor if they have not noticed any of these things. You may think this is ridiculous advice since you might expect the doctor to detect any deterioration in mental health, but we know that GPs and hospital doctors often 'miss' the appearance of symptoms of mental illness in patients. They are even more likely to do so in a person with a physical illness because their concentration will be focused on managing that.

You can help by giving a clear account of your relative's mental health before the physical illness started, or before this relapse of their long-term medical condition, and exactly what you have noticed recently. It is helpful to be as frank as possible about your relative's personality, intellectual abilities and day-to-day habits before they fell ill. Doctors call this kind of background information from a carer an 'informant history'.

Here are a few hints about how to behave when you are with a person who is panicky, depressed or confused.

Panicky. Being with an anxious or panicky person can be hard work. They may not want you to leave them, even for a moment. They may be so busy trying not to be sick with fear that they can hardly speak. Your approach here should be as calm as possible. Acknowledge that your relative is feeling dreadful but offer support by reminding them that this is a *feeling* and that it will pass. Panic is extremely unpleasant but completely harmless. If your relative has had panic attacks before, remind them that they passed with time. A person experiencing panic may be preoccupied with terrible fears of sudden death, an epileptic fit, wetting themselves, a heart attack or collapse. Their body will feel odd due to dizziness, breathlessness, a racing pulse, diarrhoea and tingling. Explain to your relative that these bodily changes are part of the panic.

Depressed. People who are depressed can be hard to spend time with for a number of reasons. They tend not to say much or do much. They may be irritable and rejecting of company. It can be difficult to be with their despair especially when it continues day after day. The thing to remember is that they are not choosing to behave like this. The slowness, the silence, the irritability are all part of the illness and your relative cannot overcome them by any effort of will on their part. The worst thing to say to your relative in this situation is to 'snap out of it', or 'pull yourself together, we all get low'. Your relative will be acutely aware that they cannot overcome how they feel by an effort of will and this is very scary for them. This helplessness in the face of persistent low mood can drive a person who is depressed to thoughts of suicide.

It is also best to avoid repeatedly asking your relative how they are feeling. They have probably felt varying shades of being low for weeks so there is nothing new to report. Instead try gentle distraction and diversion or agree a very small manageable target for each half-day. For example, going to the shops each morning may give a focus and purpose to that part of the day and is a reason for bothering to get up and dressed.

Depression disrupts concentration and time passes painfully slowly for someone who is depressed. Filling a day when you can't concentrate on anything diverting is a real problem. Simply being with your relative is valuable providing that no criticism is voiced.

The final thing to remember is that depressive illness distorts a person's judgement so everything seems pointless and utterly hopeless. Do not get drawn in to these despairing lines of thought. You cannot jolly your relative out of them. Remind them that their judgement is being affected by the depression, but that the illness will pass. If you can bring yourself to discuss openly any suicidal thinking with your relative this can be a relief for them and does not increase the risk of suicide. However, always let professionals know if someone is suicidal so that this can be managed as carefully as possible.

Confused. The confused person feels lost. They may not be clear where they are or what time or date it is. Even if you gently tell them they will probably have forgotten in a matter of minutes and so will ask you again. This can be frightening for the confused person or they may seem oblivious to their problem. They may think they are at home or at work when they are actually in hospital. They may think the nurses are their relatives or colleagues or that the nurses are trying to harm them. The golden rule for being with a person who is confused is to accept and tolerate their confusion. Do not directly challenge them or repeatedly contradict them. If they are getting worked up and wanting to leave, distraction is the best approach. Simply move on to a new topic. Confused people sometimes drift in and out of a light sleep in the daytime and are more awake and active at night.

Tips for carers

- Find out as much as you can about the nature of the physical and mental conditions your relative faces and share this with them in terms they can understand.

- Your relative or friend may not have the energy to get information leaflets or contact organisations or local groups themselves so your help may be very important.

- You can be an advocate for your relative, insisting on timely senior opinions, asking questions about options, and bringing unwanted side effects of treatment to the attention of health professionals.

What is the outlook?

The outlook for the mental health problems discussed here varies enormously. Adjustment disorders; for example, will usually settle with time without any professional help although counselling may speed up the recovery. Depression and anxiety may wax and wane with the progress of a long-term medical condition. In severe depression, especially in later life, there is a risk of premature death by suicide, unless prompt effective psychiatric treatment is arranged. Delirium can also indicate a life-threatening problem and needs expert medical and nursing management to help ensure a good recovery.

CHAPTER 9

Eating Disorders

Gill Todd, Wendy Whitaker and Kay Gavan

Elizabeth Reeves had anorexia nervosa at secondary school and became severely ill when she left home to go to college. On medical grounds she was advised to return home where her mother looked after her. Since attending a specialist eating disorders unit Elizabeth has recovered and is now a healthy weight. Mr and Mrs Reeves talk about their daughter's illness and how it affected them.

Mrs Reeves: When Elizabeth came home from college she shut out everyone except me. Her father was a 'nuisance' because he needed my time – it's a very selfish illness.

Mr Reeves: That in turn created a very intense relationship between Elizabeth and my wife. It's very difficult for someone else to share some of that burden. With the best will in the world I certainly tried but my daughter made it impossible.

Mrs Reeves: On a typical day I was woken up at 2am by the noise of my daughter dusting, brushing the dog, going for walks or sweeping outside. The dusting and so on only started after she became very ill, but she was always a perfectionist. You knew that she would do everything the same each morning. From the time I got out of bed I knew that she was just going to go on and on. It wasn't just nagging – she wanted reassurance the whole time. If you did something that didn't go along with her timing, then you were in trouble. We had to go for a four-mile walk, then we'd have lunch and then out for a walk again. We'd come home and have our meal on the dot of five. Originally we clashed because I thought it was quite unnecessary to do all these things so often and always at the same time, but then we were advised to avoid confrontation and it did become easier just to go with the flow.

I had to eat with her because then I could see what she was eating but I didn't dare say anything about it. At one stage she completely took over the cooking for everyone which was hard because I'm a mum and a housewife and that was my role. It sounds feeble as if I was letting her get away with it but it really was the only way of getting through the day. I only regained my place when she went into hospital.

I do charity work one afternoon a week and I used to make myself go because that was my outlet. You were always afraid of what you'd come home to but you have to get away sometimes. Occasionally, when things were really bad I'd just go to a friend's and bawl. It was so intense that it took my whole life away from me for years.

Mr Reeves: It's a dreadful thing to say but we got to one time when we almost wished it would stop. She'd lost the will to live and at that point, to us, there was no hope. Now she's turned the corner and can have some sort of quality of life, to think we ever thought such things is terrible. You had to be there during those last days before she went into the specialist unit to be able to understand that.

Mrs Reeves: With our friends, they divided into two sets: one group I could talk to and let off steam, although they couldn't fully understand. But with another group, the majority, it was 'Well, Elizabeth will just have to shake herself out of it'. There were only two who were really behind the family who weren't ashamed to be seen with us. I must admit it was a dreadful sight, particularly when I was pushing her around in a wheelchair. We became very aware of everyone looking but we had to carry on as if life was normal.

Mr Reeves: But then we'd have to say that the medical profession weren't that helpful either until we got involved in the specialist unit. The local facilities and support services weren't very good or supportive and you felt pretty lonely. The only time they seemed to take it seriously was when Elizabeth was days from dying. She got to the point when she was literally skin and bones and virtually lifeless. That was when she got referred to the specialist unit and they were great.

Most of all, we wanted somebody in whom Elizabeth could put her trust, and we felt that Pat, her social worker, proved to be that lady. You always felt that when times were tough, if anything went wrong, Pat was going to save us. She would always listen. I think it was when the relationships between Elizabeth and Pat and us and Pat developed that things started to change. We'll never forget her for what she did for us.

Mrs Reeves: People in the same situation need to be more demanding than I was with the medical profession. I went along with what they were doing and saying and I think in my heart of hearts I knew that we were just wasting time. Be like a terrier at someone's ankle and get the proper care – the specialist unit.

What are eating disorders?

There are three broad types of eating disorders:

- anorexia nervosa
- bulimia nervosa
- binge eating disorders.

Contrary to popular belief they are not 'slimmers' diseases', but sometimes they can be triggered by dieting as this distorts the body's normal eating behaviour. They are often long-term, severe mental and physical illnesses which affect both the individual and their family and friends. The distinction between the three illnesses is not always clearcut and people may experience the different disorders at different times. However, there are differences in the causes, course and response to treatment of the different illnesses.

Anorexia nervosa

The essential features of anorexia nervosa are:

- Refusal to maintain a minimal normal weight (see Figure 9.1). Someone suffering from an eating disorder during childhood may not gain their expected weight while they are growing and this will affect their height.
- Deliberate weight loss with avoidance of fattening foods. Sufferers are often preoccupied with food and can prepare elaborate meals for other people. In addition they may exercise excessively, vomit and use laxatives.
- Distortions and misconceptions about weight and body size; for example, sufferers believe that at five stone they are fat, and they have an intense fear of fatness or gaining weight.
- Loss of menstrual periods, or failure to start periods (or in males the failure to develop physically into adulthood). This can lead to the

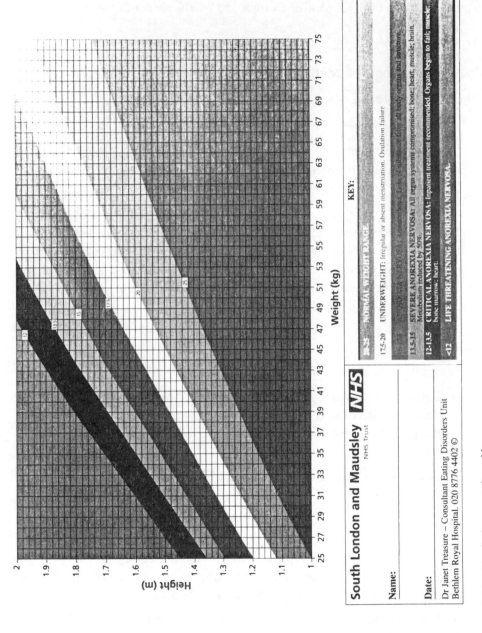

Figure 9.1 Maudsley body-mass index table

long-term risk of suffering from osteoporosis, stunted growth and infertility in adulthood, but puberty is often completed normally if a person reaches their healthy weight.

People with anorexia tend to have very low self-esteem and a lack of confidence. They may also be 'perfectionists' which makes them very effective at losing weight. Anorexia nervosa has one of the highest death rates of all mental illnesses due either to the effects of starvation – for example, through heart failure – or through suicide.

Bulimia nervosa

People with bulimia usually maintain a near-normal body weight, but their sense of themselves is unduly influenced by body shape and weight. As a way of dealing with what they perceive are unacceptable feelings such as insecurity, vulnerability, anger or sadness, sufferers binge on a large amount of food (often fatty or 'bad' foods such as sweets and biscuits). They have a preoccupation with and craving for food and also feel unable to control their eating during these binges.

After a binge a person has feelings of self-disgust and a fear of weight gain and so may take extreme action to try and rid their body of food by vomiting, misusing laxatives, fasting or excessive exercise.

As bulimia is more easily kept a secret than anorexia, the family and friends are often unaware of the problem. Devious, deceptive behaviour and mood swings are common. Individuals may develop other addictive behaviours; for example, alcohol dependence. If they feel repulsed by their behaviour and fear rejection by others, social isolation or an inability to form close, trusting relationships may follow.

The repeated vomiting causes distressing physical effects: eroded enamel on the teeth, stomach pains, dehydration, poor skin condition and lethargy. Disturbances of the body chemistry can affect body mechanisms, such as control of the heartbeat. People with bulimia often know the harm they are causing themselves and want to change but at the same time feel powerless to do so due to their fear of weight gain.

Binge eating disorder

Like bulimia, binge eating disorder is characterised by frequent, out-of-control eating either as binges, constant picking, comfort eating or just having larger portions than needed. Unlike bulimia, sufferers do not vomit or purge afterwards, although they may often attempt to diet – which inevitably fails. As a result they are usually above a healthy weight and are often overweight or obese (BMI>30). Like people with bulimia they have difficulties with poor self-esteem, lack of confidence and they may be out of touch with their own emotional needs. Obesity has very real and damaging effects on physical health, personal relationships and career prospects.

How common are they?

Anorexia nervosa is most common in adolescent girls, while bulimia nervosa starts most commonly in young women. Female sufferers outnumber male sufferers by about ten to one. Some groups are at a higher risk of developing anorexia, in particular ballet students and jockeys, both of whom need to maintain their weight within certain limits.

What are the causes?

There is no one cause which can be linked to developing an eating disorder. In terms of normal body weight, genes (which we inherit from our parents) play a part, and so do cultural and family patterns of eating.

Current research suggests a person's genes may predispose them to the disorder, with traumatic events sometimes being the trigger. Factors maintaining the illness include having obsessive compulsive disorder, being a perfectionist and difficult family relationships.

How do we treat eating disorders?

Anorexia nervosa

The main factors which any treatment programme would consider include:

- age at which the illness started, especially in relation to puberty
- current age
- length of time the person has been ill
- what treatments have been tried and their effect
- how much the sufferer's weight has fallen
- how quickly weight has been lost
- whether other family members suffer from eating problems.

Along with weight restriction some people have problems related to obsessive compulsive disorder, panic attacks, phobias, anxiety, or their physical health (associated with prolonged starvation). Someone affected by one of these other conditions may feel that even if they recover from anorexia, they will never be fully well and this can affect their motivation to improve, so making their eating disorder more difficult to treat.

Most people can be helped as outpatients and they are only admitted to hospital if their weight falls to a dangerously low level. In a very few cases compulsory treatment under the Mental Health Act (1983) is necessary if there is immediate risk to a patient's life. As anorexia can have such damaging physical effects on the sufferer all treatments must initially focus on weight gain as the main goal.

Many patients find this emphasis too constricting and so treatment should always include (along with a feeding programme):

- psychological treatments to find out how ready the person is to change and help them move along in thinking about what stops and what helps change; this is termed 'motivational enhancement therapy'

- cognitive behavioural therapy for help with social difficulties

- education with information about the illness; consideration about schooling for younger sufferers

- dietary information and practice at buying, preparing and eating regular meals

- family work in which carers are able to express their concerns about being with the sufferer and gain help with the day-to-day difficulties of living with the disorder

- medical investigations into bone density, brain function and hormonal status as well as checks on body functioning.

Depression can be a side effect of starvation or may be more long-term and deep-rooted, perhaps in unresolved grieving or learned sadness – growing up in an enviroment where there is already depression or a very negative view of the world. This can be treated with antidepressant drugs or psychotherapy. Antidepressants alone tend not to work until a person has reached a reasonable body weight and their hormone system is beginning to function.

Among the team of professionals treating someone with anorexia, an in-depth knowledge of eating disorders is very important and matters more than whether, for example, they specialise in the treatment of children and adolescents or adults. The involvement of different professionals – a nurse, doctor, social worker, occupational therapist, psychologist and dietician – is helpful in addressing the variety of problems.

There is debate about whether inpatient treatment is more effective than outpatient treatment. What we do know is that, for young people under 18 who have been ill for a short time, outpatient family work is more effective than inpatient treatment. So long as weight gain is happening and medical tests are showing weekly improvements then outpatient treatment can continue. However, severely underweight people will find it very difficult to persuade a professional to treat them as an outpatient because of the danger of sudden death. We think that people with an eating disorder do best if they are treated separately from people with other forms of mental illness.

We still do not know how long treatment should last, how much weight gain should be achieved before an inpatient is discharged and what type and how much therapy is necessary for which people.

Bulimia nervosa and binge eating disorder

We know more about the treatment of bulimia than binge eating disorders. Treatment is usually as an outpatient on a one-to-one basis with a therapist trained in brief psychotherapy. Group therapy can also be helpful. The therapy could be 'cognitive behavioural therapy', 'cognitive analytic therapy', 'interpersonal therapy', 'motivational enhancement therapy' or a combination of these, although each therapy has specific aims and requires the therapist to undergo specialist training. Outpatient as opposed to inpatient treatment is preferable because it helps the patient stay in their own surroundings and gives the therapist 'real-life' information about the problem. Self-help manuals without any therapist involvement may also be useful. Of course, success does depend on a person reading the manual and completing the homework.

Most drug treatment involves antidepressant drugs. These have a more modest effect than brief psychotherapy and generally drugs are less acceptable to sufferers than 'talking' therapy. However, if a talking therapy is not working well in the first month, taking an antidepressant as well can help.

How do eating disorders affect families and friends?

When someone is diagnosed as having an eating disorder, their family may experience difficulties in accepting the diagnosis. The sufferer often rejects and denies the diagnosis, saying they are well. On the other hand carers may feel that professionals do not take their views seriously if they suspect weight loss is due to an eating disorder.

It is common for the family to blame themselves for the eating disorder, and this can be heightened by a fear of being judged to be bad parents by professionals and by the wider community. Sometimes families keep the illness secret from other relatives for fear of criticism. They may feel labelled as 'the anorexic family' as if they have lost any other identity.

As a carer you may be faced with disturbing behaviours and this is often made worse by the sufferer's refusal to acknowledge that there is a problem. Families can become isolated from their community and friends because of the stigma attached to the illness, and also isolated from their child who may refuse to acknowledge being ill. Food and meal times become a battleground as carers experience difficulty in finding a balance between discipline and support, when the damage that the sufferer is doing to their health is foremost in their minds.

Parents may feel they have lost their child to the illness, and in their powerlessness believe that they have failed their child in some way. Carers often report feelings of worthlessness and rejection and use phrases such as being 'hopeless and helpless', 'on edge all the time', or 'walking on eggshells'. A particularly strong image is of being in a dark tunnel with no end in sight. Parents may go through the whole spectrum of emotions – anger, guilt, despair, fear – in a way that can lead to a sense of feeling shell-shocked or even besieged. There may also be problems with other members of the family feeling angry at the effect the illness is having on all of them. Siblings may feel neglected and this can divide loyalties within the family.

What can families and friends do to help?

If you suspect a person is suffering from an eating disorder, contact your GP for a medical assessment to rule out other medical conditions. If the GP is unfamiliar with eating disorders you may request a referral to a psychiatrist who will be able to assess the condition and, if necessary, refer your relative or friend to a specialist eating disorders unit. The Eating Disorders Association is an excellent resource for families and sufferers. They provide telephone helplines, a support network and self-help groups throughout the country. Making contact with others experiencing similar problems can be a big help. Often by the time a sufferer admits they have a problem the illness will have had a serious effect on their physical and psychological health, as well as affecting their social life, education or career. It is therefore worth considering how you can help at an early stage.

The confusion caused by eating disorders can make living with such an illness extremely difficult. The sufferer's behaviour may appear to be deliberately selfish and provocative but it is important to remember that anorexia is an expression of distress and unhappiness and not something that the sufferer can 'just snap out of'. Try to avoid confrontational attitudes and attempt to maintain a non-judgemental stance. The anxiety and sadness caused by anorexia often causes communication problems within families. In spite of the stress caused by such feelings it is important that you listen to your relative's point of view. Research findings suggest that the illness is not the fault of the family, but once anorexia has developed, the family and friends can be a great support.

When a child suffers from anorexia nervosa, it is important to provide a framework of rules for the family. Make sure that you and your partner are in agreement with any rules which are put in place and then set aside a time away from meal times to review these ground rules on a regular basis. Basic rules could be as follows (adapt these rules if the sufferer is a partner or friend):

- Every family needs to set limits for unacceptable behaviour.
- Share responsibility for your child equally.
- Try to ensure that your child is moving towards independence.
- Create an environment where only one person speaks at a time.
- Make sure everyone understands what is being said.
- Respect the views of others, even if you disagree with them.
- Remember you are a parent and not a best friend.
- You too can make mistakes and get things wrong – say so.

Tips for carers

- Given that sufferers are often sensitive, caring people, there may be a temptation to unburden oneself upon them; don't do this.
- Don't be hurt if your child or partner refuses to discuss their treatment with you. It is healthy for people to have some secrets, but try to avoid family secrets, for example previous marrages, half brothers or sisters, deceased siblings, suicide or devorce.

- Remember to continue with your own life and to give time to yourself, your partner and other children.

What is the outlook?

With anorexia, the earlier it started and the longer it continues without being successfully treated, the worse the outlook. Also the more weight lost, the greater the speed at which weight loss occurs and the longer the time the person has remained underweight may be indicators for a lower chance of recovery. In bulimia more severe bingeing and vomiting, a slower response to treatment and additional problems such as self-harm may lead to a worse outlook. In anorexia and bulimia there is some improvement in over a third of sufferers and another third make a good recovery. We know little about the outlook for binge eating disorder.

CHAPTER 10

Drinking Problems

E. Jane Marshall

Elsa has been married to Mark for 20 years and has had a long career in nursing. Elsa's husband has always been a heavy drinker, but his drinking has become much worse in the last decade. They have a teenage daughter.

'I didn't realise that Mark was a heavy drinker until several months after we were married. I was from a non-drinking background and going to pubs wasn't really part of our life together. We've always been very busy – I'm a bit of a workaholic – and I just didn't realise that he was secretly drinking.

Mark's health has never been that good but several years ago it got much worse. I had to take voluntary redundancy because he was so ill and drinking so heavily. I have to do everything around the house myself, all the organising and all the worrying. He can wire and plumb a house but the trouble is he never finishes anything and I can't depend on him to earn a living. It didn't seem a problem when my daughter was little because he was really wonderful at looking after her at home and I was working. I suppose I should have dealt with it then.

His being drunk has become more of a problem as my daughter has got older. She goes absolutely berserk over it and she gets very angry, particularly with me. She thinks that I should be able to solve the problem. Mark is actually a very good and loving father but he doesn't have insight into what his drinking does and the effect on her. I've always tried to be honest with her and said that he can't help it and that he's trying to get help for it and to be support-ive. I don't feel that I can tell her not to be angry because I think that she has a right to be. She would never say anything about it outside the family, and she can't bear me saying anything.

Although my daughter has lots of friends she doesn't bring them to the house in case her father is drunk and she does mind about that. I stopped entertaining at home several years ago for the same reason. Most of our friends don't know that there's a problem – they just think that we're too busy now.

All the useful medical care I've procured for my husband and myself has been through my own professional knowledge and contacts. I feel very angry that he didn't receive help a long time ago when the outcome might have been better. One useless locum psychiatrist just thought that I was a pushy wife and that Mark hadn't lived up to my expectations. At the outset I approached services very softly, even though I knew what the problems were. I have a good knowledge base and experience and they should have taken it seriously but they didn't at all.

It's paradoxical that my professional skills have been useful in getting help in the long run, but in terms of dealing with his alcohol problem and his depression they may even have had the opposite effect – I've accommodated his problems. It's not that I pretended it wasn't happening but I never forced him to go out to work and instead I did everything. I've become his mother rather than his wife and I don't want that. I get very frustrated with him. A few years ago I developed health problems including asthma and was off sick for nearly a year. Stress wasn't the cause of my illnesses but I think it undermined my ability to recover.

It was his drink driving that really brought things to a head. He would not accept that he had problems and I knew that if he killed someone he wouldn't be able to live with it – he'd kill himself. So when he came home one night I phoned the police and they arrested him for drink driving. He lost his licence for 18 months and agreed to speak to a specialist psychiatrist about the drinking.

We've got a wonderful daughter and in every other way my husband is very lovely. I am Catholic and we don't believe in divorce. We do love each other and it's very hard to think of deserting him. I have to think that things are going to be better, but there is so much pain and anxiety in living with such uncertainty...the horror of finding the person you love and respect lying semi-comatose covered in vomit; the humiliation of being a known health care professional working in this area; years of broken down untaxed vehicles outside the house until I pay someone to take them away and neighbours complaining about it; essential services being cut off and the embarrassing experience of trying to get them restored. Watching the disintegrating person unable to walk, eat, talk, day after day and week after week and listening to the self-deluding rubbish that is talked when supposedly sober...the perpetual heartache of *knowing*, no matter what I do, it's all to no avail and in the end I will still be blamed by my daughter, my husband's family and even some of my own family, for not having done the right thing, whatever that is.'

What is a drinking problem?

Alcohol consumption

Alcohol is our favourite drug. It is legally and universally available and gives great pleasure when consumed in moderate quantities. However, it also has significant chemical effects on the body and excessive consumption can give rise to a wide range of physical, psychological and social problems. Why do some people drink more than others? Why can some people get away with drinking vast quantities, while others who drink considerably less develop significant problems? What is meant by the term 'alcoholic'?

Sensible and at risk drinking

The risk of developing a drinking problem rises with the amount of alcohol consumed. It is therefore helpful to think in terms of sensible and at risk drinking. Sensible drinking is defined as 3–4 units per day for men and 2–3 units per day for women. (In the UK a unit is taken as half a pint of ordinary strength beer or cider; one glass of wine; one glass of fortified wine or sherry; one measure of spirits.) People who drink sensibly are unlikely to damage their health. Indeed, drinking at this level may reduce the chance of developing heart disease in men over 40 years and in post-menopausal women. Men drinking above 50 units per week and women drinking above 35 units per week are drinking in a harmful way and are likely to be experiencing problems as a result.

Individuals who are drinking in a harmful way should consider cutting down their alcohol consumption to sensible levels. It is a good idea to avoid drinking altogether on at least one day per week. This will reduce the risk of becoming dependent. A consultation with a person's GP, practice nurse, health visitor or even a local voluntary alcohol agency may prove helpful. Written information is available from Alcohol Concern (see Resources).

Alcohol dependence

The terms 'alcoholism' and 'alcoholic' are still used by the general public and Alcoholics Anonymous (AA). However, the term 'alcoholic' has pejorative connotations, and for some people it conjures up a picture of homeless men drinking in parks or lying in the gutter. This stereotype may prevent heavy drinkers looking for help. 'I'm not as far gone as that,' they say.

Some people come to a point where they find that they can no longer control their drinking as they once did. They 'cannot stop at one drink'. Once they start to drink they continue until they have 'drunk everyone else under the table'. Something at a very fundamental level has altered the way in which their body and brain handle alcohol. They no longer drink for enjoyment. They drink because they have to keep the level of alcohol in their blood 'topped up'. They have become physically dependent on alcohol.

The existence of alcohol dependence has been recognised for many years, and is described as follows.

NARROWED DRINKING PATTERN

This is when a drinker has lost the ability to vary their drinking. The person drinks in the same way every day, no matter whether it is a weekday or weekend, a working day or holiday. Someone who was the life and soul of the party may find themselves drinking in a solitary way at home, buying the same number of cans at the same off-licence at the same time each day. Some capacity for varying the routine still remains, but by and large the pattern becomes more rigid with the severity of dependence.

PRIORITISING DRINKING

The dependent drinker gives priority to maintaining their alcohol intake. This is more important than anything else including relationships, work, pride in their physical appearance, and their family or home life.

INCREASED TOLERANCE TO ALCOHOL

When someone drinks heavily over a long period of time their brain develops tolerance to alcohol. They can drink vast quantities without appearing to become intoxicated; that is, 'they hold their drink'. In the late stages of dependence this tolerance may be lost, in which case they can no longer handle alcohol to the same extent. The drinker usually cuts down their consumption at this stage.

WITHDRAWAL SYMPTOMS

Alcohol withdrawal symptoms usually creep up slowly, often presenting in the early stages as unexplained anxiety at lunchtime or in the late afternoon. These symptoms are linked with a fall in the level of alcohol in the blood. When the symptoms are fully fledged, the drinker experiences them on waking up every morning. Withdrawal symptoms may even wake the drinker in the middle of the night. The main alcohol withdrawal symptoms are nausea, tremor, sweating and mood swings. Other symptoms include sensitivity to sound, ringing in the ears, muscle cramps, disturbed sleep, hallucinations (seeing or hearing things which are not there) and seizures. The severity of alcohol withdrawal symptoms varies according to the severity of the dependence.

RELIEF OR AVOIDANCE OF WITHDRAWAL SYMPTOMS BY FURTHER DRINKING

Alcohol dependent individuals soon realise that a drink, or two, or three, can reduce or dispel their alcohol withdrawal symptoms. In the early stages a lunchtime or early evening drink may 'steady the nerves'. Later a person may need to drink first thing every morning, or in the middle of the night, often keeping a bottle by the bed for easy access. They are essentially trying to keep up the level of alcohol in their blood.

SUBJECTIVE AWARENESS OF COMPULSION TO DRINK

Drinkers often describe compulsive, intrusive, repetitive thoughts about alcohol that they try to resist or block in a matter not dissimilar to individuals with obsessive compulsive disorder (OCD) (see Chapter 5).

RETURNING TO DEPENDENT DRINKING AFTER ABSTINENCE

Alcohol dependent individuals who drink following a period of abstinence return to their previous level of dependence. This may take a couple of days, weeks or months. If they relapse, severely dependent drinkers usually take only a couple of days to return to their old patterns.

How common is alcohol dependence?

About 1.7 million men and 0.6 million women in the UK are drinking in a harmful way. One in 13 men and one in 50 women admit to some dependence on alcohol. Alcohol dependence may be less common in some ethnic minority communities, and more common among single and unemployed people. However, alcohol dependence is spread across the whole of society and is not confined to any one social group.

What causes drinking problems?

How much we drink is influenced by a complex interaction between a variety of factors: economic, dietary, social and cultural. Individuals vary enormously in the amounts they consume. Some drink nothing at all, some drink only on special occasions and others drink very heavily. There is no clear boundary between 'normal' drinkers and 'heavy' drinkers. We know that there is a hereditary component to drinking behaviour and drinking problems. The interaction between someone's genes and environmental factors determines whether or not that person goes on to develop a drinking problem.

How do we treat alcohol dependence?

For the majority of people with alcohol dependence, the common aim of treatment is long-term abstinence. The assessment procedure with the individual, their partner and family is the beginning of therapy as it has the potential to change the drinker's attitude, improve their commitment to changing their behaviour and clarify the goals to which they wish to work.

The *stages of change model* puts the drinker at the centre of making change happen. It includes five different stages: precontemplation, contemplation, determination, action and maintenance.

- *Precontemplation*: individuals are not considering a change in their drinking.
- *Contemplation*: individuals acknowledge a problem and are beginning to consider change.
- *Determination*: individuals are intending to take action and may have cut down on their alcohol intake.
- *Action*: individuals have started to make changes to their drinking behaviour.
- *Maintenance*: individuals seek to maintain the changes they have made in their drinking.

Much of the early stages of therapy will be concerned with helping patients to move from precontemplation to contemplation and further on to action and maintenance.

People who are dependent on alcohol are often unwilling to accept that they have a serious drinking problem. This can make it difficult for them to accept the need for treatment. Health professionals may approach this using a non-confrontational technique such as *motivational enhancement therapy*, gently nudging the drinker forward into accepting that there is a problem.

When the person is off alcohol, health professionals may use an approach called relapse prevention to help them understand the nature of their drinking problem, the cues and circumstances that trigger a craving for alcohol, and how to cope with these situations without drinking.

In the early days of abstinence, psychological problems such as anxiety, irritability, depression, jealousy, phobic symptoms and sleeping difficulties often emerge which make staying off alcohol all the harder. Sometimes in addition to the drinking people turn out to have a mental health problem such as depression or agoraphobia which also needs treatment. Recovering from such conditions can be central to tackling the alcohol problem successfully. Attending AA and staying in contact with local alcohol services can both help.

Cognitive behavioural therapy can be useful in developing social and assertiveness skills and learning how to problem solve. Couple and family therapy may be important. Medication (for example, disulfiram, acamprosate, naltrexone) helps some individuals to remain abstinent.

How does problem drinking affect families and friends?

Problem drinking has a profound effect on family life. It influences the way in which the problem drinker interacts with other members of the family and alters the family atmosphere and climate of trust. Many families remain together and 'make do' without experiencing the devastating family violence or financial problems that often accompany alcohol dependence in families. But the cost can be measured in terms of compromised lives. Two groups of relatives are particularly likely to be affected – partners and children.

Partners of men who are alcohol dependent

The wife or partner of a drinker learns to cope with his unpredictable nature by a process of trial and error. She experiences stress when he is around, even when he is not drinking. She has to be on her guard if he has been drinking. Should she speak to him? Should she challenge him and risk being hit? One way of coping is to adopt a low profile, to withstand the onslaughts of verbal and emotional abuse and get on with everyday life, doing the housework and being on hand for the family. From time to time (or more frequently) there will be crises. The partner becomes violent and aggressive, or possessive and jealous. He is rude to a neighbour, a friend, or another member of the family.

Emotionally she experiences anxiety, fearfulness, misery, self-doubt and blame. She has conflicting feelings towards her partner, feeling affectionate and loving towards him when he is sober, and furious and angry towards him when he is drunk. These feelings are set against the background of some real practical problems. Such problems include the risk of violence or eviction, having no money to pay the bills, complaining neighbours, constant arguments with her partner and his lack of physical hygiene and regular wetting of the bed.

It takes time for a woman to come to terms with the fact that her partner has a drinking problem. In the early days she may be reluctant to admit that this might be the case. She may try to control or prevent his drinking. She copes with the intoxication. She alters her behaviour to accommodate her partner, and the daily routines become organised around his drinking pattern. The family becomes socially isolated. The children do not invite friends to play. People are not encouraged to call. The parents no longer entertain. When these strategies do not work there is a sense of hopelessness, coupled with anger. 'Something must be done.' At this stage the woman may persuade her partner to seek help. If this does not succeed, she can either leave the relationship or continue like a fly caught in a spider's web. Many women feel that they have no choice.

Children

The effect on a child of being brought up in a family in which one or both parents have a drinking problem cannot be overestimated. The damage done will depend on the degree of emotional support provided by either parent when sober, and a variety of other emotional and social supports such as friends, extended family, school and church. The personality of the child and the age when one of the parents develops a drinking problem are both critical.

Alcohol use constricts family life, often in subtle ways. Family routines, rituals and ways of problem solving are altered. They become organised so as to blunt the destabilising effect of the drinking parent, and to offset any potentially destabilising event in family life. Important changes such as adolescence, or starting a new school or career may be overshadowed and ignored. Children learn to develop an emotional distance and to fend for themselves. They often recognise that alcohol has affected their lives adversely, but cannot point to specific effects.

Children have to cope with situations they do not understand and often think that they are responsible for their parents' problems. The drinking parent may have very changeable moods. The children are drawn into parental

conflicts. They may see and experience family violence. A significant proportion are sexually abused by parents or friends. They take on roles more suitable
for older children; for example, the 11-year-old eldest brother minding his
younger siblings for weeks on end because the parents are too drunk, too
depressed or not there at all. They may have to cope with parental divorce or
the death of a parent. Many are taken into care.

These experiences cause emotional suffering which is likely to have lasting
effects on personal development and the ability to form trusting relationships.
Children from such families are prone to anxiety and low self-esteem. Girls are
more likely to have high levels of depression in childhood and adolescence,
and boys to display anti-social behaviour. Other risks include poor performance at school and getting into trouble with the police. Children in these circumstances are themselves at greater risk of developing a drinking problem in
adulthood.

Children of drinkers often turn away from their parents and over-identify
with their peer group. This can make them vulnerable to involvement with
other young people who are themselves disturbed. Alternatively they may
become too involved in the home, feeling anxious to identify with the
non-drinking partner and unable to connect with other people.

Partners of women who are alcohol dependent

Women with serious alcohol problems are often depressed, experience high
levels of anxiety and feelings of unworthiness and have low self-esteem. They
are more likely to be married to heavy drinkers and to drink because of
problems in the marriage. They are also more likely to be left by their partners
than their male counterparts and divorce rates are high. Different men try to
cope in different ways. Roles they may adopt include the long-suffering
martyr; the unforgiving and self-righteous husband; the punishing sadistic
husband; and the 'normal' man.

Gay and lesbian couples

The problems experienced by gay and lesbian couples are similar to those in
heterosexual relationships in which one partner has a drinking problem.

What can families and friends do to help?

Research suggests that there are a number of common patterns of coping with an alcohol problem in the family. These strategies include:

- controlling
- avoidance
- inaction
- tolerance
- supportive
- emotional
- assertive
- independent.

Families are complex systems and coping patterns usually emerge in mixed rather than in pure forms.

In the following example a husband uses a combination of strategies.

Controlling. He tries to control his partner's alcohol consumption by buying alcohol for her and checking that she is not getting any extra from the local off-licence.

Avoidance. He spends long periods of time at work; he allows her to drink in the bedroom and doesn't confront her.

Inaction. He does very little to upset the *status quo*, accepts that the situation cannot be changed and does nothing about his partner's irritable behaviour.

Tolerance. He has come to accept his partner as she is and tries to protect her from the harmful consequences of her drinking.

Carers using an *emotional* strategy are angry and hurt. They articulate their strong emotions, blaming and accusing their partners of letting them down, or of not loving them.

Individuals using an *assertive* coping strategy remain calm and firm. They make their feelings clear; for example, they explain that they find the drinking very distressing. They also refuse to accept their partner's reasons for drinking, or to cover it up.

Partners using an *independent* coping strategy try to get on with their own lives. They organise family life without waiting to get the views of the drinker, and begin to look after their own needs.

Assertive and independent coping strategies may be difficult to initiate, but carers usually find them liberating. Young people often use avoidance as a coping mechanism, particularly as they reach adolescence and are able to spend more time away from home. Supportive, assertive and independent coping strategies are generally advised by self-help groups, while tolerant, controlling and emotional strategies are not.

Friends may be keen to help but back off when their advice is not taken. They are appalled that someone they know stays with a husband who regularly beats her. They prefer to avoid the friend who turns up drunk at the school gates to collect her four-year-old child.

As a friend you can help if you know about the problem and are prepared to take the time to listen. You need to be sensitive enough to know when advice or information might be acceptable. At this point you may need to offer practical help to enable the problem drinker to obtain treatment.

Unfortunately treatment services in the UK do not routinely offer help and support for family members in their own right. *Family approaches* have been more widely adopted in the US. Such approaches include groups for wives/partners; couple groups; couple or family therapy; relatives' groups; and individual help for relatives. As a family member you yourself might benefit from getting help even when your drinking relative is not in treatment. In the UK Al-Anon offers such help and is extremely successful (see Resources).

Families can be helped to reflect on their situation, and discussing their ways of coping may lead to behavioural change. Partners and children should be able to seek help for themselves. This is a flexible and sensible approach. You may find that *sharing* the problem lightens the burden and brings a sense of relief. Recognition that there is a problem may give you confidence to tackle it. You may learn to recognise ways in which you have been coping, for example, being self-sacrificing and tolerant; trying to modify the problem; or being distant and maintaining independence from the problem drinker. Wives often make significant reductions in self-sacrificing behaviour after discussing ways of coping with a counsellor. These changes are likely to improve your own well-being and you can then plan to modify your ways of coping.

Once family members have come forward, it may be easier to encourage the problem drinker to come for help. Additional strategies can be discussed and planned. *Community reinforcement training* emphasises changes in behaviour more strongly, with the drinker getting additional support provided they remain abstinent.

Helping children

Children need someone to listen to them in a supportive way, and sometimes help to understand that they were not to blame for their father or mother's drinking. They may also need help to come to terms with a range of emotions, including anger, anxiety and disappointment. Although they will have worked out personal coping strategies they may benefit from discussing how best to manage in certain situations. Self-help groups such as Alateen can be very helpful, not least because they bring children into contact with others experiencing similar problems (see Al-Anon Family Groups in Resources).

Tips for carers

AS A FRIEND OR FAMILY MEMBER

- Be prepared to listen.
- Adopt a non-judgemental and accepting stance.
- Do not condemn the problem drinker or take sides.
- Offer help with practical issues.

AS A PARTNER

- Remember you are not responsible for your partner's drinking.
- You do not have to be a tower of strength.
- Try to pursue your own interests and your own life as much as you can.
- Confide in a trusted friend.
- Seek help for yourself from your GP, Al-Anon or other supportive person.

AS A CHILD

- Remember it is not your fault.
- You cannot change your parent's behaviour by being good or bad.
- Try to think of your parent as they were and separate the drinking from the non-drinking person.

- Consider confiding in another responsible adult such as a teacher.
- Seek outside help; for example, phone Alateen or ChildLine.

What is the outlook?

It is now clear from research that even severely dependent drinkers can recover. The role of factors outside the treatment cannot be overstated. Personal characteristics, the family and the wider social context all contribute to recovery. About two thirds of individuals receiving treatment show some improvement.

CHAPTER 11

Drug Misuse and Dependence

Claire Gerada and Sarah Welsh

Lynne's son Dean had been using a range of drugs for several years until he went to prison and started smoking heroin. He is now 30, dependent on heroin, and has been living at home on and off. Lynne is divorced and also has two young sons to look after. Dean was receiving treatment through a 'treatment and testing order' on which his mother got him accepted by having him arrested for theft, but he has recently lapsed from this.

'Dean lived with me on and off until last year. God only knows how I managed – he stole *everything*: TVs, videos, stereos, perfume, money, the kids' Nintendos…so we'd have a row, I'd kick him out, then he'd come back and we'd have the tears.

Never knowing when the police are going to be calling on your door – because there was always a warrant out on him for something – it was like living on a knife-edge; 12 years of hell. The only time Dean doesn't ask for money is when he's asleep. And if he asks and I don't give he takes anyway. He will go out and you'll be scanning the house. You may not notice it and then one of the boys will say, "Where's my new game gone?"

Up to the age of 13 you couldn't have faulted Dean – he was a lovely kid. He had a beautiful home and went to a private school; he had all the trappings and was very lucky. It makes no difference what background they come from. He wouldn't go to school and at the age of 15 he stole my car so I had him prosecuted. I went to social services for help but they turned their back on him even at that age.

It was down to him that he went to prison originally, but now it's a vicious circle because if he can't get his heroin through nicking off me he's going to nick outside. If he nicks outside he'll be arrested and back in prison in which case he'll be on more heroin, so then he's really hooked, he comes out of prison and he wants more. This has been going on for years.

Seeing him deteriorate physically makes me feel very angry and hurt. He used to be very good-looking; he'd walk into a pub and all the girls would look, but now he's let himself go. He looks like a tramp — and that gets him down. There was a time he wouldn't go out of the house with his shirt creased. I want to shake him, to wake him up and make him realise he's killing himself. I even took him to the grave of an alcoholic he'd known. There's nothing I haven't shown him.

Dean says to the two kids, "Oh, can I just borrow your TV? You can have it back again tomorrow." You know that's not going to happen, but kids are gullible. They've got mixed views on him; they love him as a brother but Josh is angry with him. Then, when Dean's here and there's the tears they both melt, as I have, as anyone would, but I think he's cried too many tears now.

I feel as if Dean's a leech – he's taken everything from me both mentally and physically. I'm exhausted now and I want an end to it. Sometimes I just want to go into a little corner and hide because I've had enough.

What I can't bear is negativity. "Oh, he's never going to change," because you always in your heart hope that he will see sense. And everyone around you is saying, "You're wasting your time. You know he's going to kick you in the teeth." You want to believe he won't, and what does he do? He kicks you in the teeth and then you feel humiliated. "Fancy putting up with it again! I must be mad." All my friends are very sympathetic though. They're angry with Dean because of what he's done to me but they understand the whole situation because they're mothers.

The hardest struggle was to get the professionals on my side. Our GP practice was very unsympathetic. Then, you need to get your son or daughter to say to the people who are helping them, "You can discuss anything at all with my parents." The parents must also go along to the meetings with their son or daughter. And all of you must be honest – it's no good them lying to themselves that they've only got a habit of £20 a day when they've got a habit of £100 a day, and it's no good Mum burying her head in the sand. Otherwise she'll think it's not that bad.

Detox is the only answer for Dean now but of course you have to go through the whole palaver with the clinic: "We need to know that Dean is motivated before we can recommend him for detox." All the addicts are saying they want to come off it; how can you judge which ones mean it and which ones don't, because they're all good liars?

Any parent has got to try and look beneath the surface and see the boy or girl they had before the drugs. And every now and again you'll see that nice person – it's usually when he's had his hit, mind you – and that will give you the strength to go on. He's not allowed in the house now but I've said to him, "You go back onto the treatment and testing order, and I'll be with you 100 per cent of the way. I'll be there to help you, but you've got to meet me half way." And I can stick to it if he leaves me alone, but it's very difficult to turn your son away when he's at the front door crying.'

What are drug misuse and dependence?

Many people use medication or other substances (including coffee, alcohol and tobacco) in various ways to try to experience pleasure, or to help with unpleasant emotional or physical feelings. At what point the use of a substance becomes misuse is not clearcut, although in most cases it can be thought of as when the drug use causes problems – physical, psychological or social – to the user, their family or indeed to society.

In this chapter we will cover the use of drugs outside that recommended by doctors or pharmacists. Most people who use drugs do so without coming to any harm. However, there can be risks even with occasional use, such as an accidental overdose, unwanted side effects, infections and problems associated with intoxication, such as car accidents.

People who use drugs very regularly may develop a dependence syndrome or addiction. This is when a person experiences some or all of the following changes:

- a strong desire or compulsion to take the drug
- difficulty in controlling drug-taking behaviour (difficulties in resisting the drug, stopping use once started, and controlling the amount used)
- a withdrawal state when drug use has ceased or been reduced. This varies according to the type of drug used (see below). A person may experience the characteristic withdrawal problems for the drug or may use more drugs to try to prevent or relieve the withdrawal.
- increased tolerance to the drug, so that larger amounts are needed to achieve the desired effects
- progressive neglect of other pleasures or interests, and increased time spent getting the drug or recovering from its effects
- persistence with drug use in spite of clear evidence of harmful consequences.

Once dependence has developed, a person will probably find it more difficult to cut down or stop drug use without help.

Drugs and their effects

CANNABIS OR MARIJUANA

Cannabis is the most commonly used illegal drug. The effects of cannabis are quite variable and can depend on the person's mood. Most people describe feeling relaxed but if a person is feeling anxious or unhappy, cannabis may make these feelings worse. Other effects include slurred speech, reddened eyes, and impaired concentration, memory and physical co-ordination. These effects wear off as the drug is cleared from the body over the next 24 hours or so. Some people find that pre-existing problems such as depression and anxiety worsen with cannabis use. The effects on concentration and memory can make school-work more difficult, and therefore young people who have problems with learning are at greater risk of harm.

Serious overdoses are not common. They are likely to make the user feel very anxious, frightened and paranoid. There is not a clear withdrawal state after stopping cannabis use, and it is safe to stop suddenly, although some regular users will notice changes in their mood and sleep when they do so. As cannabis is often smoked with tobacco, the health risks include all those associated with cigarette smoking.

BENZODIAZEPINE DRUGS; FOR EXAMPLE, DIAZEPAM (VALIUM), TEMAZEPAM AND OTHER TRANQUILLISERS

These drugs have been prescribed by doctors since the 1970s for anxiety or sleep problems. Although most people who use these drugs do so because a doctor gave them a prescription, there is also widespread illicit use, particularly among people who also use illicit drugs such as heroin.

Overdose with a benzodiazepine causes drowsiness, or even a coma, and slows down breathing. Withdrawal problems vary from mild anxiety and sleep disturbance to a severe state of fear and confusion. There is a risk of fits if a person stops these drugs after regular long-term use. The health risks of benzodiazepines are mainly those associated with dependence and overdose, as well as the effects on concentration and co-ordination.

Some drug users take benzodiazepines with other drugs to boost the effects, or to help them to come down from drugs that make them feel high, reducing the unpleasant effects of a drug wearing off. Benzodiazepine use with other drugs such as heroin can be extremely dangerous, and overdose in these situations can cause death.

STIMULANTS; FOR EXAMPLE, AMPHETAMINES, COCAINE AND ECSTASY

People generally buy amphetamine as a white powder (amphetamine sulphate) or as tablets called dexamphetamine ('dexies'). It is usually taken by mouth, snorted, or rubbed into the gums. Some people prepare the powder for injection and use it that way. The effects include making a person feel excited, happy and energetic, and in less need of food and sleep. Other effects include anxiety, paranoia and aggression. Amphetamine causes a rise in blood pressure. High doses of amphetamine on its own can cause a distressing state of anxiety and panic. It can also lead to a psychotic illness, which closely resembles schizophrenia. This usually resolves gradually after the person stops taking amphetamine, but it may need psychiatric treatment. Overdose of amphetamine with other drugs can be very dangerous. Regular users may experience depression and sleep disturbance when they stop using the drug.

Cocaine comes in many different forms, though mostly people buy it as a white powder. It is usually sniffed or 'snorted' but can also be injected. 'Crack' is a form of cocaine that has been treated with chemicals to make lumps called rocks which can be smoked in a pipe or heated to make vapour to inhale. The effects of cocaine are very similar to those of amphetamine, but may happen more quickly as a powerful 'rush'; they also wear off more quickly. The problematic effects are similar to those of amphetamine. Occasionally, the sudden rise in blood pressure caused by cocaine can lead to a stroke. As cocaine lasts such a short time in the body, many cocaine users experience a brief but very unpleasant comedown after use, with a severe feeling of depression. Like amphetamine, people can generally stop their use of cocaine safely without any clear withdrawal symptoms, but regular users may experience depression and sleep problems.

Ecstasy is closely related to amphetamines in its actions and effects. It gives the user a surge in energy and causes a sense of well-being. These effects make it particularly attractive to younger people and so it is commonly used as a dance drug among people in their teens and twenties. Under the influence of this drug people can go on dancing for several hours. A small number of people who use the drug have serious side effects, such as liver damage, strokes and paranoid feelings. One of the most serious effects of this drug is its toxic effect on the brain, making users more susceptible to chronic depression.

HEROIN (DIAMORPHINE) AND OTHER RELATED DRUGS

People usually obtain heroin in powder form, mixed or cut by the dealer with other substances such as chalk dust or other drugs. It can be taken by any route, such as orally, snorted, smoked or injected. The commonest routes are by smoking and injection. Its effects are to produce a 'rush' or sense of intense pleasure followed by drowsiness. Heroin is highly addictive, with the dependent user needing to take the drug several times a day. Medical complications include constipation, respiratory problems and low blood pressure. In overdose the drug can produce coma, arrested breathing and death. Other problems are associated with the life style needed to obtain the drug and with injecting (see below).

INJECTING DRUGS

Injecting drugs carries a number of important risks. As the drug goes straight into the bloodstream, there is a higher chance of sudden accidental overdose. Infections, such as HIV and hepatitis, can be introduced into the body by sharing injecting equipment with someone else who has these infections. Bacteria on the skin introduced into the body through injecting can cause abscesses and life-threatening illnesses, such as septicaemia (an infection attacking the body via the blood) and endocarditis (an infection damaging the valves of the heart). Injecting can damage the veins themselves, which may become scarred and close up, or get blocked with blood clots (thrombosis).

These serious physical health risks are the reason why many treatment programmes for drug misusers concentrate on trying to help a person stop injecting, even if this means switching to a less dangerous way of taking drugs rather than stopping altogether. Agencies that supply clean injecting equipment for drug users and advice about safer injecting techniques also aim to reduce the risks to health.

How common is drug misuse?

We do not know how many people use illicit drugs, although by all accounts the numbers have increased considerably over the last two decades. Current estimates suggest there may be between 50,000 and 150,000 heroin users and an unknown number of people who use other illicit drugs in the UK. Drug use – in particular the type of drug taken – goes in fashions, with different drugs becoming popular at different times. The late 1980s saw the appearance of ecstasy and other hallucinogenic drugs, and the 1990s saw the beginning of crack cocaine use. Heroin use has always been present, but numbers are increasing especially among the young, and this is reflected by an increase in young people presenting for treatment.

What causes drug misuse?

There is no single cause of drug misuse. Drug users come from many diverse backgrounds and to try to simplify the causes does no justice to the complex interplay between environmental and individual factors. However, we can draw out certain factors that may increase the chance of a person starting to misuse drugs. Drug use is more common in young people, more often linked to social deprivation and school failure and more likely to be found in someone with inconsistent parenting. It is both a cause of and result of social exclusion and identifying a single causative factor is too simplistic.

Factors increasing the chance of heavy long-term drug use may include a combination of disturbed family relations, childhood neglect, poverty, homelessness and behavioural problems when growing up.

For carers it is important not to overplay any one factor and certainly not to label an individual as having an 'addictive personality' which can deter a successful outcome to treatment.

How do we treat drug misuse and dependence?

Many people are able to make changes in their drug use simply by learning more about the effects of drugs and the risks involved; others may need more help.

Counselling or talking therapies

A specific type of counselling is called motivational work. Here there is an acknowledgement that people often make changes in steps, rather than all at once, and that it is natural to feel uncertain about making changes. The therapist will help someone to make decisions by discussing the advantages and disadvantages of a particular course of action (such as stopping drug use, or cutting down gradually, or making some simple changes first to avoid the riskiest aspects of drug use). In this way a person gets advice and feedback, help in setting his or her own goals, and choices about how to achieve them. This may seem like slow work to relatives and friends who are worried and want the person to stop all risky drug taking immediately but the changes people make are often more lasting if they are convinced themselves that the change is the right thing. Relapse prevention is a type of therapy in which the person learns to identify or anticipate circumstances that may trigger drug use and so find different ways of dealing with them. These may be moods caused by, for example, loneliness, anxiety or conflicts with other people, or may relate to social pressures from other drug users.

Medication

Medication can help people stop their drug use safely and comfortably, a process sometimes called detoxification. Medication is usually not necessary for people stopping use of cannabis, amphetamines, cocaine, ecstasy, or glue and other solvents. However, sometimes a doctor will suggest a short course of treatment to help with any depression or sleep problems while the person adjusts to stopping these drugs, especially in the case of cocaine withdrawal.

Stopping heroin can cause a withdrawal syndrome, which is unpleasant but not generally dangerous. Some people manage to get through it without help from medication although most people find medication helpful. There are many strategies for using medication to help detoxification. One way is to help control symptoms as they arise; for example, taking medication for diarrhoea and sickness.

A second way is to use a drug that is similar to heroin and to cut down the dose gradually to minimise withdrawal symptoms. Methadone is the most commonly used drug in these circumstances as it lasts for quite a long time in the body, so the person feels comfortable with only one or two daily doses and does not have the ups and downs associated with heroin use. Detoxification using methadone can be planned over a short period (such as ten days), or more slowly over several weeks or months. A third strategy is to use a drug that helps prevent some of the withdrawal symptoms that occur by blocking these effects. One such drug is called lofexidine.

Longer-term medication, or maintenance, is sometimes prescribed for people who have become dependent on heroin or similar drugs. This is sometimes called substitute prescribing, since it involves giving a prescribed drug to substitute for an illegal drug; again methadone is the most commonly used drug. Maintenance treatment is often chosen for people who have tried to stop using heroin several times but have not succeeded, or for those who want to make some positive change but do not yet feel ready to be drug-free. Methadone treatment has to be carefully supervised, since methadone itself is sometimes misused and is sold illegally. It can be dangerous if taken as an overdose, or mixed with other drugs. For these reasons, treatment centres will ask people to attend every day to take the medication under supervision. A regular methadone prescription gives someone the opportunity to stop using illegal drugs and move away from committing crimes, and therefore to be more able to spend time dealing with major areas in their life such as housing and getting work.

Other treatments

Self-help groups, such as Narcotics Anonymous, offer the fellowship, support and advice of other users, friends, carers or families who have had similar problems.

More intensive therapies can help people make major changes in their lives that can go along with stopping drug use. Some treatment centres offer day programmes consisting of group and individual counselling along with other activities promoting positive changes. Residential rehabilitation programmes, which involve staying for several weeks or months in a drug-free environment with other former drug users, allow people to build on skills to help maintain a drug-free life in the future. These programmes are a big commitment for someone to take on but can be highly successful.

How does it affect families and friends?

Most drug users are young and not cared for in the way that one might imagine for a person with a mental illness. Carers are often the parents or a partner who find it difficult to know how to help or what to do. Feelings of impotence in the carer may translate into anger and frustration. Do not feel guilty about these feelings. They are a response to the grief of seeing a loved one hellbent on self-destruction. The best way forward involves developing some understanding of how to help and when to let go. You may want to try and share the pain with others. Remember, your relative or friend's problem is not your fault.

What can families and friends do to help?

If carers and families improve their own knowledge about drug use this makes it easier to understand the reasons why someone is using drugs, and the associated problems and difficulties that go with this use.

When you try to advise your relative or friend, he or she may object to your 'interference'. If this happens, it may be best to back off a little and try to listen to your relative's point of view. Look at the section on 'motivational' work earlier in the chapter. You can try to take this approach yourself, by encouraging your relative to think about the advantages and disadvantages of making changes, rather than pushing one particular course of action. Knowledge of the sorts of help available locally can help you both choose what to do next.

Give your relative or friend time to think, and be supportive and encouraging of any small change even if you had hoped for more. For example, people sometimes feel disappointed if their relative stays on a methadone prescription. In these circumstances, it is fine to talk about future plans for stopping methadone, but it is important to recognise and support the positive changes someone has made and to acknowledge that slow progress is better than a return to previous problems.

You can also help your relative with relapse prevention. Ask how you can help. For example, some drug users find that boredom or loneliness triggers a lapse, and that help with finding company and activity is useful. Others find that they have to avoid certain areas where there are people selling drugs. You can try to help with planning how to get on with day-to-day tasks while avoiding these areas. Even if things do not go well, preparing yourself to deal with medical emergencies and mobilising your own network of support can be very important.

Tips for carers

- Learn as much as you can about the drug or drugs your relative or friend is using.

- Think about what the motivating factors are for your relative to carry on or to stop using drugs and discuss together.

- Accept that your relative may not be able to stop drug use completely, but encourage any reduction or switch to safer use.

- Discuss the treatment options available together.

- If your relative or friend has stopped using drugs, help them to stay drug-free by looking together at things that might trigger a return to the drug use.

What is the outlook?

Not everyone who takes drugs continues to use and becomes dependent. Many young people pass through an experimental stage, perhaps using cannabis and stimulants to 'keep up with their peer group'. If drug use does become persistent, again, as a carer, don't panic. The first step is to help your relative or friend recognise they have a problem, and then seek help, hopefully through a sympathetic general practitioner, or voluntary sector 'street' agency.

CHAPTER 12

Personality Disorders

Jane Tiller

Angela Reed has been diagnosed with a personality disorder and has been severely ill with depression and symptoms resembling schizophrenia. She and her husband Glyn have two grown-up children.

'From experience I can tell when my wife is getting unwell. Sometimes she gets agitated and she won't stay in one place for long or she'll cry. When she was first ill we tried to cope ourselves. I didn't know what sort of help was available – perhaps it was lack of education or awareness or maybe lack of understanding about what she was going through with the illness. Now I encourage her to seek help because it's not going to get better by itself. Her usual reaction when she gets ill is that she doesn't need help. Maybe it's the illness, maybe it's pride. Asking for help is the hardest thing for her.

Angela first went into hospital under section and losing your liberty is not a pleasant thing to happen, so she wasn't grateful to me. But afterwards she didn't hold a grudge because she understood that it had to be done. Now she appreciates more that someone has to take the leading role in getting her help.

There was a conflict between her care team and myself over whether she should be looked after at home. One night I found a knife under her pillow and asked her what it was for. She said it was to stab me while I was asleep. I explained the situation to the care team and they were concerned, but not greatly and thought it might be attention-seeking behaviour which is part of the illness and her personality. But how can you be sure? They didn't think it necessary for her to go into hospital but I did not feel secure enough to have her at home so we came to an arrangement. If she's well enough and she isn't under section she comes to the house in the daytime but she doesn't live with me any more. I don't think she's entirely happy with the arrangement but perhaps she understands the situation.

When Angela comes home in the day we spend several hours together. Since she's been ill her world has shrunk whereas mine still continues as before but I understand that that is her life now. She talks about her fellow patients and although it's not necessarily relevant to me I make time to listen. I may contribute my views if she has any questions about things that are happening. Angela depends on me not just for material things but for giving my opinion because since the illness her decisions are not necessarily sensible ones and she needs advice. I listen to how she is feeling and what she sees in the future. She can feel enthusiastic for things tomorrow but not necessarily the day after tomorrow so I can't make long-term plans.

We weren't particularly sociable people before the illness – we preferred our own company – though we didn't have a problem meeting people if we were invited out. Now of course my time is limited. Sometimes family members come round to the house but not friends.

Living apart has made a big difference even though you don't stop worrying and she often gets herself into difficulties; she phones me saying that she's going to kill herself and I have to act on that. Sometimes it seems to me that it's necessary to take action but the other agencies don't necessarily see it the same way. You care for someone so much, you're trying to prevent the worst possible scenario and you come up against a brick wall. They give you advice that she'll be OK but you're left to deal with it, to live with it or walk away from it. Sometimes they do take my concerns seriously but other times I get the impression that they think that because I'm closely related to Angela maybe I am too sensitive. They haven't said that in so many words but I can tell from their reaction. Many times I've been to the clinic and passed between doctors and at the end of the day they go home and you are left to deal with the situation.

I cannot regard our relationship as that of a normal husband and wife. Angela depends on me like my children, but other than that there isn't any real relationship – that is the sad truth. She sees me as a carer, as a part-time husband, and as the father to our children. When she is well enough and she thinks things through she does get frustrated. Now that the children have grown up we could have had a different kind of life but that's just bad luck. If I went down that road, I'd end up getting depressed myself; there are too many questions and not enough answers.

The only advice I would give is that if you really care about someone ill in your family you should stick by them. I know it's hard – it's a damn sight easier to walk away – but if you go and form a relationship with someone else, you're still going to wonder how she is, whether she's well. If you have children, they are a common contact point and at some time or other you're going to be in contact with each other. At the end of the day this person is the mother of my children; we had good times as well as this horrendous time we're having now. And what sort of an example would it be to our children if their father deserted their mother just at the moment she needed him? So you have to consider every aspect and that is the basis of my decision.'

What are these disorders?

Although efforts are underway to address the stigma that can be attached to having a psychiatric diagnosis, the diagnosis of a 'personality disorder' may be particularly distressing. Recent media and government preoccupation with dangerous people with severe personality disorder has tended to reinforce this view. To counter this, sufferers and carers need information about these conditions.

The term 'personality disorders' refers to a group of conditions that have a number of characteristics in common. Personality disorders tend to develop in childhood or adolescence and they shape the way in which people generally react to circumstances, and how they relate to others. The result is that these people show consistent but extreme patterns of behaviour and emotions. This usually, but not always, leads to some problems in social relationships or at work and causes a person to feel distressed. Most psychiatrists do not see personality disorder as being like mental disorders such as schizophrenia; people with personality disorders have the same character traits (e.g. worry, indecisiveness, shyness, suspiciousness, impulsivity) as most of us, but to a more extreme degree.

There is no test available to help a doctor decide whether someone has a personality disorder. Instead the diagnosis is made by identifying characteristic groups of behaviours and symptoms. There are nine specific personality disorders described by the World Health Organisation (see Table 12.1), but these categories are not mutually exclusive and there is considerable overlap between them. Some people meet the criteria for more than one personality disorder. There are however three main groups of personality disorder, termed for convenience Clusters A, B and C (see Table 12.1). The type of problems experienced by sufferers is very different between clusters.

Table 12.1 Classification of personality disorders

Personality disorder categories	Features of each personality disorder	Group of personality disorder	Problems experienced by sufferers
Paranoid	Suspicious, sensitive, argumentative, stubborn, self-important	Cluster A	Tendency to be socially withdrawn and have difficulty in forming close relationships. May hold odd ideas and beliefs and be suspicious of people's motives.
Schizoid	Emotionally cold, detached, humourless, introspective		
Dissocial	Disregard of others' feelings, impulsive actions, lack of guilt, failure to learn from experience	Cluster B	Experiencing intense emotional responses both positive (e.g. enthusiasm and euphoria) and negative (e.g. depression and rage). This can lead to ill-judged or impulsive and reckless behaviour. Generally able to form relationships but have difficulty maintaining them because of the strength of emotional reactions.
Impulsive	Emotionally volatile, sometimes very angry and violent		
Borderline	Impulsive behaviour, suicide threats or action, feeling of 'emptiness', emotionally volatile		
Histrionic	Self-centred, short-lived enthusiasms, unrestrained emotional displays		
Anankastic	Stubborn, lacking emotion or humour, indecisive, inflexible, judgemental	Cluster C	Have difficulty with relationships due to high levels of anxiety which can result in avoiding social contact. This anxiety may inhibit trying out new things and so getting the most out of life.
Anxious	Persistent anxiety, discomfort in company, cautious, timid, lacking self-esteem		
Dependent	Compliance with others' wishes, lack of self-reliance, avoidance of responsibility		

How common are they?

We do not know exactly how common these disorders are but it is thought that about one in ten people meet the criteria for a personality disorder. This is not surprising as many of the features are normal responses, although out of proportion to the circumstances. Personality disorders are more common in urban than rural populations and are less common in older people. In people going to their GP with psychological symptoms, about one third will have a personality disorder as do up to half of all people attending psychiatric outpatients clinics. Higher than expected rates of personality disorder have been found in people who have harmed themselves and in prison populations.

Cluster A disorders occur in fewer than one in a hundred people. The Cluster B disorders are a little more common. Histrionic and borderline conditions are found in up to one in fifty people. Borderline personality is most common in women aged 19 to 34 years. Dissocial personality is found in about one in thirty people and is most common in younger men. Cluster C disorders are less common and found in between one in fifty and one in a hundred people.

What are the causes?

The causes of personality disorders are not known, but there are many theories. Personality itself has quite a large inherited component and this has led to research studies into the genetics of personality disorders. Patients in Cluster A have a relative with schizophrenia more commonly than would be expected by chance alone and it is likely that there is a genetic link between these conditions. Similarly, there appears to be a genetic link between obsessive compulsive disorder and anankastic personality disorder.

Although there is a genetic contribution to variations in personality, differences are due as much to a person's surroundings and life experiences as to their genes. Dissocial personality disorder is found less often in some countries, such as Japan and Taiwan. These societies discourage impulsive behaviour and emotional displays and it has been suggested that this environment is responsible for the low frequency of dissocial personality disorder. There is some evidence that borderline personality disorder may also be less common in cultures with stricter social codes.

When considering personality and the conditions in which someone has grown up it is important to be aware that this involves much more than the family upbringing. Only one child in a family may be affected even though all the children were brought up in a similar way. The explanation for this is that the experiences unique to the individual (unshared environment) rather than the family environment (shared environment) may be most important in shaping personality.

It is likely that a person's genes and the environment are important. For example, one view of borderline personality disorder suggests that sufferers are born with an inherited, increased emotional sensitivity to traumatic events such as bereavement, and take longer to recover from them. If the environment a child finds him or herself in does not help them cope with any trauma that person may go on to develop a personality disorder. The modern world and life style may make it harder for children with greater emotional needs to get the support they require.

Some research studies have found that more adult women with borderline personality disorder were victims of child abuse than average and it is suggested that this trauma may have led to the development of the disorder. Yet children show a surprising ability to bounce back from adversity and the majority of abused children grow up into adults without any psychological problems.

The effect of traumatic events may be cumulative, so the extent to which children recover from them will depend on a combination of their genetic predisposition to developing a personality disorder, and the severity and number of difficulties they encounter. Even if they have no, or very few, genes predisposing them to developing a personality disorder, they may still do so if their experiences are severe enough to overcome their resilience.

How do we treat these disorders?

Personality disorders are commonly associated with other forms of mental illness such as depression and anxiety and these conditions are likely to need treating, usually with medication. Patients may also have developed problems with alcohol or drugs requiring specialist help. There is some evidence that people with a personality disorder have a worse outlook for recovering from their mental illness than those without.

In the past it was thought that personality disorders could not be treated, but this view is changing. However, it is true that there is no quick fix and treatment is often long-term and may be difficult. There is no one clearly identified treatment, in part because there is no one clear cause. Both medication and psychological treatments have been used with some success.

Medication is aimed at reducing troubling symptoms rather than curing the disorder itself. There is some evidence that suicide attempts and repeated self-harm may be reduced if patients are treated with one of the selective serotonin reuptake inhibitor antidepressants (SSRIs). For people who have persecutory beliefs antipsychotic medication may be helpful. Low doses of antipsychotic medication can also be used in people with borderline personality disorder. Mood stabilisers may help some people with problems of poor self-control or aggression.

A large number of psychological therapies have been used with some success in people with a personality disorder. These include cognitive behavioural therapy, cognitive analytical therapy, dialectic behavioural therapy, dynamic psychotherapy, interpersonal therapy, group therapy and family therapydrinking 28–9

. At present there is not enough evidence to recommend the use of one therapy over another. Therapeutic communities have also been able to help some people with a personality disorder, especially those more severely affected.

How do they affect families and friends?

Sufferers with a Cluster A disorder can cause problems for carers because of their unusual behaviour, or because they are not emotionally warm and expressive and so do not respond as expected to other people and situations. Carers may feel uncertain about how to respond to their relative's strange beliefs: should they argue against them or should they pretend that they share them? Some carers of people with a Cluster B disorder describe the experience as an 'emotional roller-coaster'. Carers may become concerned about their relative's rage, depression or self-destructive impulses. These personality disorders have been found to be linked to sexual and marital problems, job difficulties, physical disability, self-harm and drug or alcohol problems. Patients with dissocial personality disorder may be frequently in trouble with the police. Carers of people with a Cluster C disorder may find themselves getting frustrated by their relative's dependency and fear of trying new things or by their excessive preoccupation with detail.

What can families and friends do to help?

These disorders can take their toll on carers as well as their relative. It is very important that as a first step carers look after themselves. It is easy to become so involved in trying to help your relative that you neglect your own health and well-being. Your relative's key worker or doctor should be able to provide you with more information about the condition and how it affects people. It may be helpful to join a carers' support group to meet others in the same position (see Resources).

Most people with a personality disorder are painfully aware of their difficulties and like most of us want to be accepted and valued. Encourage your relative to feel good about him or herself and to focus on and develop positive qualities and talents. It is important for sufferers to have hope for the future and not to give up. It can be a great relief to feel that someone believes in them.

As a general rule it is helpful to be as clear as you can with your relative about what you are able to do for them and to carry this out as consistently as possible. Most sufferers value honesty provided it is expressed considerately. Some people place demands on their carers that the carers are not able to meet. For example, some carers find that they are taking calls throughout the night from a distressed relative. In this type of situation you can try to help your relative develop alternative and more successful ways of coping, such as keeping a list of 24-hour telephone helplines by the phone to use after 10pm.

People with a personality disorder are often inflexible in their responses to life's difficulties. They may find themselves making the same mistakes and repeating the same unsuccessful solutions to problems. Carers may be able to help a person come up with, and try out, new strategies.

If social withdrawal and anxiety are a problem try not to be over-protective. Carers can take on more and more to shield their relative from the tasks or situations that they find difficult. Unfortunately, this does not help sufferers to learn that they can cope and it may exhaust and demoralise the carer. Your relative needs your encouragement to discover his or her own strengths and capabilities.

Tips for carers

- Encouragement is important. Celebrate even apparently small achievements in your relative's progress.

- Trust your own judgement in dealings with professionals; if you feel there is a serious problem, persist in making your views known until you get a satisfactory response.

- Try to maintain a positive attitude with your friend or relative.

What is the outlook?

Cluster B disorders tend to improve with age and increasing maturity. This tendency to improve with age is not generally seen in Cluster A. Cluster C is said to have the best outcome and this is usually the result of people learning to take more risks over time.

These are generalisations, and what seems to matter most for any one individual is the balance between their positive qualities and their disabling traits. People who have a special gift or talent tend to do better, as do those who are motivated to have therapy, and have the ability to trust others and the strength to face their weakness. Flexibility is an important positive trait, which can be enhanced with therapy. This allows an individual to select a more appropriate response to a situation and break out of habitual but unproductive patterns of behaviour.

If the first few attempts at treatment do not work it is important not to feel discouraged as the person may not yet be ready for treatment. Some people make substantial improvements following a change in their life circumstances; for example, developing a new role in life or forming an important relationship.

CHAPTER 13

Mental Illness in Older People

Amanda Thompsell and Marisa Silverman

Leon has known Jack Moffat for most of his life and now that Jack has Alzheimer's disease, Leon looks after him full time.

'Each morning carers come from social services to wash Mr Moffat, to change his incontinence pads and dress him. I do his breakfast and then he sits in the wheelchair for the rest of the day. I cook his lunch and every other day change his catheter bag. Sometimes I have to get up in the middle of the night if he needs changing or to use the commode, which happens quite a lot now, and once I'm awake I can't get back to sleep. There's also the house to clean, washing, ironing, shopping and the garden. I've looked after him for seven years and in that time have only had two weeks' leave; I'd like at least two days off a week, though I'd still be pottering around the house gardening or decorating. It's being on call all the time that's so tiring.

I used to get on with the social services carers but they abused my trust. Long-distance calls started appearing on the phone bill and I found things going missing from my bedroom. I've had to put locks on all the doors and the phones. Mr Moffat would prefer that no other carers came but I couldn't do it all myself. If I didn't have to look after the house as well, I could probably manage but I wouldn't want to give up gardening because I find it relaxing. At the end of the day I sit out there and try to unwind although I'm still tense because I know he's watching me – he's very demanding and spoilt.

Mr Moffat caused a fire with one of his cigarettes so I've stopped him smoking in bed on his own. One night at 2am the police called saying Mr Moffat had called in a distressed state and complained about me stopping him smoking in bed. The police have been up three times and he's made serious accusations against me. I think he wanted someone to feel sorry for him because he wasn't getting his own way.

Sometimes he tells people that he doesn't need me and can do everything himself. If he's nasty you can't be rude back – he'd be ever so hurt and it would make matters worse. I've had a few kicks in the stomach when I've changed the catheter bag – that's the dementia – so now I stand to the side where he can't reach. You have to ignore it but it's so hard. I walk into the garden, have a cigarette and count to ten and then walk back. Ten minutes later he knows he's done something but he can't remember what.

I've found the staff of the local services quite frustrating because when we arrange a meeting to discuss Mr Moffat they don't all turn up. You write down all the things that you want to say in the days beforehand and then it's wasted. We've also had some trouble with the GP not coming to the house – he and the district nurse are always passing the buck. And every time you need something different like incontinence pads, the district nurse has to come up to reassess Mr Moffat and that makes you feel as if no one believes you.

You might be thrown into looking after someone with Alzheimer's if it's family, but if it's a friend or a next-door neighbour, be very careful. Your friend may be suspicious of everyone and you need their trust. To Mr Moffat everything still costs one shilling and six, so when I tell him I can spend £200 in Sainsbury's he doesn't believe me. Get advice from a Citizens' Advice Bureau, Crossroads or from your local social services care manager before you take on someone's care.

If you do take on caring for someone you are going to be very lonely. You lose your friends because it's like being a recluse. When I do see my friends they ask how Jack is but then they don't want to know. They think that because I have chosen to look after Jack, I just have to suffer. That's not very sympathetic.

There are good days when we go through the parks with his wheelchair and he gets excited because he can't remember it so it's all new to him, but I knew Jack when he was fine and it is upsetting to see how he's deteriorated. It would worry me if I thought he was suffering. Sometimes he doesn't tell me he's in pain because he knows I'm tired so occasionally I tell a little white lie and say I've had a sleep upstairs for half an hour and then he says what the problem is. He can be considerate of my needs but it depends on what sort of a day he's had. Usually if he wants something there's no more "please" and "thank you" anymore – just a demanding call. You've got to accept that he won't be grateful but Mr Moffat was almost a father to me and now I am trying to pay back what he gave me.'

What illnesses affect elderly people?

Elderly people suffer from the same range of mental illnesses that affect younger people, including depression, mania, schizophrenia, delirium, anxiety and dementia. Any of these disorders may occur for the first time over the age of 65 or can be a recurrence of a long-standing problem. Depression, in particular, is common among the elderly and can easily be missed. Sometimes people are ready to assume that depression in the elderly is justified due to their circumstances. It is always worth you challenging such an assumption as depression generally improves with treatment.

However, in some ways mental illnesses are different in the elderly. For example, older people often have other physical illnesses which can affect the symptoms of any mental illness. They are also more likely to need medication for a physical illness with the risk of unwanted side effects which occasionally lead to psychiatric problems. Mental health professionals treating elderly people need to do thorough assessments to work out what is the cause of their problems and to rule out any underlying medical condition.

Although older adults suffer from the whole range of mental illnesses, it is the illnesses grouped under the term 'dementia' that are perhaps the most demanding on carers. In the rest of this chapter we discuss these in more detail.

What is dementia?

Dementia is not a single disease. It describes a collection of symptoms that develop in association with a number of progressive diseases of the brain. ('Progressive' here refers to illnesses that become increasingly more severe in the sufferer.) Alzheimer's disease is the most common form of dementia. Other, less common forms of dementia include multi-infarct dementia (MID), Lewy body dementia and Pick's disease.

The key features of dementia are a continuing decline in a person's memory, and ability to learn and understand. Usually there are also changes in social behaviour and general motivation and in the ability to control emotions. Carers may notice a person having difficulty finding the right word, a change in their personality or a lack of motivation. Everyday tasks may seem difficult to do or a person's behaviour may appear odd. The changes develop over six months or longer. One important point is that not only memory is affected. Although in the early stages of dementia memory problems may seem the most obvious sign, many older people experience a decline in their memory that does not develop into dementia.

For health professionals, finding memory problems and other difficulties is only the start of the process of making a diagnosis. The doctor will need to check in what ways a person is not functioning as expected. The assessment might be carried out at home so as to get a clearer picture of how someone is managing. The doctor will also want to know about past physical illnesses and current medication, and will be looking to rule out depression as a possible cause of the memory problems. If the memory problems are the result of being depressed, treatment with an antidepressant is likely to help.

The next step is likely to involve various tests, probably carried out at a hospital or clinic, including blood tests, X-rays and possibly a brain scan to discover what is causing the symptoms.

To carry out a full assessment of your relative's problems other professionals are likely to play a part. Members of the team may include a nurse, occupational therapist, psychologist, physiotherapist and social worker as well as a doctor.

Making a diagnosis is important, as the diagnosis will affect treatment and the likely outcome. In some cases the dementia may be reversible; for example, if it is due to the thyroid gland not working properly or there is a lack of a particular vitamin.

How common is dementia?

Dementia is surprisingly common among elderly people. It is likely to affect up to 1 in 20 people over the age of 65, and up to 1 in 5 of those over 80. Particularly in the early stages of dementia it is easy not to spot the problems. Both men and women may develop dementia.

What are the causes?

There are a number of factors that may increase the chance of a person developing dementia. These include:

- increasing age
- past head injury
- Down's syndrome
- history of Parkinson's disease or Alzheimer's disease in the family
- high blood pressure
- heart disease
- smoking.

The relatives of someone with Alzheimer's disease often worry about whether they too will develop the illness. Hereditary factors play a part in early onset Alzheimer's, when the disease becomes evident between the ages of 30 and 60. However, early onset Alzheimer's disease is rare and usually relatives are already aware of the family history. People who are concerned about this should ask their doctor to refer them to a specialist centre for counselling and, if appropriate, testing, but tests are not performed on those under 18. Although genetic factors increase the chance of elderly people developing Alzheimer's disease, they do not cause it.

How do we treat it?

The treatment for a person with dementia depends on the precise diagnosis.

Alzheimer's disease

A number of new drugs known as acetylcholinesterase inhibitors are available for treatment. Acetylcholine is a chemical naturally found in the brain which seems to be important in its normal functioning. There is not enough of this chemical in the brains of Alzheimer's sufferers. The acetylcholinesterase inhibitors work by slowing down the processes that lead to the breakdown of this chemical. These drugs may slow the progression of the disease, and sometimes also lead to improvements in a person's day-to-day functioning but they cannot cure the illness. They are expensive, and doctors can generally only prescribe them to people who are most likely to benefit from them. If a person gets one of these drugs he or she will need to see the doctor regularly to check whether the treatment is having an effect, and if there is no clear benefit from it, the doctor is likely to stop it. In the future there may be more new drugs that can slow down or halt the disease's development.

Multi-infarct dementia

Multi-infarct dementia has different causes from Alzheimer's disease. This sort of dementia results from brain damage caused by small strokes. As a result the treatment tends to concentrate on improving the blood supply. It might involve treating any irregular heartbeat or thinning the blood, perhaps through taking aspirin tablets.

How does it affect families and friends?

Living with or caring for someone with dementia can be a tiring and stressful experience. It is common to feel grief for the loss of the person you used to know, and to feel isolated and in need of support. With all the emotional turmoil and the pure physical strain of looking after a relative, carers often forget that they too have needs. Health professionals should be aware of your needs and consider your mental and physical health as well as your relative's. It is not an admission of defeat for a carer to seek help.

If you feel you may need more support, your doctor can put you in touch with the local carers' group run by the Alzheimer's Disease Society allowing you to meet other people caring for someone with Alzheimer's disease. If you feel you are not getting enough support you also have a right to ask social services for an assessment of your own needs. They may be able to refer you to other sources of help. Health services may be able to provide a community psychiatric nurse (CPN) to visit you at home on a regular basis to offer advice and support for your difficulties.

It is often helpful to have a break from caring. Your relative or friend may be able to go to a day centre, or have a short admission to a local authority home for a few nights. Crossroads is an agency that can provide someone to sit with your relative while you go out. It is also worth considering sharing the burden with other relatives or friends.

In some cases it may become necessary to plan for continuing, residential or nursing care; for example, if the level of care your relative or friend needs is greater than you are able to provide, or you yourself are having difficulties. Discuss with your doctor what might be the best type of placement. An occupational therapist's assessment can be helpful in working out what sort of help your relative will need. Visit any potential homes and do not be afraid to ask questions. Both Age Concern and the Alzheimer's Disease Society have helpful written advice on choosing a home. Another reference source is the booklet *Home from Home* available from the King's Fund publishing programme (see Resources).

What can families and friends do to help?

Help with making a diagnosis

An important step for the doctor making a diagnosis of dementia or any other mental illness in older adults is to get a full history of the person's problems from a carer. Questions the doctor asks you may include:

- How have these problems affected your relative's day-to-day functioning?

- Has there been any sudden decline or have the changes been gradual?

- Has there been any behaviour such as wandering or aggression that might be a risk to the well-being of your relative or others?

- Is there any history of dementia in the family?

- Is there any history of heart disease in your relative or others in the family?

If your relative appears depressed you may be asked about which came first, the depression or the change in functioning, to help the doctor work out whether the main diagnosis is depression or dementia.

Discuss your relative's treatment

It is worth discussing your friend or relative's illness with the doctor to check that the doctors are treating any underlying causes. It is also worth asking about whether one of the anti-dementia drugs might be useful. Even if there is no cure for your relative's illness, there are many things that may help you and your relative cope better with the situation and improve your quality of life. Your doctor should be able to discuss your relative's care needs with you. Other agencies, including social services, may be able to provide practical support in the form of a home help, meals on wheels, bathing service and some care during the day.

Common problems and how to deal with them

AGGRESSION

Aggression is a fairly common and distressing factor in the disease. Try to note what circumstances give rise to aggression and consider whether they could be avoided. If not is there anything you can do to distract your relative when these circumstances arise? In extreme cases, aggression may need treatment with medication.

WANDERING

A tendency to wander is a common problem in dementia. Often this is made worse by a person feeling bored. It can help to make sure that your relative has something to do and to provide some other outlet for his or her energy. If wandering is a problem, it is worth having secure locks on the doors and ensuring that your relative always carries some form of identification. You may find it helpful to inform neighbours of the problem. If your relative does wander out of the house, contact the police quickly.

INSOMNIA

Insomnia is often a problem in dementia. Establishing a structure for the day and including some daytime activity, perhaps by making use of a day centre, can help. In particular it is important to have a routine at bedtime. If problems continue the doctor may suggest some medication to help.

FALLS

If your relative has repeated falls, try to eliminate any possible obstacles such as loose carpets or items on the floor at home. Make sure your relative has appropriate footwear. Ask your doctor to check your relative's blood pressure and to review any medication. An occupational therapy assessment might be helpful in examining possible hazards around the home and to see if there are any useful aids and adaptations for your relative.

INCONTINENCE

It is always worth discussing this problem with your doctor as sometimes it may be possible to prevent incontinence; for example, if it is due to a urinary infection, constipation or a side effect of medication. Even if it cannot be stopped, there are ways to improve the situation. You may find it helpful to remind your relative to go to the toilet, or if no toilet is nearby perhaps get a commode. Special incontinence advisers can give you practical help such as supplying pads and your doctor can refer your relative to this service.

HALLUCINATIONS

Visual hallucinations – that is, seeing things that are not there – can happen out of the blue and are not uncommon. They may happen as a result of poor vision or having an infection and it is worth discussing the problem with your doctor. Often hallucinations will stop after a few weeks and are then forgotten, but they can be upsetting and it is important to offer reassurance. You may also try distracting your relative, but do not agree that the hallucinations are real. Occasionally medication is needed.

PARANOID BELIEFS AND ACCUSATORY BEHAVIOUR

Your relative may make accusations against yourself, such as accusing you of being no good, or of trying to cause harm or of stealing things. This is clearly distressing but it is important not to take it personally but to try and see it as your relative's way of making sense of the environment. For example, your relative's loss of memory increases his or her chances of misplacing things. Generally it is best not to contradict your relative but instead to look for the lost things or try distraction. In some cases medication can be helpful and it is worth discussing this problem with the doctor.

Tips for carers

- Establishing a routine can be helpful for you and your relative. Try to continue to encourage some independence in your relative; be flexible and keep tasks simple.

- Avoid confrontation. It is very easy to get angry and frustrated but it is important not to take it out on your relative.

- Due to the worsening nature of the illness, it is important to keep matters continually under review. If your relative's behaviour becomes more erratic then you will need to consider the safety of the immediate environment; for example, you may need to disconnect a gas cooker and replace it with a microwave.

What is the outlook?

Alzheimer's disease

Alzheimer's disease is the most common type of progressive, irreversible dementia. Although no two people with the disease follow the same course, it is usually divided into three stages.

EARLY STAGE

A person is likely to have lost interest in his or her usual activities, and to be indecisive and disorientated about time. Although short-term memory is reduced some people may be skilful at hiding this.

MIDDLE STAGE

The person is more severely impaired, and may have difficulty with everyday tasks, such as washing and dressing without help, or with finding the right words when talking. There may also be behavioural problems such as wandering and aggression. Carers may notice a change in personality such as increased rigidity and diminished emotional responsiveness, along with a lack of motivation. These changes can be a source of great distress, particularly if as often happens the person begins to disregard the carer's feelings.

LATE STAGE

A person gradually becomes dependent on others for all aspects of care. There is often a loss of mobility and people may be incontinent of urine and faeces. At this stage they may not recognise their families and may stop eating. All this can be a great source of anxiety for the carer.

Each individual has a different course but progression through these three stages usually takes about five to eight years.

SECTION 2
Mental Health Services

Introduction

Frank Holloway

The evolution of mental health services

Throughout the nineteenth and the first half of the twentieth century mental health care was based in mental hospitals or asylums. These were often remote from the inmates' homes. Initially asylums were a humane and optimistic response to the needs of people with a mental illness, with positive expectations of recovery and discharge. However, they rapidly became large institutions where conditions were often harsh, the doors were locked and expectations were low. After an episode of mental illness many people spent their entire adult life within a mental hospital.

It became clear in the 1960s that living in a mental hospital run on regimented lines can actually increase the disabilities of people with a mental illness. In the 1960s and 1970s a series of scandals surrounding poor standards of care in long-stay hospitals for people with a mental illness or mental handicap and the elderly further discredited institutional care. However, for all its faults the asylum was efficient at meeting a range of basic human needs for its residents. These included shelter, company, food, clothing, minimal leisure opportunities and, at least for some people, opportunities for work. Other needs were often denied to hospital residents.

In 1954 there were more than 150,000 people living in mental hospitals in England and Wales. At the turn of the millennium the number is less than 40,000. One by one the asylums have been closing as the process of deinstitutionalisation has gathered momentum. Over the last 50 years mental health services have moved from the era of institutional care to the era of community care. People now rarely stay in hospital for long periods and increasing numbers receive treatment for their mental health problems from community mental health services. In part this transformation in services has been due to the availability from the mid-1950s onwards of effective treatments for severe mental illness. Just as important has been a change in the attitudes of professionals, sufferers from mental illness and the public so that it is realised that people who have had an episode of mental illness can recover or, even if still unwell, experience fulfilled lives outside hospital.

What is wrong with community care?

It has long been recognised that the system of community care in England and Wales that has evolved to replace the traditional hospital-based pattern of services is unsatisfactory. Although the vast majority of people with a mental illness spend almost all of their time outside hospital, more money for mental health care still goes on inpatient services than in the community. Key community care agencies have conspicuously failed to work together in planning services. Even today the care system remains fragmented, with poor co-ordination between the many agencies supposed to be providing support to sufferers and carers being the norm rather than the exception. Planning for discharge after an inpatient stay has been repeatedly criticised, with some vulnerable people receiving little or no support on leaving hospital. There are also concerns that some services do not concentrate on people with the greatest need but instead provide care to the 'worried well'.

Successive governments have tried to tackle these very real problems in the organisation of community care within the context of spiralling costs, particularly in the care of the elderly. Other more direct concerns about community care have also been expressed and attracted a policy response. Rightly or wrongly community care has been blamed for the problem of street homelessness, for placing unacceptable burdens on carers, for filling our prisons with people with mental illness and for depriving people with a mental illness of the positive aspects of asylum life and as a result diminishing their quality of life. There has been a perception that vulnerable people are allowed to fall through the cracks of a confusing and fragmented service system. More recently there has been a degree of unjustified panic, whipped up by the tabloid press, that community care was responsible for exposing the public to risks of violence from the mentally ill.

Policy responses in the 1990s

In the decade since the publication of two landmark white papers *Working for Patients* and *Caring for People* in 1989, successive governments have placed considerable emphasis on mental health issues. The list below summarises some of the major initiatives from 1989 to 1996. These are set in a framework within which the purchasing of care was separated from its provision, with the intention that the purchasing health and social services authorities would work closely together in service planning.

Selected health and social care policy initiatives: 1989–1996

1989: *Working for Patients.*

1989: *Caring for People.*

1990: *NHS and Community Care Act.*

1990: *HC(90)23: The Care Programme Approach.*

1990: *Community Care in the Next Decade and Beyond.*

1991: *The Patient's Charter.*

1992: *Health of the Nation.*

1992: *Reed Committee Report on the Mentally Disordered Offender.*

1993: *Mrs Bottomley's Ten Point Plan.*

1993: *Mental Health Key Area Handbook.*

1994: *HSG(94)5: The Supervision Register.*

1994: *HSG(94)27: Discharge Guidance.*

1995: *Carers (Recognition and Services) Act.*

1995: *Mental Health (Patients in the Community) Act.*

1995: *Building Bridges.*

1996: *The Spectrum of Care.*

1996: *24-Hour Nursed Care for People with Severe and Enduring Mental Illness.*

There has been an increasingly consumerist agenda within health and social care, exemplified by the introduction in 1991 of *The Patient's Charter* and increasingly elaborate mechanisms for the investigation of complaints and untoward incidents. Broad issues of public health have been emphasised, with mental health being one of the key areas identified for action within *Health of the Nation* and the most recent white paper, *Saving Lives: Our Healthier Nation.* This has led to targets for the reduction of suicide rates in the population as a whole and among people in contact with mental health services.

The *Reed Committee Report on the Mentally Disordered Offender* underlined the government's commitment to the diversion of people with an identified mental health problem from the criminal justice system into mental health services, ironically at a time when the institutional base for mental health services was rapidly eroding as the mental hospitals closed.

Care management was introduced in social services with a remit for care managers to assess need, purchase care and monitor outcomes (the aim being that less expensive packages of community care would be purchased instead of residential care). Mental health providers were instructed to introduce the *Care Programme Approach* (CPA), within which everyone in contact with specialist mental health services would have a named key worker and a written, regularly reviewed, care plan. Arguably the introduction of separate systems for the arrangement of the health and social care of people with a mental illness in the early 1990s was a major lost opportunity, which has been corrected in the latest policy guidance on the CPA.

The CPA, an essentially organisational mechanism that attempts to ensure that people are effectively followed up by services, has continued to be the centre-piece of mental health policy.

Following two well-publicised highly disturbing incidents that took place in London in December 1992 – the murder of Jonathan Zito and Ben Silcock's foray into the lion's den at London Zoo – policy making has focused increasingly on issues of risk. Discharge guidance was published that required providers to carry out risk assessments and develop care plans prior to discharge from hospital. The 1983 Mental Health Act, a libertarian document concerned with the rights of the detained person, was amended to allow for a form of compulsory aftercare.

Throughout the 1990s there was a succession of policy guidance about the shape of mental health services and good practice. A range of financial incentives has been deployed to encourage joint working, from joint finance through the Mental Illness Specific Grant to the contemporary Mental Health Modernisation Fund. Special funding has been available targeting the general and mental health needs of homeless people, particularly rough sleepers.

Future policy directions

Selected health and social care policy initiatives: 1997–1999

1997: *The New NHS. Modern. Dependable.*

1998: *Modernising Mental Health Services. Safe. Sound. Supportive.*

1999: *Saving Lives: Our Healthier Nation.*

1999: *Managing Dangerous People with Severe Personality Disorder: Proposals for Policy Development.*

1999: *Making Decisions.*

1999: *The National Service Framework for Mental Health.*

1999: *Reform of the Mental Health Act 1983.*

1999: *Effective Care Co-ordination in Mental Health Services.*

The broad thrust of policy has changed little since the 1997 election, and the publication of *The New NHS. Modern. Dependable* (see the list below). The wilder rhetoric of the marketplace has been dropped in favour of increasing central control of health services through the mechanism of 'performance management', a strong commitment to service quality and an emphasis on evidence-based practice. The role of primary care is emphasised, with primary care groups and later primary care trusts taking on some of the functions of the purchasers.

Current and future mental health policy was spelt out in the publication *Modernising Mental Health Services. Safe. Sound. Supportive* (with the emphasis throughout on 'safe'). This was based on the sweeping assertion that 'community care has failed' and promised a series of initiatives which are now being 'rolled out'. They include:

- reform of the Mental Health Act to allow for compulsory community treatment while ensuring compliance with the European Convention of Human Rights

- proposals for managing dangerous people with severe personality disorders

- revised mechanisms for managing the affairs of people with mental incapacity

- new guidelines on care co-ordination, which decree a merger of CPA and care management

- a *National Service Framework for Mental Health*.

The National Service Framework sets out broad standards for mental health services including a standard on 'Caring about carers'. Its introduction will be tightly 'performance-managed' by the Department of Health.

For decades mental health policy has struggled to provide a legal and service framework that matches the reality of the end of the asylum era and brings coherence to the work of community mental health services. Current initiatives are a bold attempt to achieve this end. Time will tell.

CHAPTER 14

Mental Health Services

Sonia Johnson

Over the last 50 years as care in the community has developed local networks of mental health services have become more complicated. In the past the big asylums were the main source of care for people with a mental illness; now not only NHS providers but also social services, charitable or voluntary sector and private organisations provide a range of services in many different settings. Although the government has made some attempt to specify what services should be available in every area, and more recently, to set quality standards, the way in which services are organised still varies considerably from area to area. Working out how mental health services function in your locality may be quite confusing. There may be a local directory to give some indication of the range of services available, but it is often not possible to get up-to-date and complete listings and explanations.

This chapter provides information to help you understand how local mental health services work. It covers the following areas:

- general principles about service provision in England and Wales

- typical components of a local service for adults with severe and enduring mental health problems

- services for other groups of mental health service users, including older adults, children and adolescents, offenders who have mental health problems, people with drug and alcohol problems, ethnic minorities and refugee communities and homeless people.

The following list shows the types of service discussed in this chapter.

Main types of service

- services for adults (18 to 65 years):
  - inpatient services
  - community mental health teams
  - outpatient clinics
  - emergency services
  - assertive outreach and rehabilitation services
  - day care and work schemes
  - residential services
  - liaison services
- services for older adults
- services for children and adolescents
- services for offenders with mental health problems
- services for people with drug and alcohol problems
- services for ethnic minorities and refugee communities
- services for homeless people.

General principles in mental health service provision

The principles outlined in this section apply to mental health service provision for most groups of service users in England and Wales.

Services are based on catchment areas

Apart from a small number of specialised services, most mental health services are provided for the population of a specific geographical area (catchment area) and do not accept people from outside that area. The advantage of this is that services can be locally based. Catchment areas vary in size depending on the type of service. Services may be provided for the population of a sector, trust, local authority or larger area.

SECTOR

This is a term used to describe an area with a population of about 30–60,000 people. Each trust (see below) or local authority is likely to contain several sectors. In a sector there will generally be a single mental health team and one or two consultant psychiatrists providing mental health services for all adults (18 to 65 years) with severe mental health problems living in the area. The advantage of making very small areas the basis for planning services is that teams will know other professionals and agencies working in the area. Sectors may be defined by geography (often following electoral ward boundaries) or be based on GP lists, so that each team works with patients registered with a particular group of GP practices.

TRUST AND LOCAL AUTHORITY

Many of the core components of a mental health service are the responsibility of the local NHS trust. There are different sorts of trust including trusts centred around general hospitals which may include mental health services, and community-based trusts. In future primary care trusts are likely to include some mental health services.

If services are funded by social services, local authority boundaries may be used to define catchment areas. The boundaries of NHS trusts sometimes overlap with local authority boundaries (for example, the boundaries of counties, metropolitan areas or London boroughs), but this is not always the case, which can be confusing.

LARGER CATCHMENT AREAS

There are some more specialised services that may be available to people from a larger area covering a number of trusts. One example is a mother and baby service for mothers with a mental illness after childbirth.

There are a few highly specialised services which do not have a specific catchment area, but take referrals from anywhere in the country. If there is such a service which may meet your relative's needs it may be possible for your relative's local mental team or even GP to make a referral.

Services prioritise individuals with severe and enduring mental health problems

Mental health problems are very common in the general population. Most people can gain help from their GP or another member of the primary care team (see Chapter 16) or via the voluntary sector. To ensure that specialist mental health resources are targeted on those who need specialist care, policy makers, both within and outside government, have encouraged services to give priority to people with a severe and enduring mental illness. In practice this means that people with schizophrenia, bipolar affective disorder and severe dementia are high priority groups, while people with problems such as a milder depression or anxiety may be encouraged to seek help from their GP or through local counselling and therapy services or self-help groups.

Service provision is organised according to the principles set out in the Care Programme Approach

As described in the Introduction to Section 2, in the early 1990s, concerns about services becoming fragmented and failing to work together properly led to the introduction in England and Wales of the Care Programme Approach (CPA). This is a set of principles for organising care. Trusts and local authorities are required by law to apply the CPA in the care of all individuals who have a severe and enduring mental health problem and are in contact with specialist mental health services.

Basic principles in the care of each individual eligible for care under the CPA include:

- There must be an identified key worker. The key worker is often a community psychiatric nurse or social worker, but may be an experienced professional from any background. He or she is responsible for keeping in touch with the service user, offering support and responding to any major change or crisis, organising reviews, checking that all the services in contact with the person are working together in a co-ordinated way and making sure that the care plan (see below) is put into action.

- There is an identified consultant psychiatrist responsible for a service user's care. This is generally the consultant working with the team.

- There are regular reviews of the individual's needs for clinical and social care. After each review the key worker draws up a written care plan, setting out planned actions to address each need identified.

Many of the details of how CPA reviews are organised and care plans documented are decided at a local level. For people on standard CPA who simply attend the outpatient clinic, there may not be a requirement to hold formal CPA review meetings. For other people with more complex problems who see several different mental health professionals, the key worker must organise regular CPA meetings. These usually take place every six months, although they may be more frequent for vulnerable individuals who are at risk of harming or neglecting themselves or of harming others.

CPA meetings will usually be attended by the service user, their key worker and consultant psychiatrist or deputy (who will be an experienced member of staff working in the consultant's team). With the service user's agreement the key worker should invite members of the family, or other carers. The service user may decide to ask an advocate to accompany them. GPs are routinely invited, but many do not have the time to attend these meetings very regularly. The key worker may also invite other involved professionals. These may include a social worker, housing worker, probation officer or other therapist. As a result there may be a number of people present at the meeting, so you and your relative may feel quite intimidated. To help deal with this problem, it can be helpful for you and your relative to consider and discuss in advance issues you would like to see raised, and to talk to the key worker or advocate about these before the meeting. It may also be helpful to request arranging part of the meeting to involve a smaller group of people.

Issues discussed at the CPA review are likely to include the service user's current mental health, their ability to look after themselves, maintain relationships and carry out chosen activities, and any social problems such as difficulties with housing, benefits or childcare or social isolation. There is likely to be discussion about plans made at the last review giving a chance for everyone present to review how successful these were, and to consider any particular difficulties with them. Time should be spent on agreeing a care plan to meet the individual's current needs. The meeting should also address the particular needs of carers. After the meeting, the key worker will circulate a written care plan to everyone invited to the meeting. As well as giving details of a person's identified needs and plans for care, it will have contact details of the main professionals involved in the plan.

Typical components of a local service for adults with severe and enduring mental health problems

The largest component of a mental health service is the general adult mental health service for people aged 18 to 65 years with severe and enduring mental health problems. Services for adults include a number of elements.

Inpatient services

Admissions to a psychiatric inpatient ward are generally brief, with most people leaving hospital after a few weeks. More lengthy admissions only occur if there are exceptional difficulties with finding appropriate accommodation or a particularly high level of persisting concern about risk to self or others. Psychiatric units are now generally locally based, maybe as part of the general hospital.

Admission to a general psychiatric ward may be either on a voluntary basis or under a section of the Mental Health Act 1983 (see Chapter 22 for more details). In London and other big cities, sometimes there will not be a vacant bed in the local unit for a person needing admission and he or she may be admitted to another unit. A minority of individuals who are very unwell and present a significant risk to themselves or others may need more supervision and intensive care than is available on a general ward. In order to obtain this, they may be transferred to a psychiatric intensive care unit with a higher level of staffing.

Community mental health teams

For most adults with severe and long-term mental health problems, the main service providing and organising mental health care in the community is the community mental health team (CMHT). This is made up of members of each of the major mental health professions. It serves a particular sector, and is usually based locally away from other health service premises in a community mental health centre or mental health resource centre. This may be purpose built or a converted shop, office or house.

The type of work carried out by individual members of the CMHT is described in Chapter 15. Most members of the team are key workers for a number of service users under the CPA (see above). The CMHT will generally meet regularly as a team to consider new referrals, and discuss work with existing clients, especially those who may be showing signs of relapse or experiencing particular difficulties. Most CMHTs work Monday to Friday 9am to 5pm, although extended hours are available in some areas.

CMHTs work closely with other local mental health, social care and primary care services, aiming to help their clients access appropriate support and treatment. Team members will see some service users at the centre, but they also visit people at home, so staff gain a fuller picture of people's living situations and any social difficulties.

Outpatient clinics

Outpatient clinics are held in a variety of settings including the local hospital, community mental health centre or other community settings such as a GP surgery. Generally appointments are available in these clinics for assessments and ongoing treatment. An assessment may take up to an hour and a half, while follow-up appointments are shorter. At a follow-up appointment, the psychiatrist will assess a person's current mental health and social functioning, review any treatment, provide some support and consider needs for other forms of care.

As a carer it can be helpful for you to accompany your relative to the appointment and give your perspective on progress made and any difficulties encountered. If your relative's mental health is fairly stable this may be the only contact he or she has with services.

Emergency services

The provision for emergency assessment and treatment varies greatly from area to area. The new National Service Framework for Mental Health sets as a standard 24-hour access to emergency treatment for people with mental health problems, and this should lead to an improvement in the emergency help available in many areas.

Between 9am and 5pm Monday to Friday, the local CMHT and consultant psychiatrist will often be the best first point of contact in a crisis, especially for service users already in contact with the team. However, few CMHTs work 24 hours, and arrangements for out-of-hours contact vary.

Local authority social services departments have a responsibility to make an approved social worker available 24 hours a day to arrange Mental Health Act assessments, which may be requested by carers (see Chapter 22).

Within primary care there is 24-hour cover, but out of hours this is unlikely to be provided by your relative's regular GP. The local accident and emergency department also provides a 24-hour service. There may simply be a junior psy chiatrist based in the department or a larger team of mental health professionals. If your relative attends the accident and emergency department out of hours he or she is likely first to see a casualty officer who can ask the psychiatrist or other mental health professional to do a further assessment if needed.

In some areas there are specialised multidisciplinary crisis or home treatment teams. These aim to assess people at home and as far as possible try to help resolve the crisis without the individual being admitted to hospital. Instead members of the team may need to make frequent home visits to monitor a person's mental health and to offer support.

Crisis houses are another form of specialist emergency care available in a few areas. These are places in the community, often converted houses, where people with mental health problems can stay in an emergency. These vary in their aims, but some of the more highly staffed crisis houses aim to provide an alternative to hospital admission.

Assertive outreach and rehabilitation services

Assertive outreach teams provide more intensive care than CMHTs. Even a well-resourced CMHT will have difficulty persuading some people with a severe mental illness to stay in contact with services and accept treatment. This particularly applies to people with a psychotic illness who are not aware that they are ill (that is, who lack insight). Some of these individuals may be reluctant to accept treatment and are at particular risk of frequent hospital admissions or of harming themselves or others. Staff in an assertive outreach team have a smaller caseload allowing them to spend more time trying to keep in contact with service users. The number of assertive outreach teams is likely to increase in the future.

The term 'rehabilitation' covers a variety of ways of working with service users. The setting for such a service may be community-based, residential or in a day service. Rehabilitation work aims progressively to improve a person's quality of life and social functioning by helping them to develop their social and daily living skills and to cope with any symptoms and associated difficulties. To some extent all CMHTs carry out work of this sort, but in some areas there are specific services dedicated to rehabilitation work.

Day care and work schemes

A range of day services are provided by the NHS, social services departments and the voluntary sector, with a great variation found between areas. Day hospitals usually accept people for treatment for short periods when their mental health has deteriorated or they are facing major social difficulties, aiming to avoid the need for hospital admission. In some areas, different types of day hospital have developed; for example, providing longer-term rehabilitation services or group treatments for people with problems such as repeated self-harm.

Day centres allow people to attend over a longer time and provide opportunities for social contact and structured activities, such as discussion groups and creative activities. 'Drop-in centres' are less structured than day centres and focus on improving social contact and sometimes offer basic practical help. They may be run by a voluntary sector agency in some cases with users playing a major role in planning and managing them.

Helping people with a mental illness return to work is covered in Chapter 20. The services for adults with a mental health problem include projects which create jobs for particular groups of people, and help with gaining work in mainstream employment and in training and education.

Residential services

Supported residential services form another important part of the range of services people with a mental illness may need. The level of support available to residents varies in different schemes. At one end there are services offering intensive 24-hour care approaching that available on a hospital ward. At the other end, there are supported flats in which people live with the back-up of occasional visits from a housing support worker. More information about housing for people with mental health problems is given in Chapter 18.

Liaison services

Liaison services aim to meet the needs of patients in a general hospital setting such as the accident and emergency department and medical and surgical wards and clinics. Liaison staff work together with health professionals from other disciplines to treat people who have a mixture of physical and mental health problems or who seek help for physical symptoms which may be the result of an underlying mental health problem.

Other types of service for adults with severe and enduring mental health problems

Some more specialist types of service which are needed by a relatively small number of people are provided for a larger catchment area population (for example, a whole NHS region), or may accept referrals from all over the country. Examples of such a service are units specialising in the treatment of people with an eating disorder, mother and baby units, or the various types of secure unit.

In some local catchment areas there are a variety of other services available. Examples include a service for people in the early stages of a psychotic illness, a service for people with both severe mental illness and a drug or alcohol problem ('dual diagnosis') and a service for people who repeatedly harm themselves. Such innovative services are often set up on a research basis, with detailed investigation of the effects of the service.

Services for other populations

Services for older adults

In the same way that there are local services for adults aged under 65 years, there are also specific local services for older adults. The age limit varies, but typically these services are for people aged 65 years and over. A major part of the work of these services is in the care of people with dementia and with complex physical as well as mental health problems. Staff will work with people living in their own homes, as well as working with nursing and residential homes.

Services for children and adolescents

The range of mental health problems experienced by children is rather different from those of adults and there are specific local services for children and adolescents with mental health problems. Children may experience delays and difficulties in their development, emotional or behavioural problems and the consequences of child abuse. Staff will work closely with families and schools. Admission to hospital is rare.

The extent to which adolescent services are separate from those for younger children varies from area to area, as do the age boundaries between child and adolescent and between adolescent and adult services.

Services for offenders with mental health problems

Chapter 21 describes the network of services available for people who have a major mental health problem and have committed a significant criminal offence. These include a range of types of secure unit. Increasingly, forensic mental health professionals are developing closer links with CMHTs and other parts of the general mental health services, so that they can contribute to the assessment and treatment of people with mental illnesses who are at risk of committing a serious offence.

Services for people with drug and alcohol problems

There are particularly large variations in the way services are provided for people with drug and alcohol problems in different parts of the country. In most areas, NHS trusts offer some services for people with drug and alcohol problems, but local voluntary sector organisations are also very important providers of drug and alcohol services. Self-help groups such as Narcotics

Anonymous or Alcoholics Anonymous may be central to the recovery of people with drug or alcohol problems. This is therefore an area in which it is especially important to seek out information from local and national directories and local service providers about the range of services available.

Areas vary in the extent to which services for drug and for alcohol problems are separate from one another. Most provide services offering individual assessments, advice and treatment for people with drug or alcohol problems, treatment and self-help groups, facilities for treating those in the first stages of withdrawal from alcohol ('detoxification') and clinics for people prescribed methadone or other substitute medication. Residential rehabilitation services allow for admission over an extended period and are usually run by a voluntary sector agency. Local drug and alcohol services or social services may be able to help find funding for such services.

Services for members of ethnic minority communities and for refugees

There has been increasing concern that members of ethnic minority communities in the country may not be well served by mental health services (see Chapter 27). Issues include the high rates of compulsory admission among the African-Caribbean population, the lack of satisfaction with services of this group, suspected high levels of untreated mental health problems and under-use of services and concerns that professionals lack understanding of cultural differences. As a response to these concerns a number of community services have been set up for members of particular ethnic minorities. There have also been training initiatives intended to raise awareness of cultural issues among mental health professionals generally.

Service planners are only just beginning to consider the substantial needs for mental health care which are likely to exist among refugee communities in the UK. A particular need among these groups is for treatment for post-traumatic stress disorder.

Services for homeless people

There are high levels of mental health problems among homeless people. However, services often find it difficult to maintain contact and provide appropriate treatment for these people and, particularly in inner city areas, specific services for the homeless mentally ill have developed. The staff work intensively to make contact and keep in touch with their clients and to meet their needs, which are often a complex combination including basic practical needs for housing and money, physical care needs, and needs for treatment of both mental and physical health problems.

Does community care work?

This chapter has explained the variety of services available for helping people with a mental illness. Although most areas do have in place the essential elements of a comprehensive mental health service, there are considerable variations in the way the different services are provided across the country. Initiatives such as the National Service Framework for Mental Health and the NHS Plan are an attempt to ensure that the essential elements of a mental health service are available throughout the country.

There has been much discussion in the media over the last ten years about the 'failure' of community care. Can you trust current services to support and treat your relative or friend? Research studies have looked at how well community care works; their results indicate that most people with a severe mental illness can live safely and achieve a reasonable quality of life through the help of community mental health services and with only limited contact with inpatient services.

Advice for carers

As a carer it is essential that you know about what is available locally where your friend or relative lives. Promising innovative models of care have been introduced or are planned in many areas, and if successful may become more widespread in the future. There is also increasing weight given to the views of carers and service users, and you may wish to find out how you can make your views known about current services, or get involved in working with service planners in looking at options for new services.

CHAPTER 15

Mental Health Professionals

Wendy Maphosa and Emma Staples

Community mental health teams (CMHTs)

Mental health professionals usually work in teams. These teams include mental health nurses, psychiatrists, social workers, occupational therapists and psychologists. The team works together to assess the difficulties with which a person and their family need help. Different members of the team have different skills.

CMHTs are usually based in the community, separate from the hospital. People receiving help from the team come to the team base to see their key worker or other health professional, and team members may visit them at home. If someone needs admission to inpatient care, the CMHT will stay in contact with the inpatient unit to allow continuity of care.

A key worker is the key person involved in someone's care. He or she will liaise with all the other professionals involved, including staff in primary care such as the GP. The key worker may be a community psychiatric nurse, social worker, occupational therapist, psychologist or psychiatrist.

In order to provide co-ordinated care, the different members of a mental health team need to communicate with each other. This will usually be done at regular weekly meetings, when the team meets to discuss the progress of individuals under their care. Once or twice a year there will be meetings (under the Care Programme Approach) when professionals providing care to a particular individual meet and review plans. The individual concerned and often a family member will be invited to this as well.

The role of different mental health professionals

Community psychiatric nurses (CPNs)

CPNs are trained nurses with extensive experience of working with people with mental health problems. They may visit people living in their homes, or see them in the community team base or, if someone is admitted to hospital, visit them on the ward.

CPNs are involved in:

- assessing a person's needs, and planning and evaluating the care being provided

- providing the first point of contact for individuals and their families

- communicating, liaising and linking up with other agencies providing care for that individual

- providing psychological help

- helping with medication – giving advice, administering other medications such as depot medication, observing the response and any side effects of the medication

- being an advocate, helping to represent the individual's views, and referring someone on to other agencies as needed; for example, to social services if there are problems over housing, benefits or childcare

- offering education, advice and support to individuals and their relatives and friends about mental illness and how to cope with it; supporting families when their relative is ill; and helping prevent relapse or admissions to hospital if possible by working with carers.

Psychiatrists

Psychiatrists are doctors who specialise in treating people with mental illness and psychological problems. After training to be a doctor, psychiatrists follow specialist training in the areas of mental illness and psychology. A psychiatrist then completes higher specialist training in a particular speciality. Psychiatrists have different titles according to the amount of specialist training they have completed: senior house officers will become specialist registrars who in turn become consultant psychiatrists.

Psychiatrists are involved in:

- assessing a person's psychological difficulties

- working with other members of the CMHT, individuals and their families to develop a treatment plan
- treating individuals using both psychological approaches and medication
- admitting people to hospital if they are in need of more intensive support and treatment
- for people who need treatment but do not recognise their problems, the psychiatrist may be involved in assessment and treatment under the Mental Health Act (1983)
- co-ordinating and reviewing an individual's care with other members of the CMHT
- working with GPs and other primary care staff, which may include reviewing people in the GP's surgery.

Clinical psychologists

Clinical psychologists specialise in using psychological principles to assess and treat people with mental health problems. Their training allows them to offer specific psychological treatments.

Psychologists are involved in:

- providing a special perspective in assessment and treatment planning
- assessing individuals for specific psychological treatment approaches
- providing specific psychological treatments; these may include:
  - psychological therapies to help individuals with depression and anxiety
  - helping individuals with a psychotic illness to manage any unusual thoughts, beliefs and voices
  - working with individuals with an eating disorder
  - working with individuals and their families to develop programmes to help with difficult and distressing behaviour
  - running groups for individuals and their carers
  - helping colleagues with their work with specific psychological problems, such as severe reactions to traumatic events including bereavement
- evaluating psychological treatments.

Psychotherapists

'Psychotherapy' is a term used to describe a talking or psychological treatment. To some extent all mental health workers use elements of psychotherapy. Psychotherapists specialise in applying the psychological understanding of human relations to the treatment of mental distress. Psychotherapy may be offered as a treatment in its own right. For mental illness and emotional troubles that are more disabling it may be used in conjunction with medication and the support of other mental health professionals. Psychotherapy can help individuals, their families and mental health workers understand and cope with some of the difficult and disturbing feelings and impulses characteristic of mental illnesses and psychological distress. There are different types of psychotherapy: individual psychotherapy, group psychotherapy and family therapy.

Psychotherapists come from a number of different professional backgrounds. In the NHS, psychotherapists are usually psychiatrists, psychologists or social workers who have followed further specialist training in psychotherapy.

Psychotherapists are involved in:

- consultations with individuals to explore their psychological difficulties and think about the type of psychotherapy that could help

- treating people individually, in a group or with their partner or family

- working with other members of the mental health team to think about difficulties in understanding and helping some of the people under their care.

Occupational therapists (OTs)

Occupational therapists are trained to use activity and discussion based therapy. They help people with both mental and physical health problems to rebuild their confidence and develop the skills needed for their day-to-day living and occupations. This helps individuals develop the ability to care for themselves and relate to others.

Occupational therapists are involved in:

- encouraging individuals to identify their needs and interests and how to reach their goals in life

- helping individuals explore specific skills, such as:

- ◦ cooking, looking after a home, budgeting
- ◦ socialising with other people
- ◦ dealing with stress and anxiety
- helping people with painting, drawing, pottery and other activities that can help rebuild confidence and develop skills
- assessing needs, counselling, advising about employment and other activities
- liaising with other organisations to find places for individuals to receive training to help improve their work skills and return to employment.

Social workers

Social workers assess an individual's social needs, in consultation with other agencies involved in the person's care. They also assess the needs of carers. They then organise a package of care to support individuals and their families. 'Approved' social workers have had specific training in mental health and are approved by their local authority social services department to carry out special duties under the Mental Health Act in times of crisis. They will provide a mental health assessment and, if necessary, help organise admissions to hospital under a 'section' of the Act.

Social workers are involved in:

- assessing the needs of individuals and their families including:
  - ◦ housing
  - ◦ help around the home
  - ◦ a place in a day centre
  - ◦ help in applying for benefits and grants
- carrying out an assessment in a crisis.

Other important professionals

GENERAL PRACTITIONERS (GPS)

General practitioners provide mental health support to everyone under the care of their practice in conjunction with the local CMHT. They will assess a person's current difficulties and provide support and treatment. They can prescribe and monitor medication and provide physical health care. They are usually the first point of contact for individuals and their families whether the difficulty is physical or psychological. They can make referrals to other services. Many GPs have mental health professionals such as a counsellor working at the surgery.

PHARMACISTS

Pharmacists are responsible for ensuring the supply of medication, and that it is available in the right form. They have expert knowledge of the use of medicines and employ this to advise doctors and nurses with whom they work.

HOSPITAL CHAPLAINS

Many hospitals have a chapel and a chaplaincy service. The chapel can be used for private prayers and there may be religious services. Some hospitals have visiting representatives from different faiths to help in the spiritual care of patients. The chaplaincy may be able to help contact the appropriate representatives of someone's faith.

A day in the life of a CPN

Jane Martin is a community psychiatric nurse working with a community mental health team based in inner city London. The team provides care and support for people with mental health problems who live in the local area. Jane is involved in the care of about 25 patients whom she sees on a regular basis. She visits people at home or sees them at the team base or in hospital. She also works at a local general practice. She sees patients the GPs are concerned about for assessments and ongoing support. Jane supervises a student nurse who is training and accompanies her for some of the week.

Today is Friday

9.00am: Jane arrives at the community mental health team base. She meets with the other team members to hear about what has happened over the previous day and night. Together the team think about the difficulties that the patients and their families have had and make plans for the day ahead. Jane discusses her movements for the day so that the team are aware of her whereabouts. She checks to see if she has any messages to follow up before she starts her day. There is a message to contact the emergency clinic. One of her patients, Leah, attended the emergency clinic in a crisis during the night.

10.00am: Jane phones Leah and arranges to visit her at home. Before leaving the office, Jane meets with her student and prepares her for the day ahead. Then she phones a local GP to discuss someone who was recently referred to the team to get more information. She also phones the social worker involved to arrange a visit together.

10.15am: Jane and the student set off to Leah's home. This visit is to assess Leah's psychological difficulties and to find out more about the disturbing experiences she had been having. Jane spends time talking to Leah to find out what help she needs. She also meets Leah's parents to hear their concerns and thoughts. Jane discusses with Leah and her parents the support that could be offered, including going into hospital. Leah and her parents would prefer it if she stayed at home rather than being admitted to hospital. Jane offers advice about what to do if there is a crisis. She leaves telephone contacts to call over the weekend if they are worried.

11.30am: Back at the team base, Jane writes her notes about the visit to Leah's home and the outcome of the assessment. She discusses the situation with the consultant psychiatrist and they agree on a management plan for Leah should she come to the emergency clinic at the weekend. She faxes this information through to the clinic. Downstairs in the waiting room Robert and his brother are waiting to see Jane. She is already running late with her appointments. Robert is attending for his monthly review meeting with Jane and the psychiatrist. He is also due to receive depot medication for schizophrenia. His brother, who is very concerned about him, accompanies Robert. Jane spends time with the two brothers assessing how things are at home and what concerns they both have. They show Jane a letter they have received from the DSS stating that housing benefit payments will be stopped at the end of the month. After making phone calls and enquiring further it appears that Robert has not completed a form that had been sent by the benefit office. Jane spends time helping Robert complete the application. She also phones the housing officer and arranges an appointment for Robert at the housing office. Jane then supervises her student in preparing and administering the depot medication. (Robert has consented to receive his medication from the student nurse.) She spends a further ten minutes with Robert to ensure that he does not experience adverse side effects from his medication.

12.55pm: Jane grabs a cup of coffee and a sandwich before the Care Programme Approach review meeting of one of her patients, Mr Aziz, starts. She has arranged for the other team members who are involved with Mr Aziz's care to come to this meeting. In attendance are Dr Brown, the psychiatrist; Martin, the social worker; Maggie, the occupational therapist; Sarah, the family worker; and Neil from the local day centre that Mr Aziz attends. His GP was invited but was unable to come. Mr Aziz is accompanied by his wife. Jane discusses with the team her thoughts about the progress and difficulties that there have been. The couple are asked to describe how things have been for them. Each team member talks about the work they have been doing with Mr Aziz and his family and what their continued involvement could be. Issues and concerns put forward by Mr and Mrs Aziz are discussed and solutions sought. The psychiatrist reviews Mr Aziz's medication and finds out whether there are any problems with unwanted side effects. The social worker discusses his social needs such as benefit entitlement and their present housing situation. The occupational therapist reviews Mr Aziz's activities and discusses his observations with Neil from the day centre. They explore the possibility of courses for Mr Aziz to learn skills that could help him to return to work. At the end of the meeting, a care plan involving Mr Aziz, his wife and the team is drawn up and agreed upon. This will be reviewed again in three months' time.

2.00pm: Jane receives a call from the mother of one of her patients, John. John's mother is distressed and very worried because he has been talking about 'ending it all' and has not been sleeping or eating. In the past John has attempted suicide and been threatening to his mother. John's mother says that he has not been to work and it emerges that he has stopped taking his prescribed medication. He has been withdrawn and irritable, isolating himself in his room with the curtains drawn. He appears to be responding to voices. Jane had visited two days earlier and had been concerned that John's mental health was deteriorating. She links this relapse with the anniversary of John's father's death. His father died a year ago this month and John has been struggling to come to terms with this loss. John's partner has recently left him and will not allow John to see their five-year-old daughter. Jane has known John for several years and she recognises the pattern of his relapses. She offers to visit John at home because he will not come to the team base.

Jane discusses John's case with the team leader and it is decided that a joint visit with the psychiatrist and social worker is necessary. Jane telephones John's GP and informs her of the situation and tells her that they think it may be necessary to admit John to hospital for his safety. The GP has a good relationship with John and the family and Jane asks whether she could accompany them to John's home.

2.45pm: Jane phones John's mother to inform her of their visit and the possibility that John may need to go into hospital. John's mother is tearful on the phone. Jane listens to her concerns and reassures her that she has done the right thing by alerting the team to John's condition and that he will be best cared for in a safe environment.

Before she leaves the office, Jane asks the duty nurse if she can see two of her patients who are due to come in the afternoon to see her and collect their medication. Just as she is about to leave the building Jane is stopped by a colleague who wants to ask her advice about a patient she knows. She spends five minutes discussing the concerns of her colleague.

3.00pm: Home visit to John's home by Jane and the team. It takes half an hour to persuade John to come out of his room where he has barricaded himself. He refuses to speak and seems suspicious and frightened. He eventually agrees to come to hospital as long his mother comes with him. Jane organises his admission using her mobile phone. Jane considers the best way for John to get to hospital. John's mother is concerned that an ambulance will draw attention to them and she is anxious about what the neighbours will think. Jane wonders whether it would be too much of a risk for John to make his way just with his mother. John seems to have calmed down and Jane decides that they should all go together in a taxi. She alerts the emergency clinic to their arrival. Jane liaises with the nurse on duty about John's admission.

4.45pm: The taxi arrives and Jane accompanies John and his mother to hospital. The staff at the emergency clinic meet John. Jane spends some time with John's mother, who is very distressed and anxious, explaining what will happen next.

5.00pm: Jane updates the duty nurse at the team base about John. She and her student discuss what has happened. She writes notes about the visit and the outcome of the assessment and finally calls John's GP to let her know about the admission.

5.30pm: Jane heads home.

CHAPTER 16

Primary Care Services for Mental Health

Claire Gerada

This chapter describes the role of primary care in the provision of mental health services. It will guide the reader through some of the recent changes in the organisation and delivery of primary care and the ways that primary and secondary care can work together to best effect.

Organisation of primary care

Primary care is made up of all the services that are available in general practice, which include those provided by the general practitioner (GP), practice nurse and increasingly by a range of other health professionals.

Core primary care team:

- general practitioners
- primary care nurses (practice nurse, health visitor, district nurse)
- practice manager or administrator
- practice receptionists.

Examples of attached staff:

- mental health staff
- chiropodist
- physiotherapist
- welfare rights or social worker
- link or liaison workers.

Primary care is typically the point of first contact with the health service for a patient or carer. Other routes into the health service do exist, such as through the pharmacist, walk-in clinics, accident and emergency departments and NHS Direct. However, although these routes increase access to services, for most people the GP is the first port of call for their physical, social (e.g. housing and benefits advice) and psychological needs.

General practice care implies care that is provided to a registered population, over a period of time (in some cases from the cradle to the grave), usually to whole families. A typical GP is self-employed, runs a partnership and has a contract to provide General Medical Services. At least 95 per cent of the population is registered with a GP. Two thirds of people consult their doctor at least once a year. Practice size will vary according to the number of GPs. Typically there are 1000 to 1500 patients per doctor, so that a large group practice may have a list of 20,000 patients. Collectively across the country GPs perform around one million consultations per day, making them a valuable source of information about changing trends, problems with services and delays in treatment.

Primary care and mental health

About 1 in 4 adults will have a mental health problem that is severe enough to interfere with some aspect of their lives in the course of a year. However, only a small proportion (1 in 50) will be seen by specialist mental health services, and 1 in 200 admitted to hospital.

GPs spend up to a third of their time on mental health problems (see Table 16.1). Drug and alcohol problems take up more time for urban GPs.

Table 16.1 How common mental disorders are in primary care (approximate figures)	
Depression	3–6%
Anxiety states	10%
Obsessive compulsive problems	1–2%
Alcohol dependence	4%
Drug dependence	2%
Psychosis	<1%

Source: Davies, T. and Craig, T.K.J. (1998) *ABC of Mental Health*. BMJ Books.

Depression will affect nearly half of all women and a quarter of all men in the UK below the age of 70. Depression can be a major risk factor both for the development of cardiovascular disease and for death after a heart attack. Depression can also be associated with chronic physical illnesses such as arthritis. Depression in one family member may have effects on other people in the family; for example, depression in a mother may affect the development of her children. In ethnic minority groups, such as Asians and Afro-Caribbeans, doctors may miss the diagnosis of depression, and even if they do recognise it, because culture band effects may alter the clinical presentation, these groups are less likely to be referred for psychological treatments.

Attached mental health professionals

The mental health professionals undertaking clinical consultations in primary care include:

- clinical psychologists
- community psychiatric nurses (CPNs)
- counsellors
- counselling psychologists
- psychotherapists
- behavioural nurse therapists
- drug and alcohol shared care or link workers.

Clinical psychologists working in primary care are more likely than CPNs or practice counsellors to be referred people with an eating disorder, sexual problem, phobia or obsessive compulsive disorder. Patients report a high degree of satisfaction with their treatment, usually cognitive behavioural therapy, which can result in decreased use of medication.

An important role of clinical psychologists is to provide advice to GPs on how they can treat patients themselves.

Community psychiatric nurses (CPNs) tend to work in one of two ways in primary care. In the first model, nurses work from a specialist mental health base in the community or in a hospital. Most of their patients will have a severe and enduring mental illness, and many have had previous hospital admissions. In the second model, the CPN, although employed by the hospital, is based in primary care and GPs refer most of the patients directly to this CPN. The CPN's caseload in this model is larger, and includes people with a greater variety of problems – for example, neurotic disorders such as anxiety, depression, and reactions to current life crises – and fewer people with chronic psychotic problems.

Over half of the counsellors employed in primary care have had specialist training in counselling. The introduction of properly trained counsellors into primary care has led to a reduction in drug prescribing for mental illness, GP consultation rates and referrals to secondary care mental health services, as well as satisfying the needs of patients and GPs.

Primary care groups

At the moment primary care is undergoing rapid change both in its organisation and in its structure and function. The formation of primary care groups (PCGs) means that GPs are starting to work more closely together, outside the confines of their partnerships. GPs together with other PCG board members (including nursing, local authority and lay representation) will become more involved in how resources are spent, on whom, and according to what priorities.

In the future, sharing resources between practices will become the norm, all with the aim of improving care and reducing inequalities between different practices.

The role of primary care groups is

- to contribute to the Health Improvement Programme (that is, to improve the overall health of the local population)

- to develop primary care to help improve the services provided and to ensure that all GPs offer care to the same standard

- to commission primary and community services.

Primary care groups and mental health

Primary care groups have a key task in improving primary care itself. The new National Service Framework (NSF) for Mental Health emphasises this point. The NSF stresses that any patient who contacts primary care with a common mental disorder should have their mental health needs identified and assessed and be offered effective treatment, including referral to specialist services for assessment, treatment and care if needed.

PCGs are in a strong position to promote mental health and develop strategies for those at risk. This can be done by increasing awareness of and access to sources of neighbourhood support, including self-help groups, carer groups and voluntary sector agencies. The primary health care team can give practical information on managing stress as well as making a significant contribution to the physical health of people who also have mental health problems. Primary care staff can help ensure that delays in accessing specialist help are kept to a minimum by being well informed about the specialist services available.

Primary care groups should act on behalf of all their patients within a geographical area. This means that if a patient or carer is not satisfied with the treatment given, including not being able to get up-to-date treatments, they can appeal not only to their GP but also to the Chief Executive of the PCG.

PCGs are starting to join with community trusts (these currently provide services such as district nursing and speech therapy) to form larger organisations known as primary care trusts. Only time will tell how these new structures will influence local mental health services.

Conclusions

The way forward for better primary care mental health services must involve closer collaboration between service providers, better communication with service users and carers and most importantly a co-ordinated and comprehensive approach to service planning.

CHAPTER 17

Social Work Provision

Nick Hervey

Social services and carers

Social services departments have always had a generalised responsibility for carers, and carers can get help from them in a number of ways. The 1983 Mental Health Act gives a patient's nearest relative the specific right to request an assessment of a person's mental health. In practice social services staff will generally respond to a responsible request for assistance from any member of the family. If your relative needs admission to hospital, and you are the carer, in all likelihood you will be the nearest relative. As the nearest relative you have a right to be kept informed of the admission process. However, most social services departments would consider it good practice to involve any family member who is interested in the welfare of a relative, keeping them in touch with what is happening. Government legislation and strategies setting out what carers are entitled to are shown in Table 17.1.

The referral and assessment process

When you refer yourself to a social services department, or a referral is made on your behalf, it is important to ensure that you ask specifically about receiving a carer's assessment. You should be offered an appointment within a reasonable timescale, depending on the urgency of the request, and you should expect to be interviewed by appointment, in private. A good social work assessment should allow you to explore:

- your perception of the situation
- the nature of your relationship with your relative
- what caring tasks you undertake and their impact
- what kind of help you would like
- the emotional and physical impact of the caring role.

Table 17.1 Legislative and Policy Framework for Carers

Regulations and strategies	Carers' entitlements	Practical results
1991 Community Care Act	Highlighted the importance of taking carers' needs into consideration.	In practice carers' needs often take second place to the needs of the person they are caring for, or have been completely ignored.
1990 Community Care Act	Placed a responsibility on local authorities to provide better standards of information about their services and more responsive complaints systems.	To some extent has improved carers' access to services and their ability to complain on behalf of their relatives.
1995 The Carers' (Recognition and Services) Act	Aimed at highlighting the needs of carers in a more organised way. Introduced a responsibility for local authorities to provide a separate needs-led assessment for carers, whose needs had not generally been recognised under the Community Care Act.	Social services departments should now provide readily accessible information for carers in a range of languages. Should be available from all local offices.
Government's Modernisation Programme (1999)	Introduced a Carers' Special Grant intended to provide carers with increased opportunities to take a respite break.	Announcement of a new grant.
The Department of Health Circular LAC (99)13	Introduced three new special grants, for the development of partnership arrangements, preventative initiatives and services for carers. The Carers' Grant of £140 million is ringfenced until 2002.	Instituted the development of a number of practical care schemes to provide carers with respite breaks from caring for their relative.
Government's National Strategy for Carers (published in February 1999)	Local authorities and health authorities required to identify carers in their area, and their needs.	Leading to a more systematic assessment of carers' needs across health and social services.
1999 National Service Framework for Mental Health	Introduced seven key standards which local mental health services must meet, one of which is improved services for carers.	Widening awareness of the importance of assessing carers' needs across health trusts as well as social services.

You may also want to discuss your willingness and ability to continue in that role, which might involve considering what other commitments you have, such as work, education or childcare responsibilities. A social worker should explore your concerns about your relative and give you time to explain any difficulties that you may be having. The social worker should also look at your understanding of your relative's illness or disability, its likely possible development, and what strengths and ways of coping you already have.

Illness and disability often create stress in family relationships and may cause significant conflict. There may be differences in the wishes of carers and their relative. The assessment is a skilful process, which aims to support family and other caring relationships, and to assist those concerned in finding their own solutions. Conflict may arise if a family member is refusing to accept services. In this case social workers should be trying to help the family resolve the conflict, and the whole process may include other partner agencies, such as the local mental health service, voluntary organisations already involved and the housing department.

The social worker will also need to consider any cultural factors relevant to the situation. A good assessment should take into account any language, communication or comprehension difficulties, and social workers should have access to interpreters and signers.

What options are available?

Once the assessment is complete the social worker should discuss what options are available to you, and find out what your wishes are. You should receive a written copy of the assessment, which should include details about the services to be offered. If you are not offered a copy you should ask for it, and check that it reflects what was discussed with you.

There is a range of services that social workers can access for carers, and these will vary from area to area. Following the assessment, you may be offered counselling. There are special schemes for young carers who may be looking after a mentally ill parent and having to undertake a heavy burden of caring tasks inappropriate for their age. In some areas social services can access specialist help in providing family interventions for both carers and their relative, to offer information about the illness, its impact on the service user and carer, and to discuss more helpful ways for the family to manage these stresses and strains.

The new Carers' Grant specifically offers respite care for the carer. Some schemes provide a holiday away from home for the service user, giving the carer a break from caring. Other schemes offer flexible support to go into the home, giving the carer an opportunity to get out for a break. In some areas this service comes in the form of vouchers that the carer can use when they feel they need a break, and have negotiated this with the person they are caring for.

In many areas social workers are also able to give carers access to local carers' support groups. These may take many forms. Some provide educational information about mental illness and invite visiting speakers, while others offer carers the opportunity to share their common experiences and look at what they have found helpful. Many of these groups also have more informal sessions that may include social events.

There are some specialist mental health organisations offering support to carers, such as the National Schizophrenia Fellowship. This has its own Carers' Education and Support Package (CESP) which provides support to carers in groups. Another service available for service users in some areas is a crisis card scheme. Often the knowledge that your relative is carrying a card with details of what treatment they receive, your contact details, and their wishes about what should happen if they become ill will reassure you that many of the possible eventualities are covered.

Emergency services

Most social services departments also have an out-of-hours service that can be contacted in an emergency situation. It is useful to have their telephone number, as well as the number of the local accident and emergency department. The out-of-hours service may not be able to do home visits, but they can often offer helpful advice. Recently some social services departments have worked with health colleagues to set up home crisis teams and these are able to provide more practical support in crisis situations, helping users and families to avoid unnecessary admissions.

How a social worker can help your relative

Many social workers now work in multidisciplinary community mental health teams, rather than separate local authority mental health social work teams. The access point for getting hold of a mental health social worker will be known to the local authority. Social workers may have extra training in the use of the Mental Health Act 1983 to act as approved social workers (ASWs). You can approach an ASW to ask for an assessment if you are worried about the state of your relative's mental health and want to know whether they need admission to hospital.

Under the 1990 Community Care Act social workers are responsible for providing care management services. This means that after assessing your relative's needs they can identify and arrange a number of suitable services. These may involve a community support worker, day care, employment schemes, educational courses, residential or nursing care, specialist groups such as 'Hearing Voices', a travel pass, or paying for a telephone connection. The range of services available differs from area to area. Social workers may also take responsibility for co-ordinating people's care after discharge under the Care Programme Approach (CPA) system. As a CPA key worker they may offer individual counselling or psychotherapy, depending on their experience and qualifications.

CHAPTER 18

An Appropriate Place to Live

John Wade and Claire Henderson

For many people with a severe mental illness living at home with family members who are loving and supportive may work well for all concerned. But if, for whatever reason, this is no longer either possible or desirable then you may wish to explore other options for accommodation. This chapter aims to help answer some of the questions you or your relative may have about what is available.

What types of accommodation are available?

There is a wide range of accommodation in most areas for independent living ranging from privately rented bedsits or flats to council or housing association flats and houses. Council housing departments may have staff attached with specialist knowledge about the needs of people with a mental illness. Health and social services run some specialist mental health hostels and there are supported housing schemes managed by voluntary agencies such as MIND or the National Schizophrenia Fellowship.

What are the different kinds of accommodation like?

Independent living

An independent flat or bedsit could be in the private sector or rented from the council or a housing association. The accommodation is likely to be unfurnished and there will be no support provided by the landlord to help people live successfully in the flat. Your relative will be responsible for all the bills, including council tax, insurance, water charges and so on.

Privately rented accommodation is available in most areas. Make sure that your relative gets a written tenancy agreement and has it checked by staff at a Citizens' Advice Bureau before signing it.

For council or housing association accommodation – so-called social housing – people may be given greater priority if they have a supporting letter from a health professional or social worker. Most social housing is allocated on a points basis. Single men living at the family home get very few points.

The council housing department should have a list of what accommodation they have available. Your relative does not have to accept the first place they see. A single person may be offered a 'hard to let' property and not all councils give due consideration to the impact that the location of a property can have on someone's mental health. If your relative accepts an unsuitable property and then has problems living there it could affect their chances of being offered anything else in the future.

Always check and make a note of things such as the condition of the flat, the state of decoration and so on before the flat is occupied as charges may be made for any deterioration during the tenancy. It is worth asking about any decorating allowance as some councils will give either cash or vouchers towards the cost of any redecoration needed.

Supported housing

Supported housing schemes offer many different types of accommodation with different levels of support to meet different needs. All employ trained staff who are there to help your relative make a go of their new home. The staff will help with paying bills, furnishing the accommodation, keeping it well maintained and putting someone in touch with other agencies who provide additional care and support.

Supported housing services are usually provided by a housing association working in partnership with a voluntary agency such as MIND, the National Schizophrenia Fellowship (NSF), the Richmond Fellowship or the Mental Aftercare Association (MACA). Accommodation may be provided in single flats, flats with some communal areas such as a laundry or in a shared house. It may be furnished or unfurnished. Staffing levels vary from weekly visits to 24-hour cover.

In many schemes housing staff play a crucial role in helping to keep the individual tenant in touch with other agencies involved in their care and support. They can alert the family or health professionals if they become concerned about someone's mental state, and if someone gets into difficulties they may be able to mobilise extra help with tasks such as cooking, cleaning or budgeting.

In most supported housing schemes each resident has their own tenancy agreement and either their own flat, or their own room in a shared house. Residents can come and go as they please and have visitors. A few schemes have facilities for overnight guests but much supported housing is only geared up for the individuals living there.

Some supported housing schemes offer accommodation for a fixed period of time as a way of allowing the individual to gain new skills or build their confidence before moving on to something more independent. However, most offer a home for as long as the individual wants it and maintains the terms of their tenancy.

In a scheme in which there are self-contained flats within a larger building, individuals have the advantages of independent living but also have opportunities for social contact with other residents when they want it.

Hostels

Homeless hostels are not good places for people with a severe mental illness as they may be vulnerable to exploitation, stress or intimidation. However, there are many specialist hostels for individuals who do not need to be in hospital, but need a place of safety where they can regain old skills or learn new ones prior to moving on to a more permanent place of their own.

If your relative is in need of a lot of support or must move out quickly because things at home have become unbearable, they may need to spend some time in a specialist hostel or rehabilitation scheme. These are often run by health or social services. There is likely to be a mixture of qualified nursing staff and unqualified care workers there 24 hours a day. The aim of such a scheme will be to assess an individual's needs in a safe environment, and to prepare someone for living in a more permanent setting at a later stage. Staff can develop a specific package of life skills training such as budgeting and social skills, and offer counselling to help people achieve agreed goals.

A stay in a hostel can also provide a period of respite for someone already living in the community who needs a period of extra support or monitoring.

Residential care

This type of accommodation offers an integrated housing and care service to people who need a lot of support and who may be quite disabled by their illness. A place in residential care is usually funded through health and social services and as resources get scarcer so the criteria for accessing this type of accommodation get tighter.

Meals are generally provided and residents lose many of their freedoms including all but a tiny part of their personal benefits. More information about residential care should be available from your local social services office.

How much does this accommodation cost?

An independent flat in the private sector could cost from £30 a week up to several hundred pounds depending on its location, size, the facilities and so on. The rent in a council or housing association flat will be set at a level that aims to cover costs and will only increase by a modest amount each year. Rents in supported housing schemes can be high because of the additional costs such as staffing and furniture.

Whatever accommodation your relative considers make sure they know the total rent and what this covers. It may be high because it includes a charge for things they do not want or need. There are likely to be other regular costs on top of the rent, such as gas, electricity and a television licence, which need to go in the budget.

Is it possible to get help with the cost?

Housing benefit will normally cover the bulk of the rent and service charge unless the council considers the property too large or the rent too high. It is possible to ask the council how much of the rent and service charge on a property they would be prepared to pay through housing benefit. This is called a Pre-Tenancy Determination and can be done using a form available from the local housing benefit office.

Applications for Housing Benefit (and Council Tax Benefit) should be submitted as soon as someone signs their tenancy agreement. In supported housing a staff member will help your relative do this. For people living in independent accommodation there may be help available through the council or your relative can approach the local Citizens' Advice Bureau.

Before moving into any kind of independent or supported housing it is important to ensure that your relative is getting all the benefits to which they are entitled. They will need as much money as possible to live on if they are to make a go of things. Have they applied for income support or disability living allowance? Are they getting any premiums they are entitled to? Ask the social worker or a Citizens' Advice Bureau for help.

What facilities will the accommodation have?

Most council and housing association properties are unfurnished and have their own kitchen and bathroom.

Much supported housing is furnished and equipped with appliances such as a washing machine, vacuum cleaner, telephone, and so on. Schemes with a communal area often have a comfortable room with a television and video where tenants can socialise. There may be a cleaner visiting once a week; windows will be cleaned and the garden maintained.

If your relative moves to unfurnished accommodation they may be able to get a Community Care Grant from the Benefits Agency to help purchase some items. Many areas have some kind of furniture recycling scheme with good quality second-hand furniture that is cheap or free of charge. Ask the social worker or key worker for more help with this.

What sort of support will be available?

Your relative may well be getting support from a number of people or agencies; for example, a community psychiatric nurse, social worker or from a local drop-in centre. Once your relative has moved into their new home they should continue to get this support as well as help with maintaining the accommodation from the organisation managing it. However, they may need extra help with tasks they had previously taken for granted as being done by you, such as washing, shopping or cooking.

If your relative has not lived in their own place before or it was some time ago it is important to ask for an assessment of their needs by a social worker or occupational therapist. There are many different types of help available from health and social services and voluntary agencies, both to encourage and motivate people and to help them regain old skills or to learn new ones. You may need to be quite assertive to get the help your relative needs.

If your relative's care is covered by the Care Programme Approach (CPA) it is worth talking to their key worker as soon as a change in accommodation is being considered as a review may be needed before any assessments can be carried out.

Where is a good place to live?

When helping your relative find a suitable home, try to take your time. Consider issues such as the proximity of the shops, post office, GP and other important facilities. Is the accommodation on a good bus route? Is there a drop-in or day centre nearby? Is the accommodation in a different area or town? A change of GP or mental health team due to a move to a new area could be disruptive for your relative. Is the area suitable for someone with mental health problems? Is there a problem with drug taking or high crime levels?

If your relative is considering moving into supported housing, arrange for them to go and look around and talk to other people living there. Make sure they have a chance to meet anyone who might be sharing the same facilities. Try to meet some of the support staff as well as the manager. Think beforehand about the questions to ask. For example, you may want to know what happens if your relative has to spend time in hospital; what the rent is, who is responsible for providing bedding, towels and so on and whether or not your relative can have a pet, or an overnight visitor.

How can I find out what is available locally?

It can be surprisingly hard to find out what is available in the area. Try the local housing department, which should at least be able to tell you about council and housing association property. They may also have leaflets on their points and allocations systems. You may like to ask your relative's key worker to invite a representative from the housing department to attend the next Care Programme Approach review meeting to tell you more about what is available.

For information about supported housing try asking health or social services staff. If they are not aware of any try looking in the telephone book or Yellow Pages. There may be a poster or leaflet at the GP's surgery, or in the library or Citizens' Advice Bureau with a contact number. Drop-in or day centre staff may also be able to help. Ask other mental health service users or carers.

Do not give up! As you will probably already be aware, communication between agencies is often not as good as it could be. Not all professionals know about all the available facilities, so it is worth continuing to ask different people and continuing to explore options yourself.

Is there anything else to think about?

- As with any change of accommodation, do not rush into anything.

- Ask as many questions as you can and talk to other tenants and carers.

- Try to visit several times if possible, perhaps at different times of day.

- Find out about the area and what facilities are close by.

- Read any tenancy agreement carefully and get specialist advice if you need it.

Finally...

Do not be too disappointed if things do not work out first time. This does not mean that it may not be worth trying again in the future or considering a different option. Many people have to make several attempts before finding the type of accommodation that suits them or having the confidence or skills necessary to live there.

CHAPTER 19

Benefits

Claire Henderson and Rory O'Kelly

Poverty is likely to have a harmful effect on people's mental health and it is important that people with a mental illness claim all the benefits to which they are entitled. The stress created by problems with benefits, such as when they are wrongly stopped, or are promised but then do not arrive, may contribute to a person having a relapse of their illness.

The social security system creates many difficulties for people with a mental illness and their families, and also for mental health service providers. Simply providing information on what benefits are currently available to those with a mental illness and their families will be insufficient for them to succeed in claiming everything to which they are entitled. The frequent changes in social security policy ensure that guidelines on what is available rapidly go out of date.

This chapter will give an outline of the current system for claiming benefits for people with a mental illness, but it is important that carers and users of services also seek advice on their particular situation. Speaking to your relative's key worker at the outset about any issues over benefits will facilitate the involvement of the professionals who can provide supporting documentation.

Due to the problems over claiming the different benefits to which a person may be entitled, it is not surprising that service users and their carers frequently under-claim social security benefits.

An outline of the available benefits

Benefits for people with health problems are payable broadly on three grounds:

- incapacity for work
- disability
- low income.

Although these are distinct concepts, they often go together.

People who are incapable of work may receive Incapacity Benefit (IB) if they have paid enough National Insurance contributions, Severe Disablement Allowance (SDA) if they have not paid contributions but are accepted as at least 80 per cent disabled, and Income Support (IS) if they have low incomes and assets. Some 'premiums' that increase the rate of IS depend on disability or long-term incapacity.

People with disabilities may be able to claim Disability Living Allowance (DLA). This is made up of two 'components': the mobility component for people who have difficulty walking, and the care component for people who need personal care or supervision. There are different rates for both components, depending on the level of need. DLA does not depend on income or assets and can be paid whether or not a person is working, but in practice, those who are able to work are not very likely to qualify for the care component.

Benefits for low income include Housing Benefit (HB), Council Tax Benefit (CTB) and help with prescriptions, optical and dental charges and hospital fares. They can be paid to people whether or not they are working although those who are not working and who get IS will receive the additional benefits automatically, while others have to claim them separately. There is also a specific benefit, Disabled Persons' Tax Credit (DPTC), for people who are working but have a low income because of a disability.

Your relative may also be entitled to a freedom pass. This allows free travel on public transport and is available via social services.

The main benefit for carers is the Invalid Care Allowance (ICA) which can be claimed by people who are not working more than a minimum amount and who look after someone who gets at least the middle rate of the care component of the DLA. Carers can also claim IS on the grounds of low income and there is a special 'premium' for them as well.

This is a very simplified account. The full rules are more complex, particularly for special groups such as those who can do some work, but not very much; those who need some care, but not continuous care; and those who may be entitled to several different benefits, but do not know which can be paid together.

Under-claiming of benefits

Up to half of the people with a mental illness who are in contact with services may not be claiming all the benefits to which they are entitled. Do not assume that your relative is getting their full entitlement simply because they have been under the care of a mental health team for some time. Your relative's key worker or others giving your relative advice on benefits may not always pursue a claim until their clients are getting everything to which they are entitled. With ongoing changes in the benefits available it is worth you keeping up to date with developments and asking what the implications are for your relative.

People wanting to claim different benefits face a number of difficulties. Dealing with the benefits system can be demoralising, time-consuming and expensive. Your relative may already be feeling demoralised by their illness and its impact, or have problems with motivation, attention or concentration, and as a result find the claim forms too long and complex to complete. Listing the things they are unable to do because of illness is likely to be depressing for your relative, and as a carer you may need to be reminding your relative of more positive aspects of their life.

Some claim form questions are difficult to answer for people with mental health problems because they appear directed towards someone with a physical disability. This is particularly the case if the illness fluctuates so that they are more able at some times than at others.

Once a claim form has been completed you or your relative may need to chase up the Benefits Agency (BA). Your relative may not be able to afford the cost of the repeated telephone calls, particularly when their calls are put on hold for a long time. If your relative's claim is rejected, most people will assume that the BA has made a correct decision, but specialist benefit advisers often appeal successfully against such decisions.

Both carers and professionals who are making claims on behalf of another person but are insufficiently familiar with the system face similar problems. They may not know how to make a claim in a way that best explains that person's disabilities to the BA, they may have insufficient time to chase up the claim and they may be too likely to accept a rejection when more complete information could lead to a successful claim.

Carers and professionals may also worry that clients will have 'too much' money and that this will be counter-therapeutic. If someone has a history of drug or alcohol abuse, there may be an understandable fear that extra money from benefits will be spent on this. As a result a key worker may deliberately not claim for someone, or a doctor may refuse to provide a letter of support. However, for people with drug or alcohol problems there is no evidence that they spend more on these substances when they have just received their money than at other times. Ideally, more constructive ways to help those with substance abuse problems should be offered by mental health services.

Professionals frequently express a worry that being on a high level of benefit will discourage people from returning to work. This is particularly likely if someone's wages will be low, and there is a concern that if the person stops work again they will not be able to claim this level of benefit next time. Again, there are more constructive approaches to this problem. For example, in conjunction with local employers, mental health services are developing more attractive work placements, such as supported employment schemes and social firms (see Chapter 20). Government legislation may also influence the ease with which people can gain employment after an episode of mental illness. The Disability Discrimination Act 1995 now requires that firms employing over 20 people make 'reasonable adjustments' for people with mental or physical disabilities. The minimum wage may also provide a greater incentive to work. However, greater flexibility in the social security system would give further help with this problem.

Another concern that arises when people with a mental illness receive benefits and live independently is the potential for exploitation by others. Those wishing to extort money may target them. Again, professionals have a role in helping to protect people from such activity. Carers concerned that this is happening should discuss this with the person's key worker or other involved professional.

How can users and carers ensure they receive their full benefit entitlements?

When making a claim with respect to a relative or friend, there are several things to remember:

1. If your relative has a key worker, get them involved early on as they will be able to advise.

2. Make sure your relative's GP knows about their mental health problems and in what ways they are disabled by them. The Benefits Agency usually only contacts one person for supporting evidence, and this is usually the GP.

3. The Benefits Agency has to take into account any other evidence submitted beyond what it requests from the GP, but it is up to the applicant to submit it. Especially with the DLA, there is often

important information that cannot be conveyed using the claim form alone. Your relative or you as a carer can write a covering letter and send it in with the claim form. This will also help the person dealing with the form by telling them at the start what the problems are.

4. If you write the covering letter, explain who you are and that this is your account of the problems. You can also describe what it is that you and others have to do to care for your relative. Your account may differ from that of your relative; for example, if he or she denies they need help with something but you know that they do. This is not a problem; just make it clear that this is your perspective and that it differs from that of your relative. However, if your relative is adamant that he or she does not want to reveal something and would rather give up the benefit, then you will have to accept this, as your relative must consent to making the claim.

5. If you are filling in the form for someone else, make this clear by writing 'he' or 'she' and attach a covering letter explaining who you are and that you have filled in the form on behalf of your relative or friend (see 3). Do not write 'I' as if you were the person wanting to claim the benefit, as this will be unclear to the Benefits Agency staff.

6. Some people believe they must stress any physical problems they have in order to make a successful claim because of the apparent bias towards physical problems on the form. If your relative has an important physical illness or disability that is known to their GP and it is likely to affect the claim then this should be stated. However, if their main problem is a mental illness and this is the reason for the claim then it is best to make this clear. Otherwise the Benefits Agency staff will be confused about which illness is causing the disabilities on which the claim is based.

7. The claim form is not a quiz in which you have to answer every question in the hope of giving a 'right' answer. If the question is irrelevant to your relative's case, write 'not applicable' (N/A).

8. Remember to discuss your relative's benefits with the key worker at Care Programme Approach meetings, or if there has been a change in the benefits system or in your relative's circumstances. Another resource for you to consult may be the local Citizens' Advice Bureau,

while some voluntary sector organisations employ specialist advisers in local offices.

CHAPTER 20

Employment

David O'Flynn

A paid job or training may be something that you as a carer think would help a person with mental health problems, or you may be worried that once someone has had problems, they should avoid employment. Work can be paid or unpaid, part-time or full-time, and includes training and education. Work, whether paid or unpaid, can have value for people with mental health problems. Paid employment and 'good' jobs are likely to become increasingly important for two reasons. First, the likely future of the welfare state with an increasing emphasis on work, and second, the expectations of people with mental health problems who want to have lives outside the mental health system and traditional day centres, and in the community and the world of work.

Access to the labour market is difficult for many, and so a number of alternatives to paid employment have been developed. These should be considered when a person's mental health is stable, maybe after an admission or once other treatments are established, and long-term problems (disabilities) are known. There can be many such issues — poor confidence and self-esteem, lack of motivation, sedation from medication and agoraphobia — all of which make work difficult.

Unemployment and employment

Unemployment is a very common experience for people with mental health problems, especially for those with a major mental illness, who are on medication or have been in hospital. Over four in five people with a diagnosis of schizophrenia are unemployed. This figure is even higher if people have other disadvantages, such as belonging to an ethnic minority, or having a criminal history. Unemployment is usually detrimental to people's mental and physical ill health, with the risk of poverty, dependence on welfare, social isolation and boredom.

Paid employment in the right job (a 'good' job) has many benefits. For people with mental health problems these include increased income, being occupied, having social contacts, a social role other than that of a 'psychiatric patient' and an improvement in self-esteem and confidence. There may also be an improvement in symptoms. People often lose their jobs when unwell, or they may not want to return to a job that they feel is a cause for their mental health problems (many modern commercial organisations and places of work are technologically demanding and stressful).

For some people their jobs are harmful to their mental and physical health, and can even be a cause of their ill health. For a few, unemployment may be beneficial, the demands of available work outweighing the benefits of employment, and their needs are better met with creative leisure.

Paid jobs are important for carers for similar reasons, particularly for income and social contacts outside the home, reducing the isolation that comes with caring. The recent government policy document 'Caring About Carers' stresses the importance of flexible employment practices and support services; for example, allowing time off in a crisis, or access to a telephone to call home.

Why people are unemployed

There are a number of reasons why people with mental health problems do not have paid jobs – often termed 'barriers to employment' – which are less related to people's abilities or their symptoms.

Mental illness may start in late adolescence or early adulthood, and have a recurring pattern of relapses that disrupts a person's educational and employment history. Any long periods of unemployment will show on a CV, and make it difficult to be selected for interview, let alone get a job. At times of high unemployment, these effects are more marked.

There is discrimination by employers towards all people with disabilities, particularly those with mental health problems. This may in time change with new legislation. The Disability Discrimination Act 1995 requires employers to make 'reasonable adjustments' to jobs and places of work. Many of these adjustments are cheap and easy, as has been demonstrated in the US. Examples are changes to job descriptions or flexible hours, or the provision of a quiet workplace.

Organisational policies and prejudices often affect those who are in work, giving less access to training, promotion and career development to people with a record of mental health problems. Mental illness and treatment may make people seem different, and many employers and employees are not yet ready to accept people who were until recently segregated and excluded in mental hospitals.

While the social security benefits system is central to the well-being of people with mental health problems, the regulations limit people's options. The many 'benefit traps' result in a rapid loss of income on returning to work, making all except well-paid jobs inaccessible, and these jobs are probably not available to those trying to enter or return to the labour market. Part-time employment for more than token wages may be impossible without ending up financially worse off. In particular, housing benefit rules can make returning to employment difficult (and for people living in supported housing with high rents, almost impossible). However, some of these issues are being addressed under Welfare to Work policies.

People may find work difficult due to the consequences of their mental health problems; for example, having poor motivation or low self-esteem, or the effects of treatment such as sedation. However, people can work well in spite of major continuing problems, such as hearing voices, as there is no clear relationship between symptoms and functioning. Mental health professionals often do not know this, and can advise against employment, viewing it as stressful and detrimental, being unaware of the value of work for people with mental health problems.

Alternatives and progress to paid employment

For the above reasons, paid employment may not be an option for many people, particularly those whose problems are severe. However, the benefits of employment – especially the social and psychological ones – can follow from any work (paid, low-paid or unpaid), from education and training, and from recreational and creative opportunities. There is a range of models (see Table 20.1) providing opportunities to meet people's varying needs, and for some, providing a progression towards paid employment in the open labour market. They may create jobs in the mental health system and in the third sector of not-for-profit businesses. They may also train and support people in open, mainstream employment and education.

Table 20.1 Work projects

Job Creation

Sheltered work	Low-paid, part-time work, widespread, may be hospital or day centre based.
Sheltered mobile crew	Small teams offering low-paid, part-time work, usually on the open market (e.g. garden maintenance or house decorating).
Clubhouse	Independent community mental health projects, emphasis on empowerment and work. Includes TEP (see below).
Social enterprise	Low-paid, part-time work, emphasis on quality of work and environment, training and power sharing.
Social firm	Not-for-profit, high street businesses, aim to create jobs for disadvantaged people. Full wages and equal opportunities for mixed work force. Prominent in Italy and Germany.
Consumer-run business	US version of social firm, in which all people in the business are consumers of mental health services.

Open Employment or Education

Assessment/ Counselling	Work with the individual to ascertain abilities, aptitudes, aspirations and potential.
Vocational training	Segregated specific skills training (e.g. information technology) leading to job searching in the open labour market.
Supported education	Support in community, further and higher mainstream education.
Employment training	Approaches adapted from employment services, e.g. job clubs, CV writing, job search skills. Includes employment agencies.
Transitional employment programme (TEP)	Short-term (e.g. six months) trials in jobs not needing qualifications or experience. Aims at eventual 'transition' to the open labour market.
Supported employment	Supports a person in choosing a job in the open market, getting such a job, keeping it and developing his or her career.

All of these models have three interconnected aims: *recovery* (of mental health), *rehabilitation* (learning skills, acquiring qualifications and good employment behaviours, such as time-keeping) and *reintegration* (to a place of work, to the social life of the project, to the labour market). There is an emphasis on 'user involvement' in the running of these projects. All of these approaches may help people recover, learn, and join in community life, but we do not know which approaches are best for which people.

The provision and quality of these models in the UK is patchy and varies from area to area (see Resources). They are provided by community work projects or work schemes, as small units or programmes available in traditional day centres, and by health or social services, and the voluntary sector. They differ from traditional day care with their emphasis on work, pay if possible, and on a person's abilities rather than their disabilities and symptoms. The four models that are currently most influential in the UK are the clubhouse, social firm, supported employment and supported education.

As people go to work and learn how to work, they recover and are often able to lead fuller lives. Some people may get back to paid employment. Most will need two or three approaches, either together, or consecutively. For example, someone might work a couple of days in a social enterprise, while being supported at college to learn computing skills, enabling them to look for a job in a couple of years' time, armed then with some employment experience and a national vocational qualification. Progression is essential to avoid the negative effects of long-term day care (reinstitutionalisation). Any earnings will need welfare advice.

How the carer may help

Helping people back to work may not be easy. People need encouragement and support in trying different options, in identifying their aims, and accepting their limitations and changed aspirations. Their capacity to work can vary from day to day, and this may need some understanding. They may need to try different options, or may fail in their efforts initially. Finding local work projects may not be easy, and you may need to research the options in your area with your relative. Remember to stay optimistic and understanding.

Possible sources for further information might include:

- health and social services: GP, mental health professionals such as key worker or doctor, social worker
- library or Citizens' Advice Bureau (see Resources)
- employment service: job centres (who have disability specialists)

- local and national voluntary organisations: for example, MIND, National Schizophrenia Fellowship, Shaw Trust, Richmond Fellowship (see Resources)

- internet: for example, http://www.socialfirms.co.uk (which gives access to the Ermis database set up in 1997 tp provide information about training and employment apportunities for the 'socially excluded') or http://www.schizophrenia.co.uk

CHAPTER 21

Forensic Psychiatry

Alec Buchanan

'Forensic' means 'to do with the law' and forensic psychiatrists are psychiatrists whose patients come to them usually not through GPs, but through the criminal justice system. Forensic psychiatrists provide advice to the courts and the probation service as well as inpatient care to people who need to be looked after in secure conditions. Depending on local arrangements that vary from one part of the country to another, they may also look after some people who are living at home but who have been in a secure unit in the past. They give advice to general psychiatrists and may also be involved in court diversion schemes, which try to ensure that people with mental health problems who have committed an offence are assessed and if necessary receive treatment.

Court reports

If your relative or friend sees a forensic psychiatrist it will probably be in one of these situations. If this is not the case, you may wish to ask the forensic psychiatrist to explain to you and your relative what their role is. If your relative or friend is seeing a forensic psychiatrist so that a report can be prepared for a court, there are two things which both of you will need to bear in mind. First, when a psychiatrist sends a report to the court he or she loses control over what happens to it. They are not in a position to promise confidentiality of the kind which you would normally expect from a doctor. Second, the forensic psychiatrist is working for the court. Whereas you would usually expect a doctor to be influenced primarily by the needs of their patient, a doctor writing a court report also has to take into account the needs of the court. These considerations do not usually pose any particular problems. You should, however, try to make sure that your relative understands them, has a lawyer and that the lawyer knows about the appointment with the doctor.

Secure hospitals

If your relative has a forensic psychiatrist as his or her consultant it probably means that they are being looked after in a secure unit. Although some people feel understandably upset that their relative is in this situation, secure units are in many ways more humane environments than ordinary wards. Usually they have not suffered from a shortage of resources to the same extent and, as a result, they are better able to offer facilities such as recreation, a library, education and employment training. There are currently three high security hospitals in England and Wales (Broadmoor, Ashworth and Rampton) and a number of smaller units called regional (or medium) secure units.

You may wish to find out the name of your relative's consultant psychiatrist (often referred to as the RMO, the Responsible Medical Officer, under the 1983 Mental Health Act) as well as their primary nurse and social worker. People usually spend longer in secure units than on ordinary wards and the quality of information you receive will depend, in part, on the relationship you are able to establish with these key members of staff. You should have no difficulty in making contact with them but, if you do, the first thing to do is persevere. It is part of their job to involve carers.

One thing that will strike you if your friend or relative is in a secure unit is the amount of attention and discussion devoted to 'tribunals'. Most people who are in a secure unit in England and Wales are there under an order made using the 1983 Mental Health Act (see Chapter 22). Similar legislation applies in Scotland and Northern Ireland. This Act was passed in order to make clear the circumstances in which a patient could be detained in a hospital and to ensure the protection of that person's rights.

People detained in any hospital can appeal to the Mental Health Act Review Tribunal against their detention. If they make an appeal the doctor and social worker from the hospital, as well as an independent psychiatrist whom you or your relative appoint, must write reports and appear at a legal hearing usually called a tribunal. These meetings are chaired by a lawyer, and one of the other members of the tribunal will be a psychiatrist who works in a different hospital.

Because there are only three high security hospitals your relative may be in hospital a long way from where you live. Visiting can be time-consuming and expensive. You should consult with the welfare department of the hospital, or with staff on your relative's ward, about getting some financial help towards the cost of travel.

When you visit you will notice that the security arrangements are in some ways similar to those used by a prison. Bags are searched and you will probably have to pass through a scanner, such as airports use, which will look for concealed objects. Before visiting it is worth checking not only whether you can come, but also about what you will be allowed to bring in to the hospital and leave with your relative. For example, it is usually better to put money into your relative's hospital account than to give cash to him or her.

Regional secure units have to deal with some of these problems too, but as there are more of them you are likely to have to travel less far when visiting. There is also less emphasis on security.

Assessment of risk

In some cases a person is under the care of a general psychiatrist but will see a forensic psychiatrist because the general psychiatrist would like their advice. Usually this will concern one or more aspects of their behaviour, particularly if someone is thought to pose a risk to other people, including you. Forensic psychiatrists tend to be asked questions of this kind because the nature of their work gives them experience of a large number of people who pose such risks and they may be able to offer some new ideas. This advice can be very helpful to the local team, especially if they feel at a loss as to what to do next.

The team may be concerned about possible risk but it is not always obvious what they should do about it, especially when the concerns remain after a person has in other respects responded to treatment. You will want to make sure that all aspects of risk have been adequately considered, including the risk your relative presents to him or herself. You may also wish to satisfy yourself that, in the effort to respond adequately to any risk that exists, other aspects of your relative's needs have received proper attention.

Moving on from a secure unit

Most patients who are detained in high security hospitals and regional secure units are subsequently released and go on to live in the community. It may be important for you to remind your relative of this, as the length of stay in a secure hospital may seem long and time can pass slowly. It will be easiest if you and your relative are able to agree with the team treating your relative as to a plan for the future. If all goes well, the plan should lead to your relative going to a less secure hospital and then on into the community.

If this is not possible your relative's lawyer may be able to advise you as to what the most likely outcome is and how best to make sure your views are heard. Whatever the likely outcome, however, your relative will benefit from continued contact with one or more people from outside the hospital even if their illness sometimes makes it difficult for them to show this.

CHAPTER 22

Mental Health Legislation

Frank Holloway

Why do we have mental health laws?

There are few countries that do not have laws governing the care and treatment of people with a mental illness. Since the rise of the asylum in the nineteenth century the main focus of mental health law has been the process by which people are admitted and detained in hospital against their will. The compulsory admission to hospital of people with a mental illness is one of the very few situations sanctioned by the European Convention on Human Rights in which a person can lawfully be deprived of their liberty without having been accused or convicted of committing an offence.

Interestingly the earliest English legislation regarding mental health that is recorded, which dates back to the Middle Ages, related to the management of the property of those who were incapable of dealing with their own affairs, in order to ensure that people with mental disability were not exploited. As any carer concerned with the financial affairs of someone with a mental illness will be aware, this aspect of mental health law is less well developed and user-friendly than the law surrounding compulsory admission.

Medical ethics sets a high priority on respecting the autonomy of the individual patient. In general medical practice paternalistic interventions for an 'incapable' patient are, as a matter of common law, justified providing these are in the person's best interests. All mental health legislation has to strike a balance between respecting the rights of the individual as the best person to make decisions about their needs and the requirement to intervene when the individual is incapable of making decisions or presents a risk to the community at large.

Different countries strike this balance differently. In some the threshold for compulsory admission is high. Taken to extremes this can lead to people 'rotting with their rights on'. The law also evolves over time to take account of changes in the treatments available and the way that mental health care is delivered. Most recently mental health legislation has had to grapple with the reality of community care and confront the issue of compulsory care and treatment outside, rather than, as before, simply inside the hospital.

The Mental Health Act (1983)

Mental health care in England and Wales is currently governed by the Mental Health Act (1983), subsequently amended in 1995 to introduce powers of compulsory aftercare. (There are separate Mental Health Acts for Scotland and Northern Ireland that differ in detail.) The Act is divided into paragraphs, which are called 'sections': provisions are known by the number of the relevant section or subsection. The main provisions are summarised below.

The Act is supported by an explanatory memorandum and a statutory Code of Practice. In addition mental health law is regularly interpreted by judges and complemented by practice guidance produced by the Department of Health.

Key elements of the 1983 Mental Health Act

Part I (Section 1)

The scope of the Act is defined. It applies to people with a mental disorder: i.e. mental illness; mental impairment and severe mental impairment; and psychopathic disorder. Dependence on alcohol or drugs is not a mental disorder in the meaning of the Act.

Part II (Sections 2 to 34)

The procedures surrounding compulsory admission to hospital and guardianship are laid out. To be admitted patients must suffer from a mental disorder 'of a nature or degree which warrants detention of the patient in hospital' *and* 'he ought to be so detained in the interests of his own health *or* safety *or* with a view to the protection of others' (Section 2). Admission for assessment (Section 2) or treatment (Section 3) requires two medical recommendations and an application, signed by the nearest relative or an approved social worker. Emergency admission (Section 4) requires a single medical recommendation and an application. Patients already in hospital may be detained (Section 5). Section 25a allows for compulsory aftercare of detained patients (supervised discharge).

Part III (Sections 35 to 55)

Contains procedures for the detention in hospital of patients concerned in criminal proceedings or under sentence.

Part IV (Sections 56 to 64)

Sets out procedures governing patients' consent to treatment. Informal patients and patients detained under emergency sections (Section 4; Section 5(2) and (4); Section 135; and Section 136) and Section 35 may only be treated against their will under common law.

Part V (Sections 65 to 79)

Defines the composition, role and functioning of Mental Health Review Tribunals. Tribunals consider the appropriateness of a patient's continuing compulsory detention in hospital, receiving evidence from the medical team and an approved social worker and evidence given by and on behalf of the patient.

Part VI (Sections 80 to 92)

Sets out powers for the removal and return of detained patients who have absconded within the UK.

Part VII (Sections 93 to 113)

Identifies procedures governing the management of property and affairs of patients who are under disability by reason of mental disorder which involve the Court of Protection.

Parts VIII, IX and X (Sections 114 to 149)

Contain miscellaneous provisions. These include a duty on the health and local authorities to provide aftercare to detained patients (Section 117); the establishment of the Mental Health Act Commission, which has a duty to oversee the welfare of detained patients and the implementation of the Act (Section 121); powers to obtain a warrant to enter premises where it is believed a person suffering from mental disorder is being ill-treated or, living alone, is unable to care for himself (Section 135); and powers for the police to convey a mentally disordered person found in a public place to a place of safety for assessment (Section 136).

There is a useful website designed primarily for professionals, the Hyper-guide to the Mental Health Act: http://www.hyperguide.co.uk/mha/index.htm

Mental health law is complex and continually evolving. The 1999 edition of the standard textbook on the subject, which is by no means comprehensive, runs to 700 pages (Jones 1999). National organisations such as MIND and the National Schizophrenia Fellowship can provide advice and support to carers grappling with the complexities of mental health law. Locally the approved social worker and other professionals will have expertise that should be available to any concerned carer. Free legal aid may be available to the detained patient and their nearest relative, both of whom have a right to information on how to contact a suitably qualified solicitor.

In contrast to the complexity of legislation and guidance, the basic principles governing compulsory admission and treatment are quite simple. The Act gives information about:

- criteria which must be met to justify compulsory admission
- people who will be involved in the process (the patient, one or more doctors, an approved social worker, the nearest relative)
- opportunities for appeal against detention
- consent to treatment of detained patient and how lack of consent can be overridden
- provisions for the aftercare of detained patients.

Most importantly detained patients have rights, which are overseen by an independent body, the Mental Health Act Commission. Patients can appeal against their detention to non-professional hospital managers and to the Mental Health Review Tribunal, which is a type of court presided over by a lawyer. Patients who challenge their detention are eligible for legal aid.

Under the Act admission can occur in an emergency (for up to 72 hours), for assessment (for up to 28 days), for treatment (for up to six months in the first instance) or, under Part III of the Act, in the context of criminal proceedings. The basic criteria for admission are that the person should be suffering from a mental disorder (a broad term that excludes pure drug or alcohol abuse and sexual deviation, but must be specified further to justify long-term detention). This must be of a nature or degree that warrants admission in the interest of the patient's health or safety or the safety of others. These difficult judgements are the responsibility of the two recommending doctors (one in an emergency) and the applicant, usually a specially trained approved social worker, involved in the assessment process. The Act also allows the nearest relative to be the applicant, but this is no longer felt to be good practice. The police can bring people they feel are mentally disordered to a place of safety for assessment. Patients who are already in hospital voluntarily can be detained, in an emergency, by a single doctor or nurse, pending a full assessment.

Consent to treatment

Except in strictly defined circumstances medical treatment can only be given with the patient's consent, which must be voluntary and be based on adequate knowledge. Over the age of 16 only the patient can legally give, or withhold, consent. People with a mental illness can be treated against their will either under the specific provisions of the Mental Health Act or, in quite restricted emergency situations, under the common law. If people lack decision-making capacity the treatment of physical illness is currently governed by the common law (not the Mental Health Act), which requires doctors to provide treatment that is in the person's best interests.

Rights, roles and responsibilities of the nearest relative

The Mental Health Act acknowledges the crucial role of the carer. In law this role is currently confined to the nearest relative, a person very strictly defined by the Act (see below). Importantly a cohabitee or a long-term homosexual partner can act as the nearest relative. The nearest relative can request an assessment for admission from the local social services department. He or she must, if practicable, be consulted about compulsory admission and must agree to admission under Section 3 (admission for treatment, which can last up to six months). If the nearest relative objects to this then admission can only occur if they are 'set aside' (i.e. displaced as the nearest relative). Displacement, which is very uncommon, requires a county court judgement that the nearest relative is mentally incapable or is behaving unreasonably or without regard to the welfare of the patient or the public.

The nearest relative can request discharge of the detained patient from hospital, which can only be blocked by the consultant psychiatrist if there is an immediate risk of harm to the patient or others (a much higher threshold than the criteria for admission in England and Wales). The nearest relative also has rights to apply to a Mental Health Review Tribunal to seek the patient's

---

The nearest relative

  (a) husband or wife

  (b) son or daughter

  (c) father or mother

  (d) brother or sister

  (e) grandparent

  (f) grandchild

  (g) uncle or aunt

  (h) nephew or niece

To identify the nearest relative this list is taken in order with the oldest at any level taking precedence. Only people living in Britain are counted. Cohabitees and homosexual partners may be counted as 'husband or wife'.

---

discharge, must be informed if the patient is discharged from detention by the consultant psychiatrist and must be consulted if compulsory aftercare is proposed. Under the Care Programme Approach carers should also be involved in all aspects of the treatment of detained patients (subject to issues of confidentiality), particularly in the development of an aftercare plan.

The future

A new Mental Health Act is planned to allow compulsory treatment in the community and to ensure compliance with the European Convention on Human Rights, which has recently been incorporated into UK law. The National Service Framework for Mental Health, published in 1999, strongly emphasises the importance of carers. Future mental health legislation in

England and Wales is highly likely to strengthen the requirements on mental health professionals to involve carers in the process of compulsory admission and, perhaps more importantly, the planning of aftercare and community support.

CHAPTER 23

Driving and Mental Health

Anne Cremona

Many mental illnesses affect a person's judgement and concentration. Drugs used in the treatment of mental illnesses may be sedating and make a person feel less alert.

Regulation by the Driver and Vehicle Licensing Agency (DVLA)

If someone with a mental illness is a driver, both that person and their doctor should consider the possibility of impaired driving performance. If either of them has any doubt about the person's fitness to drive he or she should stop driving and the case be referred to the DVLA in Swansea. It is generally the legal duty of the licence-holder to notify the DVLA of a potential problem. However, in certain conditions the doctor is also obliged to notify the medical adviser at the DVLA and possibly the next of kin; for example, with people suffering from dementia who may not understand the requirements. If there is disagreement between a doctor and their patient about the referral, a second medical opinion should be sought and the person asked not to drive until this assessment has taken place.

Once the DVLA has been informed, medical reports will be requested and a decision made when these have been received. If a licence is revoked on medical grounds, it will usually be reissued when a person is well again, providing relapse of the illness is unlikely within one year. If someone has an illness that is likely to progress or relapse, then the licence may be reissued subject to medical review in one to three years.

The DVLA provides guidance regarding medical standards of fitness to drive, based on the 1988 Road Traffic Act. There is one set of standards for a Group 1 licence that allows an individual to drive a car or a motorcycle, and a stricter set of standards for a Group 2 licence that allows an individual to drive large heavy vehicles such as lorries and buses. At present medium-sized lorries and minibuses are included in Group 1 but this will change on renewal. The DVLA does not license taxi-drivers or emergency service drivers; for these vehicles the Medical Commission on Accident Prevention recommends that Group 2 medical standards should apply. The decision on whether an individual is fit to drive is taken by the DVLA.

Mental illness and its effects on driving

Any condition that could affect a person's ability to drive safely should be notified to the DVLA. The way in which an illness affects someone may be at least as important as the actual diagnosis. A person with mild anxiety or depression who does not have impaired concentration or suicidal thoughts and is not receiving drug treatment does not need to notify the DVLA. However, someone with more severe anxiety or depression or a psychotic illness such as bipolar affective disorder or schizophrenia should notify the DVLA and stop driving until a decision has been reached. In these situations there is a chance that a person may drive recklessly, particularly if they have suicidal thoughts or delusions (false beliefs) and try to act on their beliefs.

For people with severe anxiety or depression, the DVLA usually revokes the driving licence until someone has been well for six months. If the anxiety or depression is chronic, but managed on medication that does not sedate the individual, driving may be allowed.

For people with an episode of psychotic illness, the DVLA must be notified. They will usually revoke the licence until someone has been well – taking their medication and understanding the nature of their illness – for one year. For people with a Group 2 licence someone must be well – with little chance of a further episode and no reduced concentration or alertness due to medication – for three years before driving can be resumed. In chronic psychotic illnesses the DVLA must be notified. For people with a Group 1 licence, if they are well and complying with medication but still have some symptoms they may be allowed to drive provided the symptoms do not interfere with their ability to drive safely.

Other conditions that may cause an individual to drive recklessly or aggressively should also be notified to the DVLA. These would include behavioural disorders, whether due to personality factors or medical conditions such as a head injury, and drug and alcohol misuse. If an individual is seriously disturbed or persistently violent to the extent that he or she is likely to be a source of danger on the road, their licence will be revoked. A medical report confirming that the behavioural problems are no longer present will be needed before the DVLA reissues the licence.

Substance misuse and driving

Persistent drug misuse will also lead to a person's licence being revoked. With cannabis, ecstasy and LSD, the licence will usually be revoked for six months for Group 1, and one year for Group 2 entitlement. Persistent use of amphetamines, heroin, morphine, methadone, cocaine and benzodiazepines will lead to the licence being revoked for one year for Group 1, and three years for Group 2 entitlement. Individuals on an oral methadone withdrawal programme may be licensed before this period.

In all these cases, someone will usually only be relicensed after a favourable independent medical report has been prepared and there have been negative urine drug screening tests to confirm no current drug misuse. It is an offence to drive while unfit through taking illicit drugs.

Alcohol misuse, with or without dependency on alcohol, is a well-known driving hazard. Persistent alcohol misuse will lead to a person's licence being revoked for at least six months for Group 1, and at least a year for Group 2 entitlement. People will only be relicensed if they can show that they have been abstinent or only drunk moderately and relevant blood tests are normal. In established alcohol dependency, people will only be relicensed if they have been abstinent or only drunk moderately for one year for Group 1, and three years for Group 2 entitlement.

As with drug misuse, individuals who have had alcohol-related fits will in addition be subject to the epilepsy regulations.

Drivers convicted of drink-driving offences with a level of alcohol of over 200 mg per 100 ml blood, or who have had two disqualifications over a ten-year period, or who have refused to give a specimen for analysis will also be subject to the high risk offender scheme. They will need an independent medical examination and satisfactory blood tests before the DVLA will consider reissuing their licence. If a person has previously misused alcohol the DVLA may issue a short-period licence.

Dementia and driving

The DVLA should be notified as soon as a diagnosis of dementia or similar condition has been made. The DVLA's policy is that people suffering from poor short-term memory, who may get lost easily and have impaired insight and judgement are not fit to drive, but the final decision will usually be based on medical reports. In early dementia, a renewable one-year licence may be issued if the patient can cope with day-to-day living. A formal driving assessment may be needed.

Medication and driving

Driving while unfit due to the effects of medication is an offence and can lead to prosecution. Any medication used to treat psychiatric illness can cause drowsiness and interfere with alertness and concentration and cause someone to be a danger on the road. It is important that a person stops driving immediately if this is the case. This may be more of an issue when starting new medication or changing the dose, especially with a depot injection. Benzodiazepines, tricyclic antidepressants and phenothiazines can have noticeable unwanted side effects. These include blurring of vision, tremor and rigidity. The newer atypical antipsychotic drugs and SSRI antidepressants have fewer side effects and may be safer for drivers. Drugs used to treat mental illness interact with alcohol so it is best for people to avoid drinking.

Conclusions

As it is the legal responsibility of the individual to report their condition to the DVLA, if there is any doubt it is best to refer to the DVLA and ask for guidance. The basic rule is that any psychiatric condition that may make a patient a danger on the road should be notified. This will normally mean any relapsing, recurrent or progressive mental illness, as well as the effect of medication.

The DVLA can be contacted at the Drivers Medical Unit, DVLA, Longview Road, Morriston, Swansea SA99 1TU.

CHAPTER 24

Other Legal Issues and Mental Health
Mind Legal Unit

This chapter covers

- disability discrimination (general)
- disability discrimination and work
- travel
- insurance
- gun licences
- voting rights
- capacity to make decisions (general)
- finances and the Court of Protection
- making a will.

Disability discrimination (general)

The 1995 Disability Discrimination Act (DDA) makes it unlawful for most employers or service providers to discriminate against someone with a 'disability'. This is defined as a physical or mental impairment that has a *substantial* and *long-term* effect on the person's ability to perform *day-to-day activities* (see below). The Act covers any mental illness that is clinically recognised; that is, a doctor has diagnosed it and the condition appears in the standard reference books.

To be protected under the DDA, the disabled person must show that the following points apply to them:

- Their 'impairment' has a significant effect upon specified activities. These include speech, hearing, etc., but also the ability to remember, concentrate, learn, or perceive danger. The impact of medication and other forms of treatment is disregarded for this purpose.

- It has had this effect for at least 12 months, or is likely to recur. A disability that has satisfied the definition in the past is covered, even if the symptoms are not present now.

Goods and services: it is generally unlawful to treat a disabled person less favourably than anyone else unless this can be justified. In addition, service providers are required to make 'reasonable adjustments' to help the person overcome any barriers caused by their disability. Some services – at present education and public transport – are exempt.

Disability discrimination and work

- Anyone who has worked for the same employer for a year or more is protected from unfair dismissal.

- The Disability Discrimination Act also applies to an employer of 15 or more staff. People who are 'disabled' as defined in the Act (see above) can claim protection from discrimination in recruitment, during employment and if the contract is terminated. They also have the right to *reasonable* adjustments of their working conditions to help overcome the effects of their disability, regardless of how long they have worked for the employer. Possible adjustments could include time off to attend doctor's appointments or access to fresh air. What is reasonable will depend on the size of the employer, the nature of the job, and so on. An application under the DDA must be made within three months of the alleged act of discrimination.

- Someone who is experiencing unreasonable stress at work should report it to their manager without delay. The employer has a duty to the welfare of their employees, and must take reasonable steps to safeguard their health once a problem has been identified. In extreme cases, the employer may be held liable for an employee's illness.

Travel

In general there is no reason why someone with a mental health problem should be required to declare it before travelling. Booking offices and travel agents are required by the DDA not to discriminate against someone with a disability, and to make reasonable adjustments to their service to accommodate a disabled traveller. For example, they should spend extra time with a confused or anxious customer, provided the office is not unduly disrupted as a result.

Once the passenger is travelling the DDA does not generally apply. However, transport companies will normally have their own codes of practice, and unjustified discrimination can form the basis of a complaint.

When travelling overseas, two further considerations may apply:

- Airlines sometimes insist that a passenger who has recently been mentally unwell should travel with a nurse, at his or her own expense. This is not in itself unlawful, although the person is entitled to complain if the condition cannot be justified.

- Countries where a visa is required usually ask for health information, and may make further enquiries of an applicant who has been detained under section. Most countries claim they would not exclude a person simply for that reason. However, someone with a mental health problem who intends to travel to a country requiring a visa should check the position as soon as possible.

Insurance

Most insurance policies require a declaration of the applicant's medical history. Failure to answer the questions honestly can invalidate the policy. This means that people with a mental health diagnosis often experience difficulty in obtaining insurance cover. Sometimes the policy itself excludes or limits cover for mental health conditions; or it may not pay out if the claim is for a mental illness (this is standard with holiday or other insurance sold over the counter). Insurance is a service and is covered by the DDA (see above). Insurers are allowed to treat applicants less favourably if their decision is based on a medical report, statistical or actuarial data, or another source on which it is 'reasonable to rely'. The decision must be reasonable 'in all the circumstances'.

If a policy is sold over the counter, and the insurers cannot assess the individual risk, it may be lawful to exclude some diagnosed conditions to keep the policy cheap. Mental health organisations can suggest companies which offer specialised holiday insurance, but they are usually more expensive.

In individualised policies, taking a blanket approach to a health condition, without considering the individual's circumstances, is likely to be unlawful.

Gun licences

In general it is an offence to possess, purchase or acquire a firearm – including an imitation – or a shotgun without having a certificate from the police. There are special arrangements for dealers and sports clubs.

The police will grant a firearm certificate to any applicant who is fit to be entrusted with a firearm and who is not prohibited from possessing one (for example, being under age), and who will not be a danger to public safety or the peace. Applicants are required to provide extensive information about themselves on the appropriate form, including whether they suffer from a medical condition or disability, or have had treatment from their GP for depression or another mental or nervous disorder. They also have to offer two referees, who are required to confirm this information. A mental health problem will not in itself prevent the issuing of a certificate but the police are likely to want further information from the applicant's GP.

Applications for a shotgun certificate are treated in a similar way, except that someone in a professional position countersigns the application, rather than the applicant providing referees.

Certificates last for up to five years, and can be renewed or revoked.

Voting rights

Every citizen of the UK, the Commonwealth and the Irish Republic who is over 18, registered at an address in the UK and not otherwise disqualified from doing so, is entitled to vote, apart from convicted prisoners and Members of the House of Lords.

Those with a mental health problem are equally entitled to vote, provided they understand what they are doing. Until recently, those detained under the Mental Health Act (1983) could not use the hospital as their voting address. However, it is now possible for all psychiatric patients, except those on a hospital order made by a criminal court, to vote from the hospital. The hospital managers should make arrangements for them to be registered. They can also vote from their home address (if they have one) for as long as they are considered resident there; this will be questioned if they are detained for longer than six months.

Capacity to make decisions (general)

An agreement is only binding if the person making it has 'mental capacity'. To have capacity a person must be able to retain relevant information, believe it, and be able to weigh up the consequences of different courses of action. Adults over 18 are presumed to have full capacity unless there is evidence to the contrary. Having a mental health problem does not necessarily mean a person lacks capacity, even when they are unwell.

Capacity to make decisions, including financial ones, is assessed in relation to the particular decision at a fixed point in time. So a person may have sufficient capacity to buy a stereo but not to take out a mortgage.

Finances and the Court of Protection

Someone who has capacity

If a person has the capacity to handle their own money, but would like to give that responsibility to someone else, they can make their own arrangements. These include issues such as a third party mandate, which gives access to bank and building society accounts, or nominating an agent for the purpose of collecting social security benefits.

More formally, someone can grant a power of attorney. Powers of attorney are either general, in which the attorney can act on financial matters exactly as the person themselves could, or limited, where a limited range of actions is delegated. They may be short- or long-term, and come to an end automatically in certain circumstances (such as the attorney no longer wishing to act, or acting outside of the person's best interests, or if the person giving the power loses capacity). Sometimes the attorney has to act in accordance with principles laid down in a trust document.

An 'enduring power of attorney' empowers the attorney to take over the management of the person's affairs if they lose capacity in the future. It may operate as a regular power of attorney until that time, but in order to continue it must be registered with the Court of Protection (see below). An enduring power can be general or specific. There are strict procedural requirements when preparing an enduring power, and the 'donor' must have sufficient mental capacity at the time it is drawn up. Before the power is registered the attorney must notify the donor's relatives. Full information can be obtained from the Public Guardianship Office in London (tel. 020 7664 7000).

Someone who does not have capacity

If someone lacks the capacity to handle their finances, there is a range of ways in which another person can take on that responsibility.

1. They can apply to be registered as the person's 'appointee' for the collection of social security benefits, pensions or salaries, by writing to the benefits supervisor, fund administrator or employer who will investigate the application. An appointee can make claims, collect and spend money on someone's behalf. Most appointees are family members or friends.

2. Tax refunds, insurance payouts and withdrawals from savings can be handled by others on a semi-formal basis in very limited circumstances and provided only small amounts are in question. In general, to handle these aspects of someone's finances, there would have to be a power of attorney (see above).

3. *The Court of Protection*: the Court of Protection is an office of the Supreme Court. It manages the finances of people ('patients') who are unable to handle their own finances as a result of their 'mental disorder'. The Court registers enduring powers of attorney, and regulates the actions of attorneys. It can grant 'short procedure orders' for patients whose assets are less than £10,000. These authorise someone to deal with the finances of patients whose affairs are straightforward. The Court of Protection also appoints receivers to manage the financial affairs of patients. A receiver can be a family member, a professional such as a solicitor, or, in limited circumstances, the Public Trustee.

   To put someone's affairs under the supervision of the Court of Protection you must apply to the Public Guardianship Office on the required form, indicating your relationship to the patient and enclosing a medical certificate to show that the person lacks capacity to manage his or her affairs.

Making a will

For a will to be valid, it must comply with various formalities such as having witnesses. The person making it must also possess 'testamentary capacity' – the capacity to make a will. The law presumes that someone has the capacity to make a will if there is no substantial evidence to the contrary. Once a will has been made, it can only be challenged after the person's death. If someone has an enduring mental health problem, and would like to make a will, they should consider seeing a psychiatrist for a capacity test on the same day they prepare their will – this will make it much harder to challenge.

If a person does not possess testamentary capacity, you can apply on their behalf for the Court of Protection to make a 'statutory will'.

CHAPTER 25

Confidentiality and Mental Health

George Szmukler

It is unfortunately common for family members who wish to discuss their relative who has a mental illness with a psychiatrist or other member of the mental health team to be told that this is not possible because of 'patient confidentiality'. The family may wish to provide information they believe would be helpful for treatment or which might prevent a worsening of their relative's condition. Or they may want to offer care or seek advice to help them cope better with the impact of the illness on themselves, other members of the family or friends. Carers may lack basic knowledge about the illness, or not know how best to deal with burdensome behaviours; they may not even know to whom they can turn for help.

If a person expressly bars contact with the family or carer, mental health professionals often find it difficult to decide when to breach confidentiality.

How professionals think about confidentiality

Carers should first understand how professionals think about the problem. They regard listening to carers as good practice; trainee psychiatrists are usually taught that an assessment of someone's mental health is incomplete until they have consulted another family member or friend for more background information; for example, what a person was like before their illness started. On the other hand, for doctors, confidentiality is a basic aspect of their relationship with patients. Confidentiality is based on:

- *privacy*, which in turn is related to the notion of *respect for the person* – people have a right to decide how information about themselves should be shared with others
- *public interest* – good medical care requires patients to be frank to enable the doctor to make an accurate diagnosis and plan treatment;

if patients could not trust clinicians to keep their 'secrets', honesty would become less likely and this would undermine medical care.

Principles governing confidentiality for doctors can be found; for example, in guidelines produced by the UK General Medical Council (GMC):

> You must respect requests by patients that information should not be disclosed to third parties, save in *exceptional circumstances* (for example, where the health or safety of others would otherwise be at serious risk).

The GMC guidelines state that disclosure may be made in the patient's *medical interest* if

> you consider that a patient is incapable of giving consent to treatment...and you have tried unsuccessfully to persuade the patient to allow an appropriate person to be involved in the consultation. If you are convinced that it is *essential* in the patient's medical interests, you may disclose relevant information to an appropriate person or authority.

Disclosure may be made in the interests of others: '...where a failure to disclose the information may expose the patient, or others, to *risk of death or serious harm*' (emphases added).

These guidelines, and similar ones for other health professions, seem to set a high threshold for disclosure by speaking; for example, about *serious harm*. In the mental health arena it is not entirely clear what is meant by such terms and the professions involved have not reached a consensus in their views. Most would agree that a risk of death or serious physical harm, either to the patient or to others, would clearly justify a disclosure aimed at preventing such harm.

Advice to carers: Ways of approaching the problem

We offer some suggestions to carers about how they can work with professionals to deal with problems concerning patient confidentiality.

Get early agreement with your relative or friend and the treatment team. We suggest that much can be achieved in avoiding later dilemmas by setting out with the treatment team at the earliest possible stage an agreement about confidentiality. This is best done when your relative is reasonably well and able to participate with you and the treatment team in a meeting spelling out the circumstances under which discussions with you can take place, and what information can be exchanged.

For example, there might be agreement that if the person shows particular early warning signs of becoming ill again, the treatment team can discuss this with the carer so as to reduce the likelihood of further worsening. It could also be agreed what help the carer might require from the treatment team on an ongoing basis in order to cope better with their relative's illness.

Learn how to discuss disclosure against your relative or friend's wishes when it might be in their 'best interests'. As mentioned above, there is no consensus about the seriousness of the harm that justifies disclosure. We suggest that carers can help mental health professionals to think through the issues at stake. Try to discuss the following questions:

- Does your relative have the 'capacity' to make treatment choices? Carer involvement can be seen as a 'treatment choice'. 'Capacity' involves a person's ability to:
  - understand the nature of the treatment being offered including the likely consequences of having or not having that treatment
  - appreciate that he or she suffers from a disorder (or at least a problem affecting their mental health) requiring treatment or special help
  - reason with the information they now have about their illness and treatment.

  If your relative or friend has serious difficulty with any of these, they could be regarded as lacking capacity (for more information see Chapter 24).
  If this is so, you might want to put forward to the treatment team a further set of considerations, such as the following, to guide them in deciding whether maintaining confidentiality is in your relative's best interests.

- What is the nature and seriousness of the harm faced by your relative and the probability of it occurring?

- Are there alternatives available that might reduce the likelihood of harm? Other people or helping agencies, to whom your relative does not at this stage object, may be able to reduce the risk of harm.

- How would contact with you or another family member or friend against your relative's wishes be likely to be received by your relative? For example, a close family with good relationships but which the patient, as the result of a psychotic illness, sees as rejecting might be regarded differently compared to one with long-standing disharmony. There may have been previous discussion with the patient implying that contact would be acceptable under the current circumstances. It might also be asked whether the patient, following recovery, would be likely to see family involvement as having been, after all, desirable.

• Is the principle of the 'least restrictive alternative' relevant? Will your involvement reduce the likelihood of even greater restrictions on your relative's freedom becoming necessary (e.g. later involuntary admission to hospital)? This principle is implied in certain circumstances, as in the requirement to consult the nearest relative before compelling admission under some sections of the Mental Health Act in England and Wales.

By talking through these issues with the mental health team, reasons for breaching or not breaching confidentiality should become clearer to all.

Learn how to discuss disclosure against your relative or friend's wishes for the sake of the well-being of other family members. At present probably few clinicians would agree to involve the family against a person's wishes out of concern for the family's well-being (short of serious, usually physical danger). This seems unfair to families and friends struggling with enormous difficulties as a result of the illness.

Ask the clinician whether he or she might have a 'duty of care', although with some limitations, towards carers, over and above that to the patient. Until recently, this question has been largely ignored. However, there is now a trend towards the recognition of the interests of carers and this is likely to grow in parallel with the expanding role of informal carers as members of the 'care team' in the community.

Some recent legislation in the UK and abroad has recognised a formal status of 'carer'. For example, in England there is a need for carers to be consulted, with or without the patient's consent, before a 'Supervised Discharge Order' under the Mental Health (Patients in the Community) Act (1995) can be implemented. Guidance from the Department of Health concerning the protection of patient information is unfortunately inconsistent over the question of whether or not carers are members of the patient's 'care team' in the community and so entitled to information relevant to the team providing that care.

We suggest there is now sufficient recognition of a *special carer status* (with its associated rights) to argue that information necessary for carers to cope adequately with the demands placed on them should be made available. This has been reinforced by one of the standards set by the National Service Framework for Mental Health published in 1999. This framework sets out the standards the Department of Health expects from its mental health services. It states that all individuals who provide regular and substantial care for a person on the Care Programme Approach should:

- have an assessment of their caring, physical and mental health needs, repeated on at least an annual basis
- have their own written care plan, which is given to them and implemented in discussion with them.

How traditional notions of confidentiality will fit with this is unclear. There is a footnote stating that 'the service user's consent should always be explicitly sought before information (about medication, other treatment and care) is passed on to their carer' and that 'if the service user is incapacitated, information may be passed to the carer if it is in the service user's best interests'.

Whatever the interpretation, the standards set in the National Service Framework provide new opportunities for carers to talk to professionals about their situation in new ways. These should be grasped.

CHAPTER 26

How to Cope with the Stigma of Mental Illness

Geoffrey Woolf

What is stigma?

Stigma was the name of a mark used by the ancient Greeks to signify something unusual or morally bad about a person. The signs were cut or burnt into the body and they advertised that the bearer was a slave, a criminal or a traitor. The branded person was marked out to be shunned, especially in public.

In modern times the word has come to refer to the disgrace itself rather than the bodily evidence of it. Two of the main elements of stigma are a sense of shame, that the bearer has done something wrong, and social distance, that the person is to be avoided.

It refers both to society's attitude to the person and to the stigmatised person's feelings about themselves. Sometimes the stigma can extend to a person's close friends, associates and relatives, so-called *courtesy stigma*. To stigmatise somebody suffering from an illness as if they have done something wrong is grossly unfair and amounts to prejudice.

Why are people with mental illness stigmatised?

The roots of stigma are diverse. It has been suggested that stigma is a projection onto others of fears we all of us have about succumbing to unacceptable behaviour and may be realated to the excessive value given to independence, self-reliance, beauty and health. Others have postulated that stigma may be a function of the notion that disabled people violate a belief that there is a just world.

In the case of physical illness, we know that people are more likely to be rejected or stigmatised if their illness is perceived as either severe or as having a behavioural cause. There have been various physical illnesses which at one time carried stigma. Examples are cancer, because it was perceived as severe and untreatable, and tuberculosis, because it was thought to be related to poor personal hygiene. As understanding and treatments have improved, so stigma has diminished.

So it is now with mental illness. We know that sufferers are misunderstood, inadequately treated and stigmatised. Negative attitudes may well result from ignorance. Mental illness may be seen as a sign of weakness, or the person may be thought in some way to have caused the illness through bad behaviour and therefore be to blame. In addition there are exaggerated beliefs of dangerousness.

Research studies show that the perception of mentally ill people as dangerous reduces with familiarity: the more contact there is, the less threatening a person seems. Experience of mental illness, direct or indirect, also weakens stereotypes.

The media has a strong influence on people's perceptions. One of the main sources of information about mental illness is through the media, especially newspapers and television. Unfortunately prejudiced reporting perpetuates negative attitudes and a lack of understanding of mental illness.

Studies of media coverage of issues to do with mentally ill people show that these people are stereotyped and portrayed almost exclusively in a negative light. Individuals suffering from a psychotic illness are often presented as violent criminals, committing murder or rape, while those suffering from a non-psychotic illness are figures of fun, to be pitied or laughed at rather than understood. The reporting of mental illness involving violence to others heavily outweighs sympathetic reports. Reports of violence tend to be headline news, but sympathetic reports are 'back-page' items.

What are the effects of stigma?

Stigma is not only deeply hurtful to people who have experienced mental illness and their carers but can also cause those stigmatised individuals to be confronted with extra difficulties. For example, stigma can give rise to difficulties in making social relationships and gaining employment. It contributes to poor resourcing for mental health services, and it discourages people from seeking help because they may have absorbed inaccurate ideas about mental illness. The adverse effects of stigma compound pre-existing feelings of shame, low self-esteem, isolation, and poor access to treatment.

Campaigns to reduce stigma

There have been a number of local, national and international campaigns to reduce the stigma of mental illness. The Royal College of Psychiatrists' *Changing Minds* anti-stigma campaign aims to reduce the stigma of mental illness through collaboration with patients, carers, health care professionals, employers, school teachers, members of the media and the general public. Information, including a booklet 'Every Family in the Land: Recommendations for the Implementation of a Five Year Strategy, 1998–2003' can be obtained from the Royal College of Psychiatrists (see Resources).

On the international scene the World Psychiatric Association (WPA) has initiated a programme to fight the stigma associated with schizophrenia. Other countries have developed their own campaigns. For example, in Australia, *Stigma Watch* monitors the media and contacts those broadcasters or publishers who make inaccurate or discriminatory reference to mental illness. The campaign encourages members of the public to send in reports of stigmatising references to mental illness from radio or TV, films, newspaper and magazine articles, adverts or websites. These are then checked, and the broadcasters or publishers who have made the stigmatising reference are contacted and asked to explain themselves. The aim is to encourage journalists to be fairer and more accurate in their reporting. Responses are posted on the Stigma Log on the campaign website, making public the journalists' reactions.

Coping with feelings of shame

> Shame is the shawl of Pink
>
> In which we wrap the Soul
>
> To keep it from infesting Eyes

> (Emily Dickinson, c.1877)

It may help to look again at your own ideas about mental illness and dealing with shame. Shame can lead to a vicious circle. You may pick up signals from other people of put-downs and rejection and then begin to see yourself as inferior to others. Once you start to see yourself as inferior you may begin to dwell on your deficits and to discount your strengths. When you begin to think in this way you start to expect ridicule, criticism, and rejection. This in turn may lead to submissive behaviour, inhibition and withdrawal, which may make it more likely that people put you down or reject you. This then feeds back into the vicious circle resulting in more feelings of shame and so on.

Helpful attitudes

You may find the following attitudes and ways of thinking helpful. Make a note of them and remind yourself of them when you need support:

'I've got nothing to hide.'

'If people stigmatise me, it is a sign of their prejudice.'

'Mental illness is an illness like any other.'

'The illness of a family member is nothing to be ashamed of.'

'No one is to blame.'

'Success for each individual may be different.'

'Mental illness can strike anybody.'

Winning ways

The way you deal with stigma and prejudiced behaviour in others can have a marked effect on how you feel about yourself and the attitudes of others. Consider the following two examples of how people who were stigmatised dealt with specific situations:

EXAMPLE 1

Not long ago, I took my daughter Ashley out for breakfast to a local restaurant. I was preparing her medications when the waitress came to take our order. When she saw the bottles of pills lined up on the table, the waitress joked with me. She said, 'What are you, a drug addict?' I replied, 'Actually, no. My daughter is a psychiatric patient, and these pills are for her.' Ashley immediately added, 'I have a mental illness and these pills make me feel better.' The waitress was embarrassed, but I was not and neither was my daughter. Since Ashley does not fit the stereotype many people have about the mentally ill, this kind of thing happens all the time. After a while, you just get used to it.

(Jean J. Beard, from http://www.familydiv.org/nothingtohide)

EXAMPLE 2

This example is adapted from John Steinbeck's *Cannery Row* (1945) which is set in the Great Depression in America.

A group of boys were playing in the street. Willard was goading Joey in front of the other children. He tried various tactics in vain; then he asked Joey where his father was. Joey explained that his father was dead. Willard asked casually, what he'd died of. Joey become silent. He knew that Willard already knew the answer to the question but he was afraid of Willard. He was choked with emotion as he explained that his father had killed himself.

Willard in a tone of mock concern, asked how he'd done it. Joey explained that he'd swallowed rat poison. At this point, Willard shrieked with laughter and asked Joey if his father had actually believed that he was a rat. At first, Joey tried to laugh along with the joke hoping that Willard would stop. However, Willard persisted. He started crawling around on the ground asking if that was what his father had done. He wrinkled his nose, crossed his eyes and stuck his tounge out, asking if that's what his father had looked like. Willard was helpless with laughter and the others laughed along with him.

> Joey now stood his ground. "He was sick all day," he explained. "For nearly a year he couln't get a job. And you know a funny thing? The next morning a guy came round to give him a job." Willard was humilliated. He tried to continue the joke but even for him it just fell flat.

(John Steinbeck, Cannery Row (1945))

In both these examples, being open and direct rather than reacting by withdrawing and feeling ashamed was very disarming and transferred the shame onto the person who was behaving in a stigmatising and prejudiced way.

Strengths and weaknesses

You may need to adapt considerably to living with mental illness, either as a carer or a sufferer. Many people who have suffered adversity learn from the experience and develop new strengths. You may need to accept some of the limitations it imposes on your life to begin to develop in new ways. Set achievable goals for yourself and your relative. It may be preferable to compare progress with other people living with a mental illness rather than with people who have not had these difficulties. Learn to value your relative's strengths rather than focus on weaknesses. Success for each individual may be different.

Education

If you feel ashamed of having a relative or friend who suffers from a mental illness, it may be worthwhile going over your own way of thinking. Find out as much as you can about the illness using information booklets, websites, litera-ture and so on. Educate people around you. Share the information you have obtained. Talk to other members of the family and friends about the illness and its effects.

Coping with isolation

> Deep in the sea are riches beyond compare
>
> But if it's safety you seek, it's on the shore.
>
> *(Saadi, Rose Garden)*

The stigma of mental illness can result in a wall of silence around sufferers and their carers. This may leave them feeling very isolated. Withdrawing may compound the situation. Contact improves the attitudes of others. Although you may risk rejection, it is important to be able to ask for emotional support or practical help when you need it

For most people, their main supports will be from family or friends but there are also various voluntary organisations such as the National Schizophrenia Fellowship, the Manic Depression Fellowship and MIND. These organisations provide local contacts and groups all over the country (see Resources).

Getting effective treatment

When mental illness is being treated with medication, non-compliance with treatment can present a serious problem. There is widespread disapproval in the public of using medication to treat mental illness, in spite of overwhelming evidence of its effectiveness. Many people believe that drug treatments not only fail to heal, but cover up and hide real problems and cause serious side effects including dependency. It is not surprising that there may be a reluctance to consult a specialist or to take medication. However, there is a range of modern and effective treatments for mental illness including medication that does not result in either distressing side effects or dependency. There are a number of other effective interventions, including talking treatments, which are available. However, you may need to ask specifically for these, and being well informed will be invaluable in getting your treatment of choice.

References

Johnson, T.H. (ed) (1975) The Complete Poems of Emily Dickinson. London: Faber and Faber.

Saadi (1997) *The Rose Garden of Saadi.* (Trans. Omar Ali-Shah.) Tractus Books.

Steinbeck, J. (1993) *Cannery Row.* Penguin Books.

CHAPTER 27

Ethnic Minorities and Mental Health

Kwame McKenzie

There are special issues and needs for carers from ethnic minority groups. Ethnic minorities are over-represented in the mental health system. Over 40 per cent of the inpatients in London hospitals are from ethnic minority groups. Some say that this is because the mental health system is racist, but the high rates are more likely to be because being a member of an ethnic minority in the UK is stressful. Stress is one of the causes of mental illness.

Reasons for mental illness

Each of us has our own strengths and weaknesses. Some people have the vulnerability to develop a mental illness when under pressure. The pressures of life can spark off a mental illness and continued stress can make it difficult to recover. Unemployment, separation from parents, financial difficulties, racial discrimination, adjusting to a new country and poor housing may all be important risk factors for developing a mental illness. For refugees, the reasons for leaving their home country – for example, war, torture or political persecution – may lead to mental illness. Whatever the reason it is clear that being in the UK for members of ethnic minorities is stressful, and can lead to mental illness.

There are other reasons why there are higher rates of mental illness in ethnic minority groups. In South Asian, African and African-Caribbean women there is a higher risk of difficulties in pregnancy and low-birth-weight babies. Statistics show that pregnancy complications and low birth weight in the baby are linked to mental illness when these individuals are adults.

In spite of this research and information, often the cause of your relative or friend's mental illness will not be clear. This may be because a build-up of stress over a long period of time has caused it so it will be difficult for you to put your finger on what has happened.

What can you do?

People who are suffering from mental health problems need the help of their families and friends. They need support, they need familiar faces, they need someone to talk to. Just being there is important.

You can help in other ways too. If you want the best care for your relative you will need to work with the doctors, nurses and other members of the mental health team. We know from research studies that when carers, patients and professionals work together as a team, a person makes a better recovery from their mental illness.

In the UK doctors and other health professionals must consider issues around confidentiality which may mean the doctor not necessarily sharing information from a patient with the carer. However, it is worth trying to work with your relative's doctor to see how you can deal with this problem so that you are included as much as possible as a member of the care team (see Chapter 25).

The 'doctor knows best' attitude does not get the best results. As a carer, you will know more about your relative or friend. You will know more about their culture. If your relative is ill, you may be better at talking to the doctor about this and about your relative's specific needs. It is important that you help the doctor and your relative to understand each other. Your role is vital to make sure your relative gets the care he or she needs. The more the clinical team know, the better the treatment will be.

This is the time when your relative needs you most, and needs you to be strong. You may have to be your relative's advocate and tell the doctor what he or she wants and does not want. At times you may have to be cruel to be kind. You may need to give 'tough love'. If you are the next of kin, you may need to help the doctor and social worker treat your relative against their will. It may be the only way he or she will get better.

At times your relative may not agree with what the doctor or nurses advise. You also may not agree, and you may need to ask them not to treat your relative in the way that they plan to. You may prefer 'talking therapies' to drug therapy. You may prefer outpatient treatment to inpatient treatment. You are important and your voice needs to be heard. However, it is vital that you listen to what the doctor and nurses say before any decisions are made. After all they do have experience in treating mental illness.

As a carer you need to educate yourself about mental illness. You need to know your rights and the rights of your relative or friend. You need to know about the different illnesses and their treatment. You need to recognise the early signs of mental illness so that you can warn your relative or friend and their doctor or nurse that things are going wrong.

You also need to understand that you have to look after yourself. If you try to do too much and you become ill yourself, you will not be able to support anybody.

Mental illness comes in many forms. It is not always easy to recognise, even for health professionals. If you think that your relative has a mental health problem, a problem with their spirits or depression, tell your doctor. Not only that, stick to your guns. Your doctor may not recognise the signs because he or she does not understand your culture.

If there is a problem, the GP is the first person to contact. However, be aware that some GPs think that people from an ethnic minority with a mental health problem should always be referred to a psychiatrist. This is not true and it is often better for common mental disorders – such as anxiety and depression – to be treated by the GP without your relative seeing a specialist. Seeing a psychiatrist can be stressful in itself.

Types of mental illness

There are many types of mental illness. The categories are based on descriptions of the problems that people are suffering from; for example, whether they are hearing voices, whether they are depressed and so on.

Some types of mental illness such as schizophrenia and depression are common to all cultures. However, the symptoms can be slightly different in different cultures. For example, in the UK many people who are depressed go to their doctor and say they are depressed. However, in the Caribbean few people who are depressed say they are depressed; they are more likely to say that they are suffering from 'pressure' or 'heaviness'. In India, lack of energy is a more common complaint than depressed mood in people who are suffering from depression. This can cause confusion and lead to the doctor missing the depression.

There have been a number of research studies of mental illness in different groups in the UK. There is a lot of information available. Below is a summary.

Schizophrenia and Africans and African-Caribbeans in the UK

The most severe form of mental illness is psychosis. Schizophrenia is a type of psychosis (see Chapter 1). For some time there have been reports that there are higher rates of schizophrenia in Africans and African-Caribbeans in the UK. The rates are 2 to 6 times higher than in the white British population. Some researchers say that this high rate is due to misdiagnosis of distress and depression as schizophrenia. There is some truth in this, but even those who are misdiagnosed as suffering from schizophrenia are likely to have a serious mental illness such as mania or depression that needs treatment. The stress of being in the UK is causing problems for Africans and African-Caribbeans. The important role for a carer is to make sure that the mental health team has all the information they need so they can make the correct diagnosis and start the correct treatment. The earlier treatment is started the better it works.

Depression in Africans and African-Caribbeans

Depression is not diagnosed as often in African and African-Caribbean patients as in white patients. Surveys have shown that this is not because depression is less common but because doctors are more likely to miss it. If your relative or friend shows the symptoms of depression it is important that they see a doctor. Depression can be effectively treated by talking to a psychologist or by medication. There is no need for your relative to suffer in silence (see Chapter 3).

The rate of suicide in African and African-Caribbean young people is rising. This may be because they are becoming depressed but it is not being recognised and treated.

The mental health system and Africans and African-Caribbeans

The statistics are chilling. If you are black you are 6 to 9 times more likely to be brought into a psychiatric ward against your will under the Mental Health Act (1983). You are more likely to be treated in a locked ward or a secure unit such. If you are black and have a mental illness you are nine times more likely to be arrested by the police.

The reasons for this are not clear. It is not as simple as racism on behalf of the services. There seems to be an interaction between the services and young black people. The services see young black people as dangerous, and African and African-Caribbean people fear the services because they think that they are going to be given medication that causes side effects and they will be locked up. They delay seeing mental health professionals until they are very ill, but because of this they are actually more likely to be admitted to hospital. If a doctor sees a young black man and thinks that he is very ill or dangerous he will be admitted and treated against his will. He will be angry about this and so will seem more dangerous. The patient fears the doctor, the doctor fears the patient and so the circle continues.

When discharged, patients who have been admitted against their will are less likely to take part in aftercare or accept their prescribed medication. They are less likely to keep in contact with the mental health team and so are less likely to get treatment early if symptoms return. This circle of fear leads to less and less contact by patients with the mental health services and more and more symptoms. It leads to the mental health system resorting to using more and more secure means of treatment such as admission to a locked ward. It leads to more contact with the police and can lead eventually to a prison sentence.

The only way that the circle can be broken is by improving communication. This underlines the importance of carers keeping an eye on what is happening and getting help before things go wrong.

The high numbers of African and African-Caribbean patients in secure units and in prison may be because they do not get good treatment early enough or are not taking the treatment that is prescribed. If you are a black person in the UK you are more likely to have problems with the police. If you are black and have a mental illness you are much more likely to have problems with the police. The only way to stop this is to try to work with, not against, the mental health professionals – to use the system, not work against it, and to get information about your rights.

Psychosis in South Asian groups

The rate of schizophrenia in Indian, Pakistani and Bangladeshi people is the same as the rate in white British groups. However, the outlook is better. Those who suffer from psychosis are more likely to be symptom-free and less likely to be readmitted to hospital. One explanation for why this happens is the extended family system with strong family ties in South Asian cultures. This further supports the belief that relatives and carers should be involved in treatment plans.

Depression and South Asian groups

Although the stress of being a member of an ethnic minority group in the UK often leads to depression, GPs may miss this problem. The diagnosis of depression can be difficult to make. Depression is an illness of the spirit and the body. There may be a number of physical symptoms such as tiredness that can be mistaken for a physical illness. There is effective treatment for depression. If you recognise the symptoms you can help your relative or friend get the treatment they need.

Alcohol use in South Asian patients

There is a serious problem with alcohol use in Asian men. Surveys have shown that they are more likely to drink heavily than white British men or African-Caribbeans. This may be due to an underlying depression. Alcohol can cause serious damage to the body and leads to physical problems that may be life-threatening (see Chapter 10). Alcohol abuse and dependence also have effects on one's life. A person may lose his job, get into debt and his marriage may suffer. Domestic violence is more common in marriages where one partner has a drinking problem.

Most people with alcohol problems will need help in coming off alcohol. Local GPs and mental health services have special workers who deal with alcohol problems.

Suicide in South Asian women

South Asian women have the highest rate of suicide of any group in the UK. No one knows exactly why this is. It is thought that the stress of being in the UK, especially the conflict between traditional ways and the different culture in the UK, leads to suicidal thinking. In addition, GPs may miss any depression, and there may be a reluctance to use telephone helplines such as the Samaritans who can help people in crisis.

If your relative or friend is desperate and you think that she may be thinking about taking her life there are a number of agencies that can be contacted. These include the Samaritans, your local GP, your local accident and emergency department and specialist services such as local Asian mental health support lines.

Refugee groups

War, torture, being uprooted from your country and leaving other family members behind can all cause mental health problems. It is also difficult to come to terms with being in a new country especially if your standard of living is not as good as before.

There are specific illnesses such as depression and post-traumatic stress disorder that develop when people have been in extreme conditions such as war (see Chapter 6). There are a number of agencies that deal specifically with refugee mental health. In particular the Medical Foundation for the Care of Victims of Torture in London offers free counselling to those who have been victims of torture. Carers can help by supporting the person who is suffering and trying to get them to admit that there is a problem and to seek help.

CHAPTER 28

Being a Carer

Kate Harvey

Over the last few decades, health professionals and policy makers have paid increasing attention to the care that families and friends provide when a person is ill. However, the focus has tended to be on carers of older people or people with physical health problems, overlooking the carers of people with a mental illness. Caring for someone with a mental illness is rather different from other sorts of caring. There is less emphasis on doing physical tasks, and the amount of care that is needed may fluctuate with the course of the person's illness. However, like other carers, carers of people with a mental illness often find their situation difficult and sometimes feel unable to cope. This chapter looks at what caring involves, the effects of caring on the carer and why these effects might vary between carers.

What does caring involve?

Caring for someone with a mental illness does not usually involve the physical tasks that other sorts of carers do, such as helping the person to wash or dress. Sometimes carers of people with a mental illness carry out practical tasks for their relative – for example, shopping or household chores – but most find that their main role is to *take responsibility* as well as supporting, encouraging and reassuring them.

Carers take responsibility in a variety of ways. They might provide their relative with a home, or organise their finances; for example, checking that they receive any benefits to which they are entitled. They might also deal with people or organisations on their behalf, such as their employer, mental health professionals, and housing or benefits agencies. Some carers are involved in their relative's treatment, perhaps by helping them to complete activities at home, or by taking part in therapy sessions. Often carers supervise their relative's medication and encourage them to attend appointments, perhaps by reminding or accompanying them. Carers often play a vital role during crises, by seeking professional help, by supporting the ill person and by providing mental health professionals with information.

Because caring for someone with mental illness does not usually involve physical tasks, many individuals do not think of themselves as carers. However, anybody who looks after a mentally ill person in the ways described above is a carer and can be affected by caregiving.

What effect does caring have?

Looking after someone with a mental illness can affect a carer in a variety of ways.

Employment

Carers who are employed sometimes find that their performance at work is affected by the person's illness. Worrying about them can be distracting and can make it difficult to concentrate. The responsibilities of caregiving can also mean taking extra time off or unpaid holiday. We know that some carers give up work because they find it difficult to balance their caregiving responsibilities with a job.

Finances

Family finances can be severely affected if the person is too ill to work. The situation is worse if the carer also has to give up work to look after their relative. Some people with a mental illness find it difficult to budget their money, and carers can find themselves lending them money or paying for things on their behalf.

Routine

Caring can disrupt the family or household's daily routine. This is especially true if the person who is mentally ill is unable to carry out activities, such as household chores or shopping, that they would usually do. Carers then find that they have to take on new and unexpected responsibilities in addition to the things they did previously. The responsibilities of caring can also disrupt other family activities, such as holidays or special occasions.

Social life and leisure activities

For several reasons, carers often find that their social life and leisure activities are affected by caring. Mental illness can make a person feel lethargic or withdrawn, and it can be difficult for carers to persuade their relative to take part in leisure activities. This may result in the carer going out less, particularly if they are concerned about leaving the person on their own. Because mental illness can make people behave strangely, some carers feel embarrassed about going out with their relative or inviting friends and family home. We know that many carers feel lonely because they are isolated.

Family life

Caring for a person with a mental illness can cause tension within families. Not only may relations with the person become strained, but also disagreements and arguments can occur between family members.

People with mental illness can often feel frustrated by their dependence on other people, and guilty about the 'burden' they are placing on their carers. At the same time, they may feel under-valued because they are unable to contribute to family life in the way that they would like. Family members on the other hand may find it difficult to cope with the ill person's behaviour. This is true both for strange behaviour, which can be difficult to understand, and for behaviour that does not seem to be an obvious part of the illness; for example, staying in bed during the day. It can be particularly difficult to cope with an ill person's behaviour if it seems to make the problem worse, such as alcohol or drug use. Carers commonly describe themselves as walking on eggshells, unsure what to do for the best.

Caring can also cause tension between family members. There may be disagreements about the best way to deal with the person's illness and unhappiness if individuals feel that they are taking on more than their fair share of caregiving responsibilities. Difficulties can also arise when the responsibilities of caregiving mean that a carer has less time and energy to devote to other family members.

Children

The presence of children can be an added difficulty for carers, not least because the sensitive task of explaining the illness to children can often fall to them. On a practical level, in addition to caring for the person with mental health problems, the carer may also have to become more involved in looking after their relative's children, perhaps even taking over responsibility for them. This may be made even more difficult if the carer is dividing their time and energy between their own children and the ill person's children. Carers may also find themselves worrying about the well-being of children in the family, particularly if a child has problems at school or seems unhappy.

Health and well-being

The responsibilities of caregiving can leave a carer with little time or energy to enjoy life, and the isolation that many carers experience can make them feel as if they are coping alone. Caring for a person with mental illness is likely to be stressful, and we know that stress can cause a variety of physical health problems, such as headaches, tiredness and difficulty sleeping. We also know that the strain of caring can have an adverse effect on carers' mental health. Many carers experience depression or anxiety. Most carers find caregiving hard going at times and occasionally feel that they can no longer continue to provide care.

Rewarding effects of caring

Although caring can have many adverse effects, it can also have rewards. It can make carers feel valued, either by the ill person or by the wider family. It can also bring individual carers closer to the cared-for person and make families feel closer together. Taking on new roles and responsibilities, although challenging, can make carers feel more confident about their abilities.

Are all carers affected in the same way?

Not all carers are affected in the same way or to the same extent and some find their task harder than others do. This is partly due to differences between different mental illnesses (for example, some illnesses are continuous while others are episodic) but it is also because of differences between carers. We know that carers who have support from their family and friends find caring less difficult than carers who have no support. This might be because they are able to share the tasks and responsibilities of caregiving with someone else, or it might be because they feel less isolated. We also know that some carers are better than others at coping with difficulties, and consequently, the focus of many interventions and support groups is on helping carers to develop more effective coping strategies.

CHAPTER 29

Psychological Treatments

Anne Ward and Stirling Moorey

As a carer, you may wish to know more about psychological approaches to mental illness in a family member or friend; alternatively, you may be feeling stressed and looking for help in your own right. In either case, psychological treatments encompass an often bewildering array of possibilities, which can be difficult to sort through and access. This chapter will describe therapies that are commonly available through the NHS. Some of these therapies will also be available through the voluntary or private sectors. However, if you do want to look privately, then it is advisable to check that your therapist is registered with a recognised accreditation body, such as the BCP (British Confederation of Psychotherapists) or the UKCP (UK Council of Psychotherapists).

Anyone referred to a community mental health team (CMHT) should have a psychological component to their treatment programme, even if the primary treatment is medication. Three types of therapy are described:

- Type A – psychological treatment delivered as part of an overall programme of mental health care, such as anxiety management or social skills training.

- Type B – a stand-alone treatment that takes the form of a set of sessions. It may be structured and problem-focused or non-directive, and is informed by more than one theoretical framework.

- Type C – formal psychotherapy, which is practised within a particular theoretical model (for example psychodynamic or cognitive) and has a well-developed form of delivery.

This chapter focuses on the main Type C therapies: psychodynamic, cognitive behavioural, cognitive-analytical and systemic (family or couple), as these are practised in a mental health setting. Other potentially beneficial therapies, such as interpersonal, solution-focused, and the art, music and drama therapies, are still only sparsely available and will not be discussed here. The process of treatment (how to access it, the assessment procedure, and the likely format of treatment) is described, and the likely content (what happens when you get there and what you might experience). There is also information about what sorts of problems typically benefit from each treatment.

Psychodynamic psychotherapy

This is usually provided by a psychotherapy department in a mental health unit, although some GP counsellors may work in this way. Referrals are accepted from GPs or other health professionals. Patients may self-refer, but funding has to be agreed by the GP or other funding body. An assessment with a senior therapist in a psychotherapy department offers the opportunity to sample the therapy, and to think further about what form of therapy would be suitable. The usual choice is between individual therapy – weekly for up to a year, and group therapy – weekly for up to two years. However, the decision might also be for family work, or referral for, say, cognitive therapy.

The individual psychodynamic psychotherapist adopts a listening stance and allows the patient to set the agenda. The focus is on the patient's conscious and unconscious assumptions about relationships, and how these are played out with the therapist. Thus past experiences resurface, and can be thought about in a live way. The therapist avoids imposing his or her own view, and the patient, in turn, is asked to live with the uncertainty aroused by this relatively unstructured situation.

Group sessions are conducted on a similar basis. Although the therapist plays an important role, other group members are also of vital importance in helping individuals assess their experience. Group therapy might be preferable for someone who finds the idea of one-to-one therapy too intense, or for someone who has benefited from previous individual work, but has residual difficulties in relationships.

In thinking about who might benefit from psychodynamic psychotherapy, diagnosis is less important than personal characteristics. Someone who wants to understand their difficulties in the context of a relationship, who does not feel the need to be rid of their symptoms instantly, and who has some ability to tolerate anxiety – without acting out in their behaviour (e.g. misusing alcohol or self-harming) – might benefit from this approach. In practice, most patients treated have neurotic or personality difficulties (e.g. depression, anxiety or relationship problems) but psychodynamic treatment can also help some people with a psychotic illness.

Cognitive behavioural therapy

Cognitive behavioural therapy (CBT) or cognitive therapy may be provided in general practice, as part of the work of a CMHT, or in a specialist psychological treatment service. Therapists are usually clinical psychologists, nurses, or, less commonly, psychiatrists specialising in CBT. Referrals are accepted from GPs or other health professionals within the CMHT. Again, patients may self-refer, but funding has to be agreed by the GP or other funding body. Within a specialist service, formal assessment involves meeting with a senior therapist who explains and illustrates the model, and decides on its suitability in each case. A course of therapy is typically between 6 and 20 weekly individual sessions.

A cognitive behavioural therapist will help a person identify specific problems to work on, and set goals for how to change. Therapy will usually involve learning methods for changing unhelpful patterns of negative thinking (cognitive techniques) and acting (behavioural techniques). This is done in the therapy session, and then practised as homework between sessions. For example, a person may try to combat depression by challenging self-critical thoughts, or someone with a phobia may try some tasks, graded in difficulty, to face a feared situation. Therapy is very much a collaborative process, with the patient contributing actively to the agenda and finding out how to become his or her own therapist. The beliefs and rules we live by often make us vulnerable to psychological problems (e.g. if you believe you must do everything perfectly, you may become depressed if you make a mistake). Although a cognitive behavioural therapist may help in understanding how these rules were learned, the emphasis is more on changing their current impact.

Cognitive behavioural therapies have been used effectively in disorders such as depression, anxiety, phobias, panic and obsessional compulsive disorders, as well as in bulimia nervosa. They have also been used with some people who have a psychotic illness and, less commonly, the techniques have been applied in groups.

Cognitive-analytical therapy (CAT)

This form of therapy grew as a result of the long NHS waiting lists for psychotherapy in the 1970s and 1980s. It is a time-limited intervention, typically 16 to 20 sessions, incorporating aspects of both psychoanalytical and cognitive therapies. It is increasingly available in NHS settings and GP counselling services, but is still much less widespread than either psychodynamic or cognitive therapies. Referral procedures vary according to the setting, but information can often be accessed through a central psychotherapy department.

The patient and therapist jointly agree on goals for the therapy. In session four, the therapist 'reformulates' a person's difficulties in the form of a letter, placing difficulties in the context of early experiences, and suggesting ways in which they may be perpetuated in the present. This also involves identifying someone's repertoire of 'reciprocal roles', that is, the typical relationships in which he or she engages, and which are likely to be repeated in therapy. Diagrammatic descriptions of mood shifts and relationship changes are often helpful in this respect. The therapist asks the patient to corroborate or modify the letter, and it is used as a working guide for further sessions. Towards the end of therapy, both therapist and patient write 'goodbye' letters, summarising the course of therapy and what remains to be done. Sessions are structured, akin to CBT, to the extent that goals, letters, diagrams and so on are kept in mind and in the sessions. However, the relationship with the therapist also permeates the therapy in a less definable manner, similar to psychodynamic work.

CAT has been described as a good first therapy for most problems. In practice, it has been used mainly for people with neurotic or personality problems, similarly to psychodynamic psychotherapy, but perhaps holding more 'disturbed' people in its more structured, relatively brief format. If necessary, someone can progress to longer-term work, usually psychodynamically oriented.

Systemic (family and couple) therapy

Systemic implies that it is the family or couple system rather than the individual that is the focus of interest. As such family therapy may naturally belong to a child psychiatry service where families are usually included routinely. However, it may also be offered by a CMHT, or referrals may be made directly to a stand-alone family therapy service, usually part of the hospital psychotherapy department. Referrals may be made by GPs, other health professionals, or be self-generated (provided funding is supported by the GP). Typically, families or couples are offered four to six sessions at two- to three-week intervals, followed by a review.

Systems theory holds that individuals interact with a system (family or partner) that affects them, and that that system is in turn affected by the individual. If one member of a family has a serious mental illness, how the rest of the family responds can determine how the illness expresses itself. In relationships, people often seek partners that in some way complement themselves, for both good and ill. Family or couple therapy offers a chance to explore these interactions in a blame-free setting, experimenting with different ways of relating to one another with the help of a therapist. There are different theoretical underpinnings to this, varying from the more psychoanalytical to the more behavioural in tone. For example, work on a specific sexual problem may be practical and focused, or it may look more at presumed underlying relationship difficulties.

Couple work is widely accepted, both within and outside the NHS; for example, through the voluntary sector organisation, Relate. Its success or otherwise depends on the couple, and their willingness to work together, rather than on specific diagnostic categories. A successful outcome may even be the decision to split up. Family work can be effective for a variety of problems, ranging from schizophrenia, in which it can reduce the relapse rate, to adolescent anorexia nervosa, in which it improves the outcome. Interestingly, despite solid research evidence to back this up, family therapy is not often suggested in routine treatment of psychosis.

Further information

Your relative or friend's GP will know how to access local services. Alternatively, your relative may already be in contact with a CMHT and can ask directly. In addition, most psychotherapy departments are willing to answer queries by phone, and some will have general information that can be sent out to you.

CHAPTER 30

Suicide and Suicide Attempts

Mike Crawford

Feeling fed up with life from time to time is a normal part of our experience as human beings. The stress and upset of life leads many people, at some point in their lives, to ask themselves if life is worth living. For most of us these are passing feelings, but for others they can build up and lead to episodes of self-harm or even to suicide. Every year in the UK about 4500 people die by suicide and many more take overdoses and deliberately harm themselves in other ways. People who experience mental distress and mental illness are far more likely to think about harming themselves or actually attempt to commit suicide. Knowing that someone you care for has these thoughts can be very distressing and place a burden on your relationship with them. This chapter explores these problems and considers ways of trying to help someone in this situation.

When someone has thoughts of self-harm

Finding out that someone you care for is experiencing thoughts of self-harm can come as a great shock. The fear that a person you care for could kill themselves is a chilling one. However, it is important to remember that thinking about harming oneself is common among people who experience mental distress and that of all the people who have this thought, very few act on it.

Professional carers are taught that when they become aware that someone has suicidal thoughts they should take these thoughts seriously. Such feelings signal that a person who is experiencing mental distress may be becoming desperate. It will often prompt the professional into deciding that further measures need to be taken to help the person with the difficulties they are experiencing.

If someone you know experiences thoughts of self-harm but has not sought professional help this may be the time to suggest that they do. If someone is already seeing their GP or other health care worker and has not discussed these feelings with them, suggesting that they do so helps to make sure that they get the care they need. At such times reassurance can sometimes be useful. Most people who go through a period of mental distress will recover and someone who is experiencing thoughts of self-harm may have begun to worry that they will not get better.

Help for people who have suicidal feelings is available 24 hours a day, both from health services and from organisations such as the Samaritans (see Resources). Many people who harm themselves have used alcohol or drugs prior to the incident and helping someone to avoid these substances may be worth doing. When someone takes an overdose, the damage they suffer will depend on the type and quantity of the tablets taken. It is not a good idea for anyone to have large quantities of old tablets in the house.

When someone has harmed themself

The most common way that people harm themselves is by taking an overdose of tablets. If this happens, urgent medical attention should be sought. Some overdoses can cause serious long-term health problems even after the person appears to have made a full recovery. Early treatment can often prevent these problems from occurring.

When a person is treated in hospital following an overdose they will usually be asked to speak to someone about the difficulties that led to the incident and to explore ways of helping with these problems. Sometimes this will include a follow-up appointment at the hospital or a local clinic. Unfortunately many people who are offered an appointment do not attend. They may feel that they would rather forget about the incident or think that talking to someone about their problems will not achieve anything. Sometimes this feeling of pessimism is part of the problems that the person is experiencing and encouraging them to attend the appointment can be helpful.

After someone has tried to harm themselves or commit suicide, there is an increased risk that they will try again in the period afterwards, although as few as 1 in a 100 people will kill themselves in the following year. The exception to this is among older people and those with long-term mental health problems, who should be in regular contact with services following an overdose or episode of self-harm.

Repeated self-cutting

A smaller proportion of people self-harm by repeatedly cutting themselves. This usually happens when the person is experiencing strong feelings such as tension or frustration. People who repeatedly cut themselves often report that harming themselves in this way helps the feelings to go away. They generally deny having thoughts of wanting to kill themselves.

Some people who repeatedly cut themselves live ordinary lives and do not experience self-cutting as a major problem. For others self-cutting is part of a wider problem that includes long-standing feelings of low self-esteem and deep-rooted sadness and is associated with other forms of self-harm such as alcohol dependence and eating problems. People in this situation often feel rejected and their behaviour can lead to a vicious cycle in which others feel forced into turning away from them. In these circumstances psychological help may be beneficial in helping the person make sense of their difficulties without feeling the need to self-harm. The approach that therapists usually use involves paying attention to how a person is feeling rather than concentrating directly on whether or not they are harming themselves.

Coping with suicide

Whatever the cause, coping with the death of someone close is always difficult. Different people grieve in different ways. Many people experience a terrible sense of loss and sadness. In the weeks following a death experiences such as thinking you have seen the person walking down the street or that you heard them call out your name can leave a person worried that they are 'going mad'. These experiences are normal and will pass. Having friends or family to talk to at such times can be a great help. For those who do not have anyone to turn to or want to speak to someone outside of the situation, organisations such as CRUSE Bereavement Care and the Compassionate Friends (for bereaved parents) can be very supportive (see Resources).

How we feel about a death is also influenced by the way the person died. When death is the result of suicide it can be especially difficult. A person may feel guilty and ask themselves questions about what they could have done differently to help. They may ask themselves how others involved in caring could have helped to prevent the death occurring. Again, asking oneself these sorts of questions is a normal part of any bereavement but this process may be intensified following a suicide. Such feelings and sometimes the reactions of others may lead to a person repeatedly asking these questions. Sometimes this is a way of trying to cope with the loss and as time passes the burden of repeatedly questioning oneself also passes.

Recent research by the Samaritans shows that almost a quarter of people know someone who has died by suicide. People who have been bereaved because of suicide need the same help and support as anyone else who has been bereaved. Further help and advice is provided in a booklet called 'Bereavement Information Pack' (see Resources).

Living with long-term risk of suicide

Most people who experience mental illness make a full recovery. Similarly, most people who attempt suicide survive and do not harm themselves again. However, a minority of people suffer from a long-term mental illness. Sometimes the illness is associated with enduring suicidal feelings and repeated overdoses or other forms of self-harm.

Suicidal thoughts and acts can complicate the care that the family and friends provide. At these times carers need to be aware of their own health needs. The support of other members of the family and friends, local carer support groups and national agencies (see Resources) can be a great help. Sometimes carers feel caught between feeling angry with the person because of the way they are behaving and guilty because they feel they are not being caring enough. At other times carers may feel manipulated by threats of self-harm. In these circumstances experiencing complex feelings such as these are an almost inevitable part of caring for someone. It is impossible to 'get it right' all the time. Sometimes a person experiencing suicidal thoughts will not want help. Even though someone has suicidal feelings they sometimes need space as well as support. Giving someone space when you are worried about them can be hard but may be the right thing to do.

Every year a minority of carers face coming to terms with the death by suicide of someone who was close to them. Research into suicide suggests that there are many social, environmental, psychological and medical reasons why people eventually kill themselves. No one person or event is ever the cause.

CHAPTER 31

Violence

Mari Anne Harty

Violence by people who are mentally ill can be an important problem. Increasing numbers of victims, including carers, seek support and treatment when a relative or friend has behaved in a threatening, intimidating or violent manner. Violence has become as much of a public issue as accidents, since both give rise to a large number of injuries and sometimes death, and both are a source of tremendous distress for those concerned.

Why are some psychiatric patients threatening and aggressive while others are not? This is a complicated subject and relates to a number of factors including a person's gender, their underlying personality, the type of mental illness, and how they are feeling; for example, whether they are frightened, irritable, suspicious, excitable or angry or a combination of these. We know that people with a mental illness who use illicit substances are more likely to be violent.

Violence is more likely to occur in the person's home where a person is exposed to any stresses in their relationships with their family than in a psychiatric hospital where there are staff to supervise patients and provide them with some structure and support.

British crime surveys confirm that a high proportion of crime is not reported to the police. The victims in many cases are too fearful to seek help from the police because of worry that their relative might regard involving the criminal justice system as a breach of confidence, or lead to their relative being further stigmatised. Carers may also fear that their relative could be convicted and imprisoned. In many cases the police are reluctant to press charges against people with a known mental illness. Offences such as arson, actual bodily harm or grievous bodily harm in which the victim has been injured are more likely to be dealt with by the police, although of course incidents still need to be reported.

It is important that you know how to cope with any aggressive behaviour by your relative. The following section explores the causes of violence by people who suffer from a mental illness and considers ways of managing aggressive behaviour.

Causes of threatening, intimidating and violent behaviour

The experience of someone you care for behaving in a hostile, intimidating or violent manner towards yourself or others is extremely distressing. Violence may arise for a variety of reasons; for example, due to a person's mental state being abnormal, an altered level of consciousness, or drug or alcohol intoxication. Violence may occur without intent or any prior planning on the part of the assailant, and it may be instrumental, criminal, or malicious. An assault may be relatively minor or more serious, ranging from verbal abuse, intimidation, and physical or sexual harassment to an actual physical or sexual assault. In the most extreme cases, physical injury or even death of the victim may result.

People who suffer from mental illness or brain damage are not immune to personal crises, and may be more susceptible than others to stressful relationships and life events. Many violent incidents may be better understood in terms of 'behavioural crises'; that is, as a response to a life event and associated stresses. Dramatic changes in behaviour can result with damaging consequences if the crisis is greater than the person's ability to cope. Anger may be displaced inwards, causing depression, withdrawal, and a wish for self-harm. It may also be displaced outwards, causing hostility and aggression, with escape via drug or alcohol abuse, psychotic behaviour or inappropriate behaviour; for example, petty crime such as shoplifting and calls for help via the emergency services.

A distinction also needs to be made between behaviours resulting from active mental illness and those associated with anti-social personality traits. Typically, behaviours that are clearly connected to mental illness can be identified by their ebb and flow with improvement and relapse in the mental illness. By contrast anti-social behaviour linked to underlying personality traits predates the onset of the illness. Here the main purpose of threats and intimidation may be to manipulate family members. When confronted, people motivated in this way often back down and offer excuses for their behaviour. However, psychotically driven threatening or violent behaviour, such as that arising from delusions (a belief held in the face of evidence to the contrary that is resistant to all reason) or hallucinations (abnormal perceptions), can be intense, bizarre, and particularly frightening. People who are actively psychotic may react aggressively to confrontation or a perceived threat, especially if they are under the influence of illicit drugs or alcohol.

The effects of violent behaviour on the family

A significant number of people with a mental illness who live at home with their families are aggressive and destructive, often subjecting their families to threatening, intimidating and violent behaviour. If the family is unable to cope in this situation everyone's quality of life will decline, morale diminishes and trust in mental health professionals goes. Families, in anticipation of their relative's violent acts, often suffer long-standing and overwhelming tension from dread, shame and embarrassment. The relative's bizarre, psychotic behaviour may occur not only in the home but also in the community, adding to the family's sense of social stigma, embarrassment and isolation. It is understandable that families experience arguments, physical threats or attacks, the destruction of property and the serious challenge of this behaviour to their safety as the main burdens of caretaking. As a result of high levels of stress-induced tensions families may feel overwhelmed and more vulnerable to violence.

The psychological effects of assault range from short-lived stress reactions lasting hours or days, to depression, anxiety and in some cases specific prolonged reactions such as post traumatic stress disorder. If a person perceives a relatively trivial attack as life-threatening at the time their response is likely to be more severe. Many victims of assault suffer from poor concentration, feelings of irritability, decreased efficiency in the home and workplace and an exaggerated startle response. For most people these problems resolve within days or weeks, but prolonged distress may also occur

What to do when someone has intimidated or threatened others

The first priority is to try to bring some calm to the situation. Do not confront your relative but ensure your own safety and the safety of your family by leaving the area. Seek help; for example, from the police, GP, mental health professional or crisis team, or other relatives and neighbours. If possible, remove anything that could be used as a weapon from the area; for example, any knives or other dangerous objects. Try to inform your relative in a firm but non-threatening manner what action you and others will take if violence ensues. Stay calm, and provide your relative with space if necessary. Make no promises that you cannot deliver.

After your relative has calmed down, it is important to review the sequence of events and symptoms that triggered their behaviour. This may help you all to identify any warning signs or indicators of a relapse of illness. In the long term, do not ignore violent acts, or deny or excuse them simply because your relative has a mental illness. All forms of violence are serious and need to be prevented if possible. It is important to seek help from mental health professionals and the police if necessary, and not deal with these incidents alone.

Preventing violence

In order to try to control and reduce violence by people with a mental illness, it is vital for you to understand the emotional needs of your relative. Communication often breaks down with the chaotic onset of a psychotic illness as the person loses contact with reality. If you become preoccupied with the stresses that result from caring for your relative, you may give priority to coping and survival over communication, understanding and empathy. Mental health professionals recommend that the four most important needs of patients that family members should be meeting are predictability, reduced stimulation, appropriate expectations, and sensitivity to a person's self-esteem.

You need to be able to identify warning signs and take them seriously; for example, sweating, agitation, mounting pressure and activity, hallucinations, delusions, and drug and alcohol abuse. You may also need to be aware of and moderate any negative attitudes, criticism or hostility you may feel and refrain from overstimulating your relative. Encourage your relative to take their prescribed medication, moderate caffeine and alcohol intake, abstain from illicit drug use, take regular exercise and maintain a regular daily routine.

Help for carers

We know that professional support can reduce the burden of caregiving on family members. Apart from education about your relative's illness, counselling should extend to all relevant concerns, bearing in mind issues of confidentiality. Families should seek and be offered assistance from services in these situations to enable them to deal with the practicalities and emotional demands of caring for a relative with a mental illness who has demonstrated hostile, threatening or violent behaviour. In some cases family members have to acknowledge and come to terms with their inability to control or cope with such behaviour. In these circumstances an alternative environment outside the home may be the best option, which can provide the necessary structure. Family counselling may be advisable to enable family members to deal with intense emotions such as feelings of anger or guilt. In these circumstances it is important to seek and obtain assistance and support from mental health services in coming to terms with the fact that this action is ultimately in the best interests of your relative and to ensure the safety of others.

Glossary

Absolute discharge: An order of the Mental Health Review Tribunal or the Home Secretary whereby a patient detained under the Mental Health Act 1983, previously subject to a restriction order or conditional discharge, is no longer subject to detention or recall to hospital.

Acetylcholine: One of the mono-amine chemical neurotransmitters in the central nervous system, transmitting impulses to the nerves or to muscles. It is important especially in the function of the peripheral nerves (to skin and muscles of torso and limbs), the internal gland secretions, and in sexual arousal.

Acute: Short-term; sharp or severe.

Adrenaline: A hormone secreted by the adrenal gland and produced in large amounts when an individual is frightened, angry or under stress; increases heart and muscular activity, as in the 'fight or flight' response to stress.

Affect (adj: affective): Mood, emotion, feeling.

Affective disorder: Group of psychoses typified by a change or recurring changes of mood; depressive or manic.

Aftercare: Community care services following discharge from hospital. Especially the duty of health and social services to provide aftercare under Section 117 of the Mental Health Act (1983) following a patient's discharge from detention for treatment. Also applies to people released from prison.

Agoraphobia: Fear of open spaces, of being outside, of large crowded spaces such as supermarkets.

Akathisia: Extreme restlessness and anxiety caused by major tranquillisers. Like other adverse effects, this sometimes occurs at low or moderate doses.

Akinesia: Absence of or inability to make voluntary movement; loss of muscle power.

Alienation: A sense of separateness, strangeness from others. Used to describe a feature of schizophrenia or of depersonalisation.

Alzheimer's disease: A form of **dementia** causing a progressive degeneration of the neurones of the brain.

Amnesia: Loss of memory. 'Anterograde' amnesia refers to events since an illness or injury; 'retrograde' refers to events prior to an illness or injury.

Anaesthesia: Lack or loss of feeling.

Anomie: Feeling of hopelessness, lack of purpose.

Anticholinergic drug: A drug used to counteract the side effects (e.g. shaking, stiffness) of major tranquillisers.

Anticholinergic side effects: Peripheral (not in the brain) effects of chlorpromazine-like drugs (e.g. constipation, dry mouth etc.).

Anti-Parkinson drugs: Given to lessen the Parkinson's disease-like symptoms of neuroleptics.

Antipsychotic drugs: Also called neuroleptics and major tranquillisers. Used mainly to treat manic states and schizophrenia.

Anxiolytic: Category of drug used to relieve anxiety. Also called minor tranquillisers. Commonly used anxiolytics are the benzodiazepines.

Apathy (adj: apathetic): Absence of emotion; reduced or lack of responsiveness.

Aphasia: Loss of ability to express meaning in speech or writing or to understand speech or writing.

Aphonia: Loss of ability to make sounds.

Apnoea: Breathlessness, temporary cessation of breathing.

Appointee: Person appointed by the Department of Social Security to receive and manage the social security benefits of a person who is unable to act or manage their own affairs.

Approved social worker (ASW): A social worker who has undertaken special training in the Mental Health Act (1983) and the Code of Practice. They will co-ordinate an assessment of a person's mental health, which may lead to an application to admit that person to hospital, or extend their detention in hospital. Alternatively, the person may be received into guardianship. ASWs are responsible for informing or consulting the nearest relative and for arranging the conveyance of a patient to hospital if necessary.

Apraxia: Inability to deal with or manipulate objects, or to perform other skilled purposeful movements, due to brain damage.

Assessment: (1) assessment of need for community care services (Section 47 of the NHS and Community Care Act 1990); (2) assessment for possible admission to hospital (whether formal or informal); (3) assessment while detained under, for example, Section 2 of the Mental Health Act (1983).

Ataxia: Loss or impairment of muscular co-ordination.

Athetosis: Slow, writhing involuntary movements.

Attorney: (See **power of attorney**).

Autism: Withdrawal into self; self-absorption; an inability to relate to others. A condition in which mental activity is controlled exclusively by the thinker without reference to external realities.

Automatism: State of mind in which a person acts mechanically without intention, or awareness. Such a state may occur during an epileptic seizure, sleep walking or hypnotic trance.

Autonomic nervous system: Body system for transmission of emotional and functional impulses, not generally under voluntary control.

Auto-suggestion: An idea suggested from within one's own mind, or the process of deriving such ideas.

Avoidance: Psychological defence mechanism in which situations, activities, or objects which represent painful events are avoided.

Barbiturate: Group of drugs, liable to cause addiction and now very rarely prescribed as sedatives. Phenobarbitone is used for epilepsy.

Behaviour therapy: Form of psychotherapy in which the therapist, usually a clinical psychologist, focuses on changing problematic behaviour patterns rather than examining underlying feelings.

Benzodiazepine: Category of anxiolytic drug.

Beta-blocker drugs: Prescribed drugs mainly to treat blood pressure problems but also used to deal with anxiety and panic.

Body dysmorphophobic disorder: Preoccupation with bodily defects or imperfections to such an extent that it causes distress or impairs normal functioning.

Borderline personality disorder: A type of mental health problem in which a person has a pattern of unstable relationships and moods, low self-esteem, fears being abandoned, may tend to self-harm and therefore have difficulty with social and occupational functioning.

Brain: The organ in the skull that is part of the central nervous system. The brain is extremely complex but in broad terms it includes the cerebral hemispheres, the cortex which covers them, the corpus callosum which bridges them, cerebellum, and four lobes (frontal, temporal, parietal and occipital), each with special functions. It is said to be the seat of intellect, feeling, and emotion. To be distinguished from the mind.

Capacity: A person has capacity if they (1) possess the ability to understand and retain information given to them and (2) are able to believe in its truth and (3) possess the ability to make a choice.

Care manager: A person responsible for ensuring that an individual gets the range of services they need.

Care programme: An individual programme, particularly after a person has been discharged from hospital or is between admissions to hospital, involving support and supervision from medical, nursing, social services staff and others, usually organised at a multidisciplinary meeting and reviewed periodically.

Care Programme Approach (see Chapter 14): A system of care required by government since 1991. It involves assessment, a care programme, a key worker and reviews.

Case conference: A meeting of professionals involved with a person's care, to plan and evaluate arrangements for care, treatment or supervision.

Catalepsy: Abnormal immobility of physical posture; a condition in which the skeletal muscles become semi-rigid and will remain in any position they are placed, for long periods, without discomfort.

Catatonia: Profound mental automatism, stupor, with immobility, or strange postures, and in schizophrenia may be followed by repetitious overactivity and destructiveness or sudden change from one state to another.

Catchment area: A geographical area, significant as certain services, e.g. health or social, may be limited to people living or working in that area.

Catharsis (adj: cathartic): A process of purging one's mind or emotions, as in reliving a painful experience to relieve underlying tension caused by it.

Cerebellum: The part of the brain under the cerebrum which co-ordinates movement.

Cerebral cortex: The outer layer of the brain particularly concerned with sensory perceptions and intellectual functions.

Cerebrum: The main part of the brain consisting of the two hemispheres, the **cerebral cortex** being the outer layer of neurones.

Cholinergic: Of the nerves and organs which are activated by the neurotransmitter acetylcholine. Cholinergic drugs increase the activity of acetylcholine or have similar effects.

Chorea (Huntingdon's): A rare, inherited disorder, typified by involuntary jerky spasms from a disturbance of parts of the brain concerned with physical movement.

Chronic: Long-term or long-standing.

Clinical nurse specialist: A nurse with advanced training and skill in a specialised area of nursing.

Clinician: A doctor caring for patients in hospital (as opposed to those in research or other medical functions).

Clouding: A state of reduced consciousness in delirium or acute toxic confusional state; in psychoses like schizophrenia there should not be clouding, and if there is, causes of delirium should be looked for.

Cognitive behavioural therapy: See Chapter 5 on Obsessive Compulsive Disorders.

Community care: Care outside hospital (including residential care, social help, medical services) for elderly people or people with mental health problems, learning disabilities or physical disabilities.

Competence: See **capacity** and **disability**.

Compliance: Obedience, willing or compelled, of a patient to prescribed treatment or other arrangements for their care.

Computerised axial tomography (CT or CAT scanning): A technique using X-rays guided by a computer, to produce images of detailed cross-sections of the brain and other organs.

Conditional discharge: An order of a Mental Health Review Tribunal or the Home Secretary whereby a patient who is detained in hospital under the Mental Health Act 1983 and subject to a restriction order to protect the public is discharged. Conditions will usually be to abide by a treatment programme, live in a specified residence and be supervised by a psychiatrist and a social worker or probation officer.

Confabulation: Imaginary inventions to fill gaps in memory.

Congenital: Condition present at birth.

Consent: As in consent to treatment; the voluntary and continuing permission of the patient to receive a particular treatment, based on an adequate knowledge of the purpose, nature, likely effects and risks of that treatment including the likelihood of its success and any alternatives to it. Permission given under any unfair or undue pressure is not consent. See **informed consent**. A patient must have capacity in order to be able to consent to treatment. See also **incapacity**. Medical treatment given in the absence of consent can constitute an assault or a battery and may amount to an action for damages in the civil courts. There may be a defence when in an emergency, urgent treatment must be given to avoid an immediate serious danger to the patient or others. The Mental Health Act (1983) also provides that in certain circumstances prescribed by the Act, treatment for mental disorder can be given to detained patients without their consent.

Contra-indication: Medical term used to warn doctors to exercise caution before prescribing certain drugs to a patient who may also have other medical problems, in order to avoid an adverse reaction.

Counselling: A process, therapy, in which one person, a counsellor, aims to help another, the client, to cope with a personal problem or a crisis.

Courts: Court of Protection (see Chapter 24): An Executive Agency within the Lord Chancellor's Department established to administer the assets of a person deemed to be incapable of managing their financial affairs and who suffers from a mental disorder. The person who is appointed by the court to deal with an individual's assets is called a receiver.

Crown Court: Deals with trials by judge and jury, appeals from the Magistrates Court and cases in which the Magistrates believe that their powers of sentence are insufficient. Can make hospital orders and restriction orders to detain a mentally disordered offender in hospital for treatment.

Family Proceedings Court: The division of the Magistrates Court dealing with children (non-criminal cases) and domestic disputes.

High Court: The higher civil (non-criminal) courts, with divisions dealing with different kinds of cases, namely Queen's Bench, Chancery, Family etc. The High Court hears cases involving substantial sums of money or those which are particularly complex. There are district registries to deal with High Court matters in the regions.

Magistrates Court: The local court dealing with criminal cases, licensing etc. The Magistrates are either three 'lay justices' or Justices of the Peace (JPs) who are not legally qualified or salaried, or else a single stipendiary (i.e. a paid, full-time lawyer). Can make hospital orders (under Section 37 of the Mental Health Act 1983) for the detention of a person in hospital for treatment.

Creutzfeldt-Jakob disease (CJD): A rare brain disease caused by a transmissible agent with a long period of incubation, mostly in people over 40 years of age. The symptoms are confusion, **dementia** and **ataxia**.

Crisis centre: A place of asylum where people can feel secure and safe and be supported through their experience of mental distress, by staff or others who have been through similar experiences.

Day hospital: A department where patients who normally return to their own home at night attend for treatment, prescriptions, occupational therapy, and other specialist services.

Deferred discharge: Order of a Mental Health Review Tribunal that a person detained under the Mental Health Act 1983 should be discharged at a future date, e.g. when suitable accommodation is found.

Delirium acute: A state of excitement, disorientation, disordered memory, clouded consciousness, typified by confusion; often associated with fever or the toxic action of drugs on the brain or sudden physical illness.

Delirium tremens (DTs): Acute delirium with tremors, anxiety, delusions; a consequence particularly of sudden withdrawal of alcohol or sedative drugs.

Delusion: False belief, held as genuine, in spite of evidence or reason to the contrary. Unsystematised delusions are spontaneous, disconnected or random. Systematised delusions are part of a complex pattern of beliefs or explanations. Delusion of grandeur is an unreal and exaggerated belief of one's self-importance or wealth or status. Delusion of persecution is a paranoid belief. Depressive delusion is a conviction of one's degradation, insignificance or sinfulness. Somatic delusion relates to the appearance or functioning of one's body. Delusion of reference is a misinterpretation of what happens around one.

Dementia: The result of chronic brain damage. It is typified by disturbances of memory, particularly of the recent past, loss of reasoning ability, disorientation of time and place, extreme emotional variability. Pre-senile (people under 65) dementia is either of the Alzheimer type (SDAT) or arterioscherotic type (usually called 'multi-infarct') in either age group. See also **Alzheimer's disease, Creutzfeldt–Jakob disease** and **chorea (Huntingdon's)**.

Dependence: Addiction to a drug or alcohol; psychological or physiological craving which is perceived as a need; personal or emotional reliance on another person for personal or physical needs.

Depersonalisation: A sense of loss of identity, estrangement from the outside world, or altered awareness in which the person believes their body seems changed in some way, or they have a sense of being an observer of themselves.

Depot: Form of medication, by injection, with slow release over a period of several weeks.

Depressant: A drug which reduces activity or function, including tranquillisers, sedatives, anaesthetics and alcohol.

Derealisation: A sense of unreality similar to depersonalisation, but in which the perceived change is in the surroundings rather than in the person or body.

Diagnosis: Deduction of the nature of an illness or disorder from symptoms, history and specific examinations and tests. Differential diagnosis is the process of determining which of two or more diseases with overlapping symptoms applies to a particular person.

Diminished responsibility: A defence to murder which, if successful, means the defendant will be guilty of the lesser charge of manslaughter. The defence is that at the time of the offence the defendant was suffering from an 'abnormality' of mind (Section 2 of the Homicide Act 1957) which substantially impaired their responsibility for the act. Contrast with **insanity**.

Diogenes sydrome: Gross self-neglect particularly in an elderly person (named after the Greek philosopher famed for living in a barrel).

Dipsomania: Recurrent urge to drink alcohol to excess, often in binges. Between drinking bouts there may be long periods of sobriety.

Disability (legal): Or acting under a disability: (1) may apply to persons under 18, or an adult who is incapable of acting by reason of mental or physical disability (see also **insanity**);

(2) under the Disability Discrimination Act (1995) is 'a physical or mental impairment which has a substantial and long-term adverse effect on ability to carry out normal day-to-day activities'.

Discharge: (1) discharge from inpatient care, usually at the discretion of the doctor in charge of a patient's care; (2) discharge from detention in hospital, or liability to be detained, under the Mental Health Act (1983) (see **absolute discharge, conditional discharge, deferred discharge, supervised discharge**); (3) release of tension or emotion.

Disinhibition: The loss or loosening of social constraints on behaviour. See **inhibition** for the converse.

Disorientation: Loss of direction or bearings in relation to one's surroundings, especially as to identity, place, day, date and time.

Dissociation: Unconscious defence mechanism whereby conflicting ideas and feelings are separated from the rest of the psyche.

Dopamine: One of the neurotransmitters. Has been synthesised (i.e. produced artificially) for use as a drug. A dopamine blockade means that the body's own secretion of dopamine as a neurotransmitter of nerve impulses is suppressed.

Dysfunction: State of operating badly, as in a dysfunctional family, in which relationships are poor, broken or causing personal distress.

Dyskinesia: Distortion of voluntary movement; involuntary muscular activities. See also **tardive dyskinesia**.

Dysphasia: Difficulty in speaking properly with lack of co-ordination and inability to put words into correct order.

Dysphoria: Unpleasant mood (e.g. discontented, anxious, depressed).

Dysthymic disorder: A chronic mood disturbance lasting at least two years, characterised by feeling low, and associated with eating/sleeping problems, low self-esteem, low energy levels.

Dystonia: State of abnormal tension, often used of muscle tension.

Echolalia: Repetition of words spoken by someone else.

Echopraxia: Mimicry of other people's movements.

Electroconvulsive therapy (ECT): An electric current passed through the brain under general anaesthetic to produce a seizure; generally used as treatment for severe depression.

Electro-encephalogram (EEG): The result of a test of electrical activity in the brain. The method of testing is called electro-encephalography.

Endogenous: Causal factors that arise within the body and not externally, thus endogenous depression indicates it arises from chemical or psychological factors not environmental causes.

Endorphin: A neurotransmitter, one of the opiate-like peptides, secreted at nerve endings and contact points to transmit messages about pain, raising pain thresholds, and inducing sedation and euphoria.

Enduring power of attorney: See Chapter 24

Enuresis: Incontinence of urine.

Erotomania: Obsessive preoccupation with sexual activities, thoughts and fantasies, or with loving an individual (in a deluded way).

Extra-pyramidal: Concerning the nerve pathways relating to posture, muscle tone and fine control of movement.

Family therapy: A form of group psychotherapy in which the whole family attends together to look at distorted and disturbing patterns of communication and behaviour that have contributed to the mental distress of one or more family members.

First rank symptoms: A system of diagnosing schizophrenia based on the division of symptoms into categories including; for example, hallucinations and delusional ideas.

Flat/flattening: As of mood or affect, disturbance of mood/affect; an impoverishment of emotional response; failure to react to stimuli.

Flight of ideas: Succession of thoughts or utterances virtually without stopping and without apparent rational links. Sometimes with clang associations (associations made on similarity by rhyme and sound) and characteristic of mania and hypomania.

Functional: Term describing a psychotic illness, schizophrenia and affective disorders, distinguishing them from organic states in which physical illness may cause psychotic symptoms.

Geriatric: Relating to old age.

Group therapy: Psychotherapeutic approach, comprising a series of group meetings of patients with a therapist, to confront, share and deal with fears and anxieties and problems in relationships.

Guardian ad litem: Person appointed by a court to represent the interests of a child in certain proceedings. See also **next friend**.

Guardianship: Power under the Mental Health Act 1983 whereby an Approved Social Worker or the nearest relative or some other suitable person can make an application for a person over 16 to be received into guardianship. A guardian will be appointed by the local authority and he or she will have specific power (not all the a powers a parent would have), namely the power to require the patient to live in a specific place, to permit access by specified professionals, and to attend day care or treatment facilities This power does not rely on **incapacity** but is most often associated with it in practice.

Hallucination: A false perception, auditory, visual or sensory; an experience without detectable basis in external relatity.

Hallucinogen: An agent that causes hallucinations (drugs, or biochemical activity), or response within a person.

Heredity (adj: hereditary): The process by which characteristics are passed from one generation to the next.

Hormone: A product of one of the endocrine glands, secreted into the blood and carried to another organ where it excites certain activity.

Hyperkinesis: Excessive movement (as in hyper-activity).

Hypertension: Excessive or abnormally high blood pressure.

Hyperventilation: Rapid deep breathing caused by stress. Over-breathing, as it is also called, lowers the carbon dioxide level of the blood and produces symptoms such as light-headedness and palpitations.

Hypochondria: Exaggerated concern with one's physical health (in anxiety neurosis) and preoccupation with the fear of having a serious illness.

Hypomania: A state typified by elation, over-activity, a sense of well-being, grandiosity in plans, pressure of speech, sleep disturbance, exhaustion, normal appetite but irregular eating times, mood swings, distractibility. Sometimes with depression, as in manic depressive psychosis, a psychosis indicated by attacks or swings of mania and depression.

Hypotension: Abnormally low blood pressure.

Hysteria: An emotional state in which there is a disordered bodily function without any physical cause. Explained as the patient converting anxiety created by emotional conflict into physical symptoms such as paralysis, loss of sensation and blindness. Also used to describe a state of loss of control over one's emotions. Often confused with histrionics (self-dramatisation).

Iatrogenic: Of illness caused by treatment.

Ideation: The process of forming ideas and images.

Incapacity: Legal disability in which a person is considered unable to make certain decisions for themselves; (1) for financial see **appointee**, **Public Trust Office**, **Court of Protection**, (2) for civil court proceedings see **guardian ad litem** and **next friend**, (3) for criminal court proceedings see **insanity**, (4) for medical treatment see **consent**, (5) for decisions about life style see **guardianship** (though not a power exclusively for people who are considered incapacitated).

Industrial therapy: The use of sheltered work in a patient's treatment to build self-esteem and skills necessary to operate in an ordinary working environment.

Informed consent: Giving consent to a particular treatment based on information which enables a person to weigh up benefits and risks. See **consent**.

Inhibition: Constraint on normal behaviour and speech, moral restraint on instinctive or emotional behaviour or on display of feeling.

Insanity: Used in criminal law to denote someone whose state of mind comes within a legal definition (1) a presumed inability to form an intent to commit a crime, see **mens rea** and **M'Naghten Rules** (2) inability to understand the nature of the trial.

Insight: Understanding, especially the ability of a person to understand the nature, cause and effect of their disorder and behaviour.

Institutionalisation: Effect on a person of long-term confinement in an institution.

Interim secure unit: Hospital or ward which provides security of a level which is between that of a medium secure unit and ordinary hospital wards; usually run by district services. Contrast with **locked ward**, **regional secure unit**, **special hospital**.

Key worker (see Chapter 15): Person named as responsible for supporting someone in need of ongoing health and social care; required part of the Care Programme Approach.

Korsakoff's psychosis or syndrome: An organic syndrome occurring primarily in chronic alcoholics and people who have had severe head trauma. Major symptoms are an inability to form new memories (anterograde amnesia), and to remember a variable period of the past prior to the illness (retrograde amnesia), leading to confabulation, inappropriate emotions and behaviour.

Labile: Inordinately mobile of mood or emotion, unstable, volatile, uncontrolledly expressing emotion.

Leucotomy (brain surgery): Separation of prefrontal lobes of the brain from the rest of the brain by cutting the connecting nerve tracts; highly controversial in use; used to reduce severe levels of tension or violent behaviour.

Life event: One of the major transitional events in one's life, including educational transition, leaving home or moving house, getting married or divorced, getting or leaving a job, retiring, bereavement.

Lithium: A chemical element. In the form of lithium salts it is used to stabilise mood swings particularly in the treatment of manic depression.

Locked ward: A ward, usually psychiatric, where patients cannot enter and leave as they choose; the doors may be physically locked or nursing staff may control entry and exit.

Major tranquilliser: Another name for neuroleptics or antipsychotic drugs used in psychiatry to try and counter psychosis.

Medium secure service/unit: Psychiatric hospital ward, usually locked, which has security lower than a special hospital, but higher than district services. Mostly managed and funded as a regional (regional secure unit) rather than local facility.

Mens rea: Latin meaning 'the guilty mind'; the state of mind (intent) which must be proved in some cases to secure a criminal conviction.

Mental disorder: A legal term referring to mental health problems or psychiatric disorders; defined in the Mental Health Act (1983) as 'mental illness, arrested or incomplete development of mind, psychopathic disorder and any other disorder or disability of mind'; four specific classsifications are given in the Act, namely, mental illness, severe mental impairment, mental impairment and psychopathic disorder.

Mental nursing home: Privately run accommodation for people with mental health problems; some homes are registered under the Registered Homes Act (1984) to receive patients detained under the Mental Health Act (1983).

Mental state examination: A method of process of examination to test for signs of phenomena of mental disorder, using categories covering appearance, behaviour, speech, thought, mood, perception, belief, cognition, orientation, insight.

Minor tranquilliser: Prescribed to relieve anxiety or sleeplessness mainly. May be addictive. See **anxiolytic**.

M'Naghten Rules: From *M'Naghten's Case* in 1843, when the court set out the conditions to be met if a defence of **insanity** was raised in criminal proceedings. Namely, a defendant is presumed to be responsible for their actions, but if they prove on the balance of probabilities that they were suffering from a 'defect of reason from disease of the mind' so they did not know the 'nature or quality of the act' or that it was wrong, then they may escape responsibility for the act.

Monoaminase-oxidase (MAO) inhibitors: A group of drugs used particularly as antidepressants, by inhibiting or inactivating the MAO which oxidise various amines in the brain.

Motivational: Adjective of motive, being the thought, emotion or impulse that causes a person to do an act; of significance especially in relation to allegations of criminal conduct.

Multidisciplinary: Meeting of medical, nursing, social services and other professionals involved in a person's care, to discuss their history, progress, outlook and plans. See also **Section 117 meeting**.

Myalgic encephalomyelitis (ME): Transient state of depression, fatigue, irritability and heightened sensitivity to environmental stimuli following infections, usually viral, and disease.

Neuroleptic: Category of drug acting on the nervous system with antipsychotic effect. See also **side effects**.

Neuropleptic malignant syndrome (NMS): Adverse effect of neuroleptic drugs.

Neurology: The science of the nervous system, including brain function.

Neurone/neuron: Nerve cell, the essential component of the nervous system, and comprising the longest cell form in the body. Neurones do not divide and reproduce and so are irreplaceable, but they are, to a limited extent, self-repairing.

Neuropathy: Inflammation or degeneration and loss of function of nerve cells.

Neurosis (adj: neurotic): Major general category of mental illness (and to be compared and contrasted with psychosis), usually of milder form, in which anxiety is the principal feature, and insight is retained. A shrinking category, as depression and anxiety are increasingly classified in their own right.

Neurosurgery: The branch of surgery that deals with the brain, the spinal cord and the central nervous system.

Neurotransmitter: A chemical substance secreted by the nerve cell (neurone) terminals to transmit impulses across the minute gaps between nerves and from them to the muscles and glands they supply. Neurones transmit and receive information. The transmitters include adrenaline, noradrenaline, serotonin, the neuropeptides, endorphins, histamine, acetylcholine, dopamine – some 50 or more in total.

Next friend: Person appointed with consent of the court to represent someone with a legal disability by reason of age or mental disorder to take proceedings against someone else. See also **guardian ad litem**.

Occupational therapy: A form of supportive therapy usually carried out in a day hospital which helps restore independent living skills.

Official Solicitor of the Supreme Court: The High Court officer and department which can act for a person who is under a disability (see **disability**) in civil proceedings if there is no suitable relative or friend to do so, and when required will make a report to the court; looks after certain funds for persons under a legal disability including trust funds and awards by the Criminal Injuries Compensation Agency; and represents patients in certain kinds of cases in the Court of Protection, such as applications for statutory wills, and gifts of a patient's property.

Opiate: Of the group of drugs derived from or related to opium, including heroin, morphine, pethidine etc. Liable rapidly to cause addiction.

Organic: A term used in psychiatry to describe a condition that is basically physical in origin, as opposed to having psychological causes.

Panic attack: Acute bout of anxiety or sense of imminent danger or doom, with sudden onset, which makes people feel overwhelmed and out of control. Panic attacks usually last for several minutes and consist of feelings of terror and phsyical symptoms such as palpitations, dizziness, trembling, shortness of breath, sweating, and fear of dying.

Paranoia (adj: paranoid): Irrational and/or extreme and persistent suspiciousness or sense of persecution.

Parasuicide: Attempted suicide.

Parkinsonism: A state of tremor, muscle stiffness, shuffling, excessive salivation. May be a drug-induced problem, as a side effect of some neuroleptic drugs.

Pathology: Branch of medicine concerned with disease and abnormalities.

Pathological: Tending to imply underlying disease; signifying a persistent, compulsive tendency as in pathological liar, pathological jealousy.

Perception: What is perceived or the faculty of perceiving; that is, of recognising and understanding what is experienced or information that is received sensorily.

Polypharmacy: The use of several antipsychotic drugs concurrently. The British National Formulary (BNF) advises against this as it is hazardous. It is more likely to cause or increase side effects, and resistance in compliance by the patient.

Positron emission tomography (PET): Technique of nuclear medicine to monitor the brain. It is used to visualise the amount of dopamine receptor blockade in a patient caused by antipsychotic medication.

Power of attorney (see Chapter 24): Authority to act granted by 'the donor' who must complete a formal document authorising a named person or persons to manage their financial or legal affairs; an enduring power of attorney is a specific kind of power which continues despite the incapacity of the donor. Once the donor becomes incapable an enduring power of attorney must be registered at the Court of Protection

Pressure of speech: Where the patient talks rapidly, with little pause.

Probation: An order made by a Magistrates or Crown Court after a person is convicted (or pleads guilty); a sentence served in the community. A probation order may have conditions attached, such as having to attend or reside in a hospital for treatment, or to see a psychiatrist by appointment. Breach of the order means the case may go back to court which may pass a fresh sentence for the original offence.

Prognosis: Forecast, estimate of course of an illness.

Prophylaxis (adj: prophylactic): Prevention treatment (e.g. by immunisation).

Proprietary name: The name a drug company gives to a drug.

Psychometry/psychometric tests: Exercises that analyse memory, intelligence, personality and a range of mental functions.

Psychopathic disorder: A legal term; a form of mental disorder, defined as 'persistent disorder or disability of mind resulting in abnormally aggressive or seriously irresponsible conduct' (Section 1 of the Mental Health Act 1983).

Psychosis (adj: psychotic): Major general category of mental illness often characterised by loss of insight and during which symptoms such as hallucinations and delusions are experienced.

Psychosurgery: Surgery on the brain. See **leucotomy**.

Psychotropic drug: One which affects behaviour, experience and other psychological functions (e.g. tranquillisers, sedatives, stimulants, antidepressants etc.).

Public Trust Office: A government agency working under the direction of the Court of Protection but separate from it. It deals with applications and enquiries for the appointment of a **receiver**, the accounts of those acting as receivers, and in some cases will, when appointed by the Court of Protection, act as receiver for patients deemed incapable of managing their property and affairs.

Rapport: Emotional contact between people.

Reactive: As in reactive depression (or neurotic depression), depression arising in response to adverse circumstances (the converse of endogenous depression).

Receiver: A person appointed by the Court of Protection to administer the property of a person who is incapable of managing their own affairs.

Regional secure unit (RSU): See **medium secure unit**.

Rehabilitation: Restoration of a person's functioning in society after a period of mental distress or physical disability.

Relapse: Recurrence or reappearance of deterioration of symptoms.

Remand: The adjournment of a criminal case in a Magistrates Court or Crown Court; or the detention of an accused person in custody pending trial or sentence; a prisoner is said to be 'on judge's remand' after conviction or plea of guilty and remanded to a later date for sentence. Before conviction or plea of guilty formally entered in court, a prisoner on remand in custody has ' privileges' as to visits, letters, phone calls, clothes etc., which are taken away after conviction or plea of guilty, even if not yet sentenced. Remand to hospital for reports under Section 35 of the Mental Health Act (1983) may be made if there is medical evidence indicating there is a good reason to suspect mental disorder, and it is impracticable for a report to be prepared while the accused person is on bail. Remand to hospital for treatment under Section 36 of the Mental Health Act (1983) may be made by a Crown Court if there are two medical recommendations.

Remission: Apparent disappearance or reduction of symptoms.

Restraint: Broad description of different types of mechanisms for limiting the freedom of a patient to stop harming themselves or others; especially used in connection with nursing on a psychiatric ward; can be verbal or physical and can include seclusion.

Schizo-affective disorder: Used when a differential diagnosis between affective disorders and schizophrenic disorders cannot be made or when symptoms of major depression combined with psychotic symptoms are present.

Section (colloquial): When someone is detained under the Mental Health Act (1983), they are often described as 'sectioned'; more accurately they are either restrained (under a holding power), admitted (for assessment or treatment), received (into guardianship), subject to an order (by a court) or a direction (by the Home Secretary) or removed (by the police).

Section 117 meeting: Meeting of medical, nursing, social services and other professionals involved in a person's care, to discuss their history, progress, outlook and plans.

Sedative: Of calming or tranquillising effect, especially used of a drug to sedate a patient.

Selective serotonin reuptake inhibitors (SSRIs): A group of antidepressant drugs which act on the neurotransmitter serotonin in the brain and thereby relieve depression. Also used for OCD and anorexia.

Self-harm: Any physical injury to oneself.

Side effects: Reactions caused as a result of taking prescribed medication. May be dealt with through separate medication to reduce effect if particularly unpleasant.

Somatisation: Expressing emotional distress through physical symptoms.

Special hospital: Hospitals for patients who are detained under the Mental Health Act 1983 and require treatment under conditions of high security because of their dangerous, violent or criminal behaviour.

Special observation (verb: to special, to be specialed): The procedure for keeping special watch on a patient while in hospital and reporting on the observation at given intervals.

Supervised discharge: Sometimes referred to as after-care supervision; gives powers to certain named professionals to ensure that a person previously detained under Section 3 or Section 37 of the Mental Health Act 1983 co-operates with the after-care services provided.

Sympathetic nervous system: That part of the autonomic nervous system concerned to prepare the body for 'fight or flight', governing reactions in states of fear. Functions by means of noradrenalin, a monoamine neurotransmitter.

Synapse: The nerve-cell junction, the point of contact where the electrical impulse is transmitted from one cell to the other by chemical transmitter agent.

Tachycardia: Rapid pulse rate above normal; often associated with drugs or anxiety.

'Talking treatment': A treatment which does not involve drugs, including psychoanalysis or psychotherapeutic approaches.

Tardive dyskinesia: A brain disorder causing involuntary movement, particularly of the mouth and tongue, often a side effect of large doses of antipsychotic medication taken over a long period of time.

Therapy: Any form of treatment, including 'drug therapy' – treatment through medication – or 'talking treatments'.

Therapeutic community: A group environment in which every detail of institutional life is organised into an all-embracing programme aimed at promoting recovery. The programme includes not only treatment processes but also interaction between members of the community, participation in community meetings, and various forms of therapy.

Thought interference: A delusion that one's thoughts are interfered with by some other person, real or imagined.

Tranquilliser: Drug used to relieve tension and anxiety or to combat psychotic symptoms without significant sedation. See **major** and **minor tranquillisers**.

Trauma: Physical injury; emotional or psychological shock with lasting effect.

Treatment: The administration of appropriatee measures, e.g. drugs, nursing care, psychotherapy, to relieve a condition.

Tricyclic drugs: Group of drugs used for treatment especially of severe depression or psychosis.

Unfit to plead: Legal disability whereby a person fails to understand the nature of criminal proceedings, or how to instruct a solicitor, or the pleas of guilty and not guilty. See also **mens rea**, **insanity** and **M'Naghten Rules**.

User: A general term referring to a person using psychiatric services.

Ward of court: A person placed under the supervision of the High Court in special proceedings, usually children but can include other persons who are said to be legally 'incapable' of acting. See **incapacity**. No steps may normally be taken to change the arrangements made for a ward of court, without the permission of the court. Arrangements include where the person is to live and with whom, going on holiday, contact with other people, consent to operations, marriage, schooling, etc. The court has to give permission for a ward (adult or child) to be admitted to hospital compulsorily, and for a child to be subject to guardianship under the Mental Health Act (1983).

Ward round: The procedure whereby the doctor and other members of staff see patients individually on visits to the ward, examine the person and their medical and nursing notes, compare recommendations with others involved in the patient's treatment programmes.

Warrant: Written authority, to arrest and detain a person, to enter premises to search for and arrest and detain a person, to search for and seize property. Section 135 of the Mental Health Act (1983) enables an approved social worker to apply to a magistrate for a warrant, so that a police constable can enter named premises (by force if need be) to remove a person to a place of safety if that person is thought to be mentally disordered and ill-treated, neglected, out of control, or living alone and unable to care for themselves.

Withdrawal symptoms: The symptoms, physical or emotional, which arise because of reducing or ceasing consumption of a drug upon which the person has become dependent.

Abbreviations

AA	Alcoholics Anonymous, a self-help group of people dependent on alcohol
ADL	Activities of daily living
ASW	Approved social worker
BNF	British National Formulary, produced by the BMA and the Pharmaceutical Society of Great Britain
CNS	Central nervous system
CPN	Community psychiatric nurse

DDU	Drug dependency unit of a hospital to deal with drug addiction
DSH	Deliberate self-harm
DTs	Delirium tremens
ECT	Electrocardiograph, the result of the measurement of heart patterns, beat, rhythm etc. by a machine called the Electrocardiogram
EEG	Electro-encephalogram
FME	Forensic medical examiner, previously known as a police surgeon
FRCPsych	Fellow of the Royal College of Psychiatrists
ICD	International Classification of Diseases now in its tenth edition. A disease will be referred to in 'ICD 10'.
LOC	Loss of consciousness
MAOI	Monoamine oxidase inhibitor
ME	Myalgic encephalomyelitis
MRI	Magnetic resonance imaging of brain anatomy. See **NMR**
NFA	No fixed abode
NMR	Nuclear magnetic resonance, imaging of brain anatomy. See **MRI**
NMS	Neuroleptic malignant syndrome
OT	Occupational therapy or occupational therapist
PET	Positron emission tomography brain scanning technique
prn	When required
RMN	Registered mental nurse, nurse qualified for psychiatric practice
SAD	Seasonal affective disorder
SSRIs	Selective Serotonin Reuptake Inhibitors, an antidepressant
STD	Sexually transmitted disease
U&E	Urea and electrolytes, relating to biochemical tests

Resources

Useful organisations

Note: there are many organisations which do not specifically deal with mental illness but may be able to help people in difficult circumstances, such as occupational benevolent funds.

Telephone numbers beginning 0800 are freephone numbers – there is no charge for these numbers and they will not appear on itemised telephone bills. Numbers beginning 0845 or 0990 are charged at a local rate. All other numbers are charged at the appropriate rate for the time of day when the call is made.

Alcohol

Al-Anon Family Groups (UK and Eire) are a self-help fellowship of relatives and friends of alcoholics who share their experience in order to solve their common problems whether the alcoholic is still drinking or not.
   61 Great Dover Street, London SE1 4YF. 24-hour helpline 020 7403 0888 Fax 020 7378 9910 Website www.hexnet.co.uk/alanon

Alateen, a part of Al-Anon, is for young people aged 12–20 who have been affected by someone else's drinking, usually a parent.

Alcohol Advisory Service offers informal counselling to individuals, couples and families with alcohol-related problems. It also provides community-based treatment.
   7 Sebert Road, London E7 0NG. Tel 020 8257 3068 Fax 020 8522 0734.

Alcohol Concern is the national voluntary agency on alcohol misuse and can provide information about alcohol and alcohol problems.
   Waterbridge House, 32–36 Loman St, London SE1 0EE. Tel 020 7928 7377 Fax 020 7928 4644 Website www.alcoholconcern.org.uk

Alcoholics Anonymous is a voluntary fellowship of people who help each other achieve and maintain sobriety by sharing experiences and giving mutual support. Regular weekly meetings are held in all parts of Britain.
   Information is widely available from AA helplines or contact AA at PO Box 1, Stonebow House, General Service Office, Stonebow, York Y01 2NJ. Tel 01904 644026 (administration) Helplines 020 7352 3001/020 7833 0022 (London) 0141 226 2214 (Scotland) 01907 6255574 (Mid-Wales) 01685 875070 (South Wales) 01639 644871 (Swansea) Fax 01904 629091.

Drinkline offers confidential advice and information to people concerned about their own or someone else's drinking. Telephone 0800 917 8282 9am–11pm Monday–Friday, 6–11pm Saturday and Sunday.

Women's Alcohol Centre. For women who are problem drinkers. Offers parents and young women confidential individual counselling, group work and acupuncture as part of a day programme as well as a residential service. Leaflets available.

66a Drayton Park, London N5 1ND. Tel 020 7226 4581 Fax 020 7354 8134.

Alzheimer's disease and elderly disorders

Action on Elder Abuse promotes awareness of issues relating to the elderly. Its helpline offers confidential emotional support to anybody (including relatives or carers) concerned about the abuse of an older person and advice on contacting other organisations, agencies and charities that could help.

Astral House, 1268 London Road, London SW16 4ER. Helpline 080 8808 8141 weekdays 10am–4.30pm Tel 020 8764 7648 (administration) Website www.elderabuse.org Email aea@ace.org.uk

Age Concern England obtains information for friends and relatives of people affected by Alzheimer's disease on support services from the NHS, social services and voluntary groups.

Astral House, 1268 London Road, London SW16 4ER. Tel 020 8679 8000 Fax 020 8679 6069.

Age Concern Cymru 1 Cathedral Road, Cardiff CF1 9SD. Tel 01222 371 556 Fax 01222 399 562.

Age Concern Scotland 113 Rose Street, Edinburgh EH2 3DT. Tel 0131 220 3345 Fax 0131 220 2779.

Age Concern Northern Ireland 3 Lower Crescent, Belfast BT7 1NR. Tel 01232 245 729 Fax 01232 235497.

The Alzheimer's Disease Society gives support to carers and sufferers through information, carers' support groups, specialist daycare services and volunteer services.

Gordon House, 10 Greencoat Place, London SW1P 1PH. National helpline 020 73060606 8am–6pm.

Alzheimer Scotland – Action on Dementia helps people with dementia, their carers and families. It also campaigns on behalf of people with dementia.

22 Drumsheugh Gardens, Edinburgh EH3 7RN. Tel 0131 243 1453. 24-hour dementia helpline 0800 317 817 Email alzheimer@alzscot.org Website www.alzscot.org

Relatives and Residents Association provides advice and support to the relatives and friends of older people who are considering going into residential or nursing home care or who are experiencing difficulties with their residential or nursing home.

5 Tavistock Place, London WC1H 9SN. National Advice line 020 7916 6055 (10am–12.30pm and 1.30–5pm weekdays) Tel 020 7692 4302 (administration) Fax 020 7387 7968.

Anxiety and phobias

ANXIA – The Anxiety Disorders Association (formerly Phobic Action) offers practical self-help support to people affected by anxiety conditions and their carers.

20 Church Street, Dagenham RM10 9UR. Tel 020 8491 4700 Helpline 020 8270 0999.

National Phobics Society exists to help those suffering from anxiety disorders i.e. panic attacks, phobias and obsessive compulsive disorders.

4 Cheltenham Road, Chorlton-cum-Hardy, Manchester M21 9QN. Tel 0161 227 9898 Monday – Friday 10am–4pm Website www.phobics-society.org.uk.

No Panic offers relief and rehabilitation to people suffering from anxiety disorders e.g. panic attacks, phobias and obsessive compulsive disorders.

93 Brands Farm Way, Randlay, Telford, Shropshire TF3 2JQ. Tel 01952 590005 Helpline 01952 590545 10am–10pm Information line only 0800 783 1531 Fax 01952 270962.

Northern Ireland Agoraphobia and Anxiety Society deals with problems of phobias, agoraphobia and high anxiety states.

29–31 Lisburn Road, Belfast BT9 7AA. Tel 01232 235170.

Stresswatch Scotland offers advice, information and materials on panic, anxiety and stress phobias with local groups.

The Barn, 42 Barnweil Road, Kilmarnock KA1 4JF. Tel 01563 574144 (administration) Helpline 01563 528910 Monday–Friday except Wednesday 10am–1pm.

Thanet Phobic Group helps with the rehabilitation of stressed and phobic people by giving moral support. It runs a postal group with members throughout the country and a magazine that provides information.

47 Orchard Road, Westbrook, Margate, Kent CT9 5JS. Tel 01843 833720/231783 Fax 01843 831724.

Triumph Over Phobia (TOP UK) is a network of structured self-help groups for people with recognisable phobia run by lay people (many of whom are ex-sufferers). Members learn how to overcome their fears by following a self-exposure programme in a supportive group environment.

PO Box 1831, Bath BA2 4YW. Tel 01225 330353.

See also 'First Steps to Freedom' under *General*

Bipolar disorder or manic depression

Manic Depression Fellowship supports people with a diagnosis of manic depression and their families and has local self-help groups.

8–10 High Street, Kingston-upon-Thames, Surrey KT11 1EY. Tel 020 7793 2600.

Manic Depression Fellowship (Scotland) is at 7 Woodside Crescent, Glasgow G3 7UL. Tel 0141 331 0344.

See also under Depression

Chronic fatigue syndrome / ME (myalgic encephalomyelitis)

Association of Youth with ME produces 'Cheers', a newsletter written by and for young people affected with ME. They also produce a newssheet for parents and carers called 'Cheers Extra'.

AYME, Box 605, Milton Keynes MK6 3EX. Website www.ayme.org.uk Email ayme@powernet.com

The Young Minds Parent Information Service provides information and advice for anyone concerned about the mental health of a child or young person.

102–108 Clerkenwell Road, London EC1M 5SA. Parent information service 0800 018 2138 Administration 020 7336 8445.

Deliberate self-harm and suicide

Bereavement Information Pack is designed for relatives and friends of people who die by suicide or other sudden death.

Available from www.rcpsych.ac.uk

The Compassionate Friends is a national organisation of bereaved parents offering friendship and understanding to other bereaved parents.

53 North Street, Bristol BS3 1EN. Helpline 0117 953 9639 9.30am–5pm Fax 0117 966 5202.

CRUSE Bereavement Care provides counselling and information through a national network of branches.

126 Sheen Road, Richmond, Surrey TW9 1UR. Tel 020 8940 4818 (head office) for details of local service. National counselling line 0845 758 5565 Open Monday, Wednesday and Thursday 3–9pm; Tuesday 3–6.30pm; Friday 3–6pm; Saturday 3–5.30pm; Sunday 3–7pm.

CRUSE: Bereavement Care Northern Ireland. 10 College Green, Belfast BT7 1LN. Tel 02890 232695 or 02890 434600.

National Self-Harm Network provides support for people of all ages who self-harm. It aims to challenge assumptions and common misconceptions about, and raise awareness of, self-harm.

PO Box 16190, London NW1 3WW. Email nshn@wobbly.demon.co.uk.

Women and Self Harm Group is a support group for women (only) who self-harm with the emphasis on self-injury. The group meets every Friday afternoon, 4–6pm, at CHRC Self Help Services, Zion Centre, Off Royce Road, Hulme, Manchester. Tel 0161 226 5412 Email 95663924@mmu.ac.uk.

Depression

Depression Alliance (formerly Depressives Associated) provides information, support and understanding to people directly or indirectly affected by depression. There is a national network of self-help groups, a range of free publications and other schemes for members.

35 Westminster Bridge Road, London SE1 7JB. Tel 020 7633 0557. Website www.depressionalliance.org

The Ex-Services Mental Welfare Society (Combat Stress) specialises in the care of men and women discharged from the Armed Services and Merchant Navy who suffer from mental health problems. It employs welfare officers throughout the UK supporting patients in the community and providing short-term residential and respite care.

Tyruhitt House, Oaklawn Road, Leatherhead, Surrey KT22 0BX. Tel 01372 841600 Fax 01372 841601 Website www.combatstress.com Email contactus@combatstress.org.uk

The Fellowship of Depressives Anonymous offers self-help for depressives, their friends and families, providing a list of helpful books, contacts for individuals via a newsletter, a penfriend scheme and local groups. It also offers advice and support for setting up groups.

c/o Self-Help Nottingham, Ormiston House, 32–36 Pelham Street, Nottingham NG1 2EG. Tel 01702 433838 Fax 01702 433843.

The SAD Association (Seasonal Affective Disorder) informs the public and health professions about SAD and supports and advises its sufferers through newsletters, meetings and network of contacts and local groups.

PO Box 989, Steyning BN44 3HG. Tel and fax 01903 814942.

Drugs

Adfam National offers confidential support and information for families and friends of drug users.

Waterbridge House, 32–36 Loman Street, London SE1 0EE. Helpline 020 7928 8900 Monday, Wednesday, Thursday and Friday 10am–5pm; Tuesday 10am–6.45pm.

The Council for Involuntary Tranquilliser Addiction (CITA) provides support and information to help people withdraw from tranquillisers.

Cavendish House, Brighton Road, Waterloo, Liverpool L22 5NG. Tel 0151 474 9626 (administration) Helpline 0151 949 0102 Monday–Friday 10am–1pm.

DrugScope aims to inform policy development and reduce drug-related risk. (It does not provide treatment or counselling.) It maintains a library of world literature on drugs open to the public by appointment with charges of £5 per visit or £2 for students or the unemployed.

DrugScope, 32–36 Loman St, London SE1 0EE. Tel 020 7928 1211 Fax 020 7928 1771 Website www.drugscope.org.uk

Families Anonymous runs self-help groups in the UK for families and friends of those with a drug problem.

UK Office, Unit 37, The Doddington and Rollo Community Association, Charlotte Despard Avenue, Battersea, London SW11 5JE. Tel 020 7498 4680, Monday–Friday 1–5pm.

Narcotics Anonymous is run by and for recovering drug addicts using the '12-step' approach through self-help groups. Information about local meetings and helpline 020 7730 0090 from 10am to 10pm seven days a week.

UK Service Office, 202 City Road, London EC1V 2PH. Tel 020 7251 4007 Fax 020 7251 4006 Helpline 020 7730 0009. Tel 020 7251 4007 (UK Service Officer) for leaflets. Email ukso@ukna.org and pinews@ukna.org Public Information Website: www.ukna.org/

The National Drugs Helpline 0800 77 66 00 is free, confidential and open 24 hours.

Release Legal Emergency and Drug Service works with people who have substance misuse problems and specialises in drug-related legal problems.

388 Old Street, London EC1V 9LT. Fax 020 7729 2599 Advice Line 020 7729 9904 Monday–Friday 10am–6pm. 24-hour helpline 020 7603 8654.

Turning Point is a national charity, which helps people with drink, drug and mental health problems. It provides a range of services including drug and alcohol education, and drop-in and residential clinics for counselling, rehabilitation and aftercare.

Head Office: Turning Point, Unit 3.05, New Loom House, 101 Backchurch Lane, London E1 1LU. Tel 020 7702 2300 Fax 020 7702 1456 Email tpmail@turning-point.co.uk Website www.turning-point.co.uk/ho.htm Turning Point has a separate website for young people concerned about drugs and drug issues: www.drugworld.org

Eating disorders

The Eating Disorders Association provides information and advice. They have a network of self-help groups across the UK.

First Floor, Wensum House, 103 Prince of Wales Road, Norwich. Adult Helpline 01603 621414 Monday–Friday 9am–6.30pm weekdays Youth Helpline (for under–19s) 01603 765050 Monday–Friday 4–6pm. Tel (administration) 01603 619090 Fax 01603 664915 Website www.edauk.com Email info@edauk.com

The Eating Disorders Club offers support and advice to members, families and friends through penpals, useful contacts, fact sheets, self-help tips, personal letters, support groups, meetings and involvement with psychotherapists and counsellors and a helpline.

Stricklandgate House, 92 Stricklandgate, Kendal, Cumbria LA9 4PU. Tel 01539 736077 Fax 01539 725561.

Overeaters Anonymous runs self-help groups for those suffering from eating disorders or overeating. Tel 01454 857158 (recorded information about local groups in south west England and Wales).

See also 'First Steps to Freedom' under General

Employment and training

ACTION MENTAL HEALTH offers assessment, training and counselling in relation to work for people with mental illness.

Mourne House, Knockbracken Healthcare Park, Saintfield Road, Belfast BT8 8BH. Tel 02890 403726 Fax 02890 403727.

National Vocational Rehabilitaion Association

Lloyds Court, 1 Goodman's Yard, London E1 8AT. Tel 020 7369 4000.

OUTSET is a national charity promoting employment and training for disabled people including those living with or recovering from mental illness. Centres in London, Luton, Wolverhampton, Bexley and Middlesbrough.

Telemax House, 15 New Bedford Road, Luton LU1 1SA. Tel 0870 200 0001 Fax 0980 200 0110.

Richmond Fellowship Work Schemes teach employment and life skills, usually to people resident with the Richmond Fellowship. It also provides care and rehabilitation to people with mental health needs, substance misuse, eating disorders and other related problems through residential facilities, day centres, advocacy, family units and community outreach projects.

80 Holloway Road, London N7 8JG. Tel 020 7697 3300 Fax 020 7697 3301 Website www.richmondfellowship.org.uk

Shaw Trust helps disabled people back into employment.

Shaw House, Epsom Square, White Horse Business Park, Trowbridge, Wiltshire BA14 0XJ. Tel 01225 716300 Fax 01225 716334.

Social Firms UK supports social firms – businesses employing people with a disability.

Kingsfield Centre, Philanthropic Road, Redhill, Surrey RH1 4DP.. Tel 01737 764021 Fax 01737 281032.

Ethnic minority organisations

African Caribbean Mental Health Association (ACMHA) is a voluntary organisation offering a variety of services, including counselling, to black clients diagnosed with a mental illness. All volunteers are from the African-Caribbean community.

35–37 Electric Avenue, London SW9 8JP. Tel 020 7737 3603 Fax 020 7924 0126.

Asian Family Counselling Services provides counselling for Asian couples experiencing marital problems.

76 Church Road, Hanwell, London W7 1LB. Tel/Fax 020 8567 5616.

Asian People with Disabilities Alliance (APDA) works to highlight the particular cultural and social needs of Asian disabled people. It provides advice/information, advocacy/cases management, respite care and other services.

The Old Refectory, Central Middlesex Hospital, Acton Lane, London NW10 7NS. Tel/Fax 020 8961 6773.

Chinese Mental Health Association exists to promote the preservation and safeguarding of mental health and the relief of people of Chinese origin suffering from mental distress in the London area.

Oxford House, Derbyshire Street, London E2 6HB. Tel 020 7613 1008 Fax 020 7729 0435.

Commission for Racial Equality is a statutory body set up under the Race Relations Act. It can help individuals with cases of racial discrimination, investigate instances of discrimination, and works to promote good race relations.

10 Allington Street, London SW1E 5EH. Tel 020 7828 7022 Fax 020 7630 7605.

Jewish Association for the Mentally Ill (JAMI) offers guidance, counselling and support for sufferers and their carers. It produces a voluntary newsletter and runs a help and referral line. A drop-in centre is open throughout the year including Jewish holidays, and one Sabbath per month.

16a North End Road, London NW11 7PH. Tel 020 8458 2223 Fax 020 8458 1117 Email Ruth@bt.click.com

Refugee Council gives practical support and advice to refugees and promotes their rights in the UK and abroad. It is an umbrella organisation for agencies and organisations involved with refugee issues and provides information on their mental health services.

3 Bondway, London SW8 1SJ. Tel 020 7820 3000 Fax 020 7582 9929.

Vietnamese Mental Health Services (formerly Project) provides relief for Vietnamese people with mental health difficulties and their families. It gives advice, counselling and information on mental health issues.

Units 21 and 23, 49 Effra Road, London SW2 1BZ. Tel 020 7733 7646 Fax 020 7274 1378.

Obsessive compulsive disorder

Obsessive Action (Support Group) is a national charity for people with obsessive compulsive disorder. It can supply further information sheets and reading lists and publishes a quarterly magazine giving details of local groups.

PO Box 6097, London W2 1WZ, 22–24 Highbury Grove, London N5 2EA. Tel 020 7226 4000 Fax 020 7288 0828 Email admin@obsessive-action.demon.co.uk

See also Anxiety and phobias

Post-traumatic stress disorder

Medical Foundation for the Care of Victims of Torture provides survivors of torture in the UK with medical treatment, social assistance and psychotherapeutic support.

96–98 Grafton Road, London NW5 3EJ. Tel 020 7813 7777 Fax 020 7813 0011.

Victim Support Schemes Organisation provides practical and emotional support for victims of crime and for witnesses regardless of whether the crime has been reported.

Cranmer House, 39 Brixton Road, London SW9 6DZ. Tel (administration) 020 7735 9166. Fax 020 7582 5712. Victim Support Line 0845 303 0900 (local rate) 9am–9pm weekdays, 9am–7pm weekends, 9–5pm Bank Holidays.

Schizophrenia

The National Schizophrenia Fellowship offers help to people with severe mental illness (not only schizophrenia) and their carers.

28 Castle Street, Kingston-upon-Thames KT1 1SS. Tel 020 8547 3937 Website www.nsf.org.uk

General

Association of Crossroads Care Attendant Schemes Ltd (also known as Crossroads) is a charity which provides trained care staff to take over caring tasks in people's homes to give carers a break. This may be a couple of hours a week or for an overnight break. It has regional centres throughout the UK and a scheme for young carers also.

10 Regent Place, Rugby, Warwickshire CV21 2PN. Tel 01788 573653 Fax 01788 565498 Website crossroads.rugby@pipemedia.co.uk

Carers Connect Scotland (CCS) is a collaborative two-year project supported by 23 carer organisations across Scotland setting up a computerised system which will help local groups to use their phone lines to share information, support and a database of good practice. CCS has created the website CARERS.net, a full package of internet connection, email, newsgroups, web hosting and a bulletin board.

Carers Connect Scotland, c/o VOCAL Carers Centre, 8–9 Johnston Terrace, Edinburgh EH1 2PW. Tel 0131 622 6666 Email CCS@carers.net

Carers National Association has a telephone helpline for carers and older, ill or disabled relatives and friends. It has branches throughout the UK, which are involved in organising social events, campaigning and putting carers in touch with each other. 20–25, Glasshouse Yard, London EC1A 4JT. CarersLine 0808 808 7777 10am–12pm and 2–4pm Monday–Friday Tel (administration) 020 7490 8818 Fax 020 7490 8824 Website www.carersuk.demon.co.uk

ChildLine provides a free and confidential service for children.

ChildLine, Freepost 1111, London N1 OBR. Telephone 0800 1111 for urgent calls. Tel 0800 884444 3.30–9.30pm weekdays, 2–8pm weekends for children living away from home. Website www.ChildLine.org.uk.

Citizens Advice Bureaux offer free, independent and confidential advice on matters including debt and consumer issues, benefits, housing, legal matters, employment, and immigration. Advisers can help fill out forms, write letters, negotiate with creditors and represent clients at court or tribunal. There are 700 CABs in England, Wales and Northern Ireland. Website: www.nacab.org.uk

First Steps to Freedom aims to help in a practical way people who suffer from phobias, obsessive compulsive disorder, those with general anxiety, panic attacks, anorexia and bulimia, and those who want to come off tranquillisers, together with help and support for their carers. It offers a helpline, telephone self-help group, telephone counselling and audiotapes (10am–10pm).

7 Avon Court, School Lane, Kenilworth, Warwickshire CV8 2GX. Tel (administration) 01926 864473 Website www.firststeps.demon.co.uk

Mental Health Foundation provides a wide range of publications and support services.

UK Office, 20/21 Cornwall Terrace, London NW1 4QL. Tel 020 7535 7400 Fax 020 7535 7474.

Scotland Office, 5th Floor, Merchants House, 30 George Square, Glasgow G2 1EG. Tel 0141 572 0125 Fax 0141 572 0246

Email mhf@mentalhealth.org.uk Website www.mentalhealth.org.uk

Mind (National Association for Mental Health) provides a national information and legal service as well as 230 local groups offering a range of support services in the community.

Head Office: Granta House, Broadway, London E15 4BQ. Tel (administration) 020 8519 2122 Fax 020 8522 1725 Helpline (in London) 020 8519 2122 ext. 275 or (outside London) 0345 660163 (local rate). Wesite www.mind.org.uk

NARMI (National Alliance of the Relatives of the Mentally Ill) provides advocacy, advice, medical information and information about government legislation. Members receive quarterly newsletters, updates on medication, the Mental Health Act and changes in housing and welfare benefits.

Tydehams Oaks, Tydehams, Newbury, Berks RG14 6JT. Tel 01635 551923 (answerphone service – all calls returned same day).

The National Debtline is open Monday and Thursday 10am–4pm, Tuesday and Wednesday 10am–7pm and Friday 1am–12 noon.

The Princess Royal Trust for Carers has nearly 100 centres across the UK, which make up the Carers Centre Network, providing information, personal counselling and support, access to respite care and other practical help to carers.

Details of the nearest Princess Royal Trust Carers Centre can be obtained from the London Office at 142 Minories, London EC3N 1LB. Tel 020 7480 7788 Fax 020 7481 4729 Email info@carers.org.

Or Glasgow Office: 215 West Campbell Street, Glasgow G2 4TT. Tel 0141 221 5066 Fax 0141 221 4623. Email infoscotland@carers.org

Website www.carers.org

The activities of the Carers Centres vary, and may not necessarily be specific to mental illness. However, if you are in Tunbridge Wells and surrounding area, Carers First runs a mental health project which can be contacted at Carers First, Mental Health Project, 2 Lyons Wharf, Lyons Crescent, Tonbridge, Kent TN9 1EX. Tel 01732 357555.

Relate National Marriage Guidance centres offer marital and couple counselling and psychosexual therapy.

Herbert Gray College, Little Church Street, Rugby CV21 3AP. Tel 01788 573 241 Fax 01788 573241 (see your telephone directory for your local branch).

Richmond Fellowship (see under *Employment and training*)

Royal College of Psychiatrists is a professional and educational organisation for all psychiatrists working in the UK and Republic of Ireland. It provides information for the general public on common mental health problems.

17 Belgrave Square, London, SW1X 8PG. Tel 020 7235 2351 Fax 020 7235 1935 Website www.rcpsych.ac.uk

The Samaritans provide a 24-hour service offering confidential emotional support to anyone who is in crisis. Tel helpline 08457 90 90 90. Website www.samaritans.org.uk.

SANELINE is a national mental health helpline offering emotional support and practical information to anyone coping with mental illness whether as a sufferer, carer or family member.

Second Floor, 199–205 Old Marylebone Road, London NW1 5QP. Helplines: London 0845 767 8000 Outside London 0345 678000.

World Psychiatric Association has initiated a programme to fight against the stigma of mental illness.

International Center for Mental Health, Mount Sinai School of Medicine of the City University of New York, Fifth Avenue and 100th Street, Box 1093, New York, NY 10029–6574, USA. Tel + 1 212 241 6133 Fax + 1 212 426 0437.

The Young Minds Parent Information Service provides information and advice on child mental health issues.

102–108 Clerkenwell Road, London EC1M 5SA. Tel 0800 018 2138.

Youth Access offers information, advice and counselling throughout the UK.

1–2 Taylor's Yard, 67 Alderbrook Road, London SW12 8AD. Tel 020 8772 9900 Fax 020 8772 9746 Email admin@youthaccess.org.uk

Publications

Caring for Carers: A National Strategy for Carers (1999). London: HMSO.

Further useful publications available from the Department of Health's Health Literature Line on 0800 555 777.

GMC (2000) *Confidentiality: Protecting and Providing Information.*

Home from Home: Your Guide to Choosing a Care Home (1998) King's Fund publishing programme. ISBN 1 85717 217 5.

Available from King's Fund Bookshop, 11–13 Cavendish Square, London W1G 0AN.

Jones, R. (1999) *Mental Health Manual.* London: Sweet and Maxwell.

Websites

Further useful organisations are listed at: mentalhealth.org.uk/helplist.htm

The Contributors

Alec Buchanan, Clinical Senior Lecturer in Forensic Psychiatry, Institute of Psychiatry, King's College London

Mike Crawford, Senior Lecturer, Imperial College School of Medicine, London

Anne Cremona, Consultant Psychiatrist, South London and Maudsley NHS Trust

Felicity de Zulueta, Hon. Consultant Psychiatrist in Psychotherapy and Clinical Lecturer in Traumatic Studies, Institute of Psychiatry, King's College London

Alicia Deale, Lecturer, Institute of Psychiatry, King's College London

Vincent Deary, Cognative Behavioural Therapist, South London and Maudsley NHS Trust

Anne Farmer, Professor of Psychiatric Nosology, Institute of Psychiatry, King's College London

Kay Gavan, Senior Social Worker, Eating Disorders Unit, Royal Bethlem and Maudsley Hospitals, London

Claire Gerada, General Practitioner, Hurley Clinic, London

Susan Grey, Consultant Clinical Psychologist, South London and Maudsley NHS Trust

Mari Anne Harty, Consultant Forensic Psychiatrist, South London and Maudsley NHS Trust

Kate Harvey, Research Fellow, Department of General Practice and Primary Care, Guy's, King's and St Thomas's School of Medicine, London

Claire Henderson, MRC Training Fellow in Health Services Research, Institute of Psychiatry, King's College London

Nick Hervey, Head of Mental Health Practice, Southwark Social Services

Andrew Hodgkiss, Consultant Liaison Psychiatrist, South London and Maudsley NHS Trust

Frank Holloway, Consultant Psychiatrist, South London and Maudsley NHS Trust

Sonia Johnson, Senior Lecturer in Social and Community Psychiatry, University College, London

Elizabeth Kuipers, Professor of Clinical Psychology, Institute of Psychiatry, King's College London

Wendy Maphosa, Carers and Families Nurse Specialist, South London and Maudsley NHS Trust

Sarah Mars, Research Fellow, London School of Hygiene and Tropical Medicine

E. Jane Marshall, Consultant Psychiatrist, South London and Maudsley NHS Trust and Senior Lecturer, National Addiction Centre

Kwame McKenzie, Senior Lecturer in Transcultural Psychiatry, Royal Free and University College Medical School, London

Mind Legal Unit, c/o Simon Foster, Mind, 15–19 Broadway, London E15

Stirling Moorey, Consultant Psychiatrist in Cognitive Behavioural Therapy, South London and Maudsley NHS Trust

David O'Flynn, Specialist Registrar in Psychiatry, South London and Maudsley NHS Trust

Rory O'Kelly, Senior Advisor, Benefits Advice Service, Mind, Croydon

Richard Parkin, Consultant Psychiatrist, Barnet, Enfield and Harringey NHS Trust

Rosalind Ramsay, Consultant Psychiatrist, South London and Maudsley NHS Trust

Marisa Silverman, Old Age Consultant Psychiatrist, South London and Maudsley NHS Trust

Emma Staples, Senior Registrar in Psychotherapy, Tavistock Clinic and Royal Free Hospital

George Szmukler, Consultant Psychiatrist, South London and Maudsley NHS Trust, and Dean of the Institute of Psychiatry, King's College London

Amanda Thompsell, Specialist Registrar in Psychiatry, South London and Maudsley NHS Trust

Jane Tiller, Consultant Psychiatrist, South London and Maudsley NHS Trust

Gill Todd, Clinical Nurse Leader, Eating Disorders Unit, South London and Maudsley NHS Trust

John Wade, Mental Health Service Manager, Bromford Housing Group

Anne Ward, Consultant Psychotherapist, South London and Maudsley NHS Trust

Sarah Welsh, Consultant Psychiatrist, South London and Maudsley NHS Trust

Wendy Whitaker, Social Worker, Eating Disorderss Unit, Royal Bethlem and Maudsley Hospitals, London

Geoffrey Wolff, Consultant Psychiatrist, Leeds Community and Mental Health Services NHS Trust

Index

abbreviations 282–3
abstinence, from drinking 113, 114
accommodation
  choosing 195
  costs 193–4
  facilities in 194
  finding 195
  support available 194
  types 190–3
accusatory behaviour 149
acetylcholine 145
acetylcholinesterase inhibitors 145
action, drinking problems 113
acute psychotic disorders 17
addiction *see* drinking problems; drug misuse
adherence therapy 23
adolescents, mental health services 168
adults, mental health services 163–7
African-Caribbeans
  mental health services 246–7
  mental illness 246
Africans
  mental health services 246–7
  mental illness 246
aggression 147
agoraphobia
  defined 51
  effect on families 57
  treatment 53–4
alcohol *see* drinking problems
Alzheimer's disease 143, 145
  outlook for 149–50
  useful organisations 285–6
amisulpiride 23t
amitriptyline 33
amphetamines 125
anankastic personality disorder 135t
anger 73
anorexia nervosa 99–101, 102
  treatment 102–4
anticonvulsants 35
antidepressants 33, 43–4, 45, 53, 64, 75, 85, 104
antipsychotics 19–21, 22–3t, 34, 138
anxiety disorders
  case story 49–50
  causes 52
  defined 51–2
  driving 221

families and friends
  effect on 57
  support from 57–8
numbers diagnosed 52
outlook 58–9
primary care 181t
PTSD 71
treatment 52–7
useful organisations 286–7
see also health anxiety
anxious personality disorder 135t
appetite, depression 41
approved social workers 175, 188–9
assertive outreach teams 166
assertive strategies 117, 118
assessments
  PTSD 75
  social services 185–7
asylums 152
atypical antipsychotics 21, 22–3t
avoidance
  drinking problems 117
  medically unexplained disorders 84, 87
  panic attacks 54
  PTSD 72

behaviour
  accusatory 149
  hostile 37
  reasonable, OCD 65–6
  see also aggression; violence
behavioural exercises 54, 55
benefits
  accommodation costs 193, 194
  available 197–8
  and employment 205
  ensuring receipt of entitlements 200–2
  underclaiming 198–200
benzodiazepines 34, 124–5
binge eating disorder 101–2
  treatment 104
bipolar affective disorder
  case story 28–30
  causes 31–2
  defined 30–1
  families and friends
    effect on 36
    support from 36–8
  numbers diagnosed 31
  outlook 38
  treatment 32–6
  useful organisations 287
bodily sensations, panic attacks 54
body mass index 100f

borderline personality disorder 135t, 137
bulimia nervosa 101, 102
  treatment 104

cannabis 124
care management 155
Care Programme Approach (CPA) 155,
  162–3, 189, 194, 235
carers
  case stories *see* case stories
  confidentiality 231–5
  effects of caring 251–3
  help for, violent relatives 266–7
  helping people back to work 207–8
  legislative and policy framework for 186t
  mental health services 170
  responsibilities 250–1
  social services 185, 187–8
  tips for
    anxiety disorders 58
    bipolar affective disorder 38
    dementia 149
    depression 47
    drinking problems 119
    drug misuse 130
    eating disorders 106–7
    medically unexplained symptoms 87–8
    mental and physical illness 96
    OCD 68
    personality disorders 139
    PTSD 77
    schizophrenia 26
  see also families and friends; relatives
Carers' Education and Support Package
  (CESP) 188
Carers' Grant 186t, 188
Carers' (Recognition and Services) Act (1995)
  186t
Caring about Carers 204
case stories
  anxiety disorder 49–50
  bipolar affective disorder 28–30
  depression 39–41
  drinking problem 108–10
  drug misuse 121–3
  eating disorders 97–9
  medically unexplained symptoms 79–81
  mental illness in elderly 141–2
  OCD 60–2
  personality disorders 132–4
  physical and mental illness combined
    89–91
  PTSD 69–71
  schizophrenia 15–16

catchment areas, service provision 160–2
CBT *see* cognitive behavioural therapy
Changing Minds 238
checking, compulsive 62
chemical messengers *see* neurotransmitters
child abuse, border personality disorder 137
children
  of alcohol dependants 115–16, 119–20
  of carers 252–3
  mental health services 168
chlorpromazine 20t, 34, 45
chronic fatigue syndrome 81, 84, 287
chronic pain syndrome 84
citalopram 44, 64
clinical psychologists
  in primary care 182
  role 173
clomipramine 64
clopenthixol 22t
clozapine 21, 22t
CMHTs *see* community mental health teams
cocaine 125
cognitive analytic therapy (CAT) 104, 256–7
cognitive behavioural therapy (CBT) 256
  for specific disorders 23, 35, 44–5, 53,
    64–5, 75, 86, 93, 104, 114
community care *see* mental health services
Community Care Acts (1990 and 1991)
  186t, 189
Community Care Acts (1992 and 1995) 26
Community Care Grant 194
community mental health teams (CMHTs)
  164, 171
community psychiatric nurses (CPNs)
  day in life of 176–9
  home visits, dementia 146
  in primary care 182–3
  role 172
community reinforcement training 118–19
compliance therapy 23
compulsions 62–3, 112
confidentiality, mental health 231–5
confusion, dealing with sufferers 95–6, 106
consent, to treatment 217
consumerism, health and social care 155
contemplation, drinking problems 113
controlling strategy, drinking problems 117
conversion disorder 82
coping
  drinking problems 117–19
  stigma 238–41
  with suicide 261–2
costs, accommodation 193–4
council tax benefit 193, 198

counselling, drug misuse 127–8
counsellors, primary care 183
counting, OCD 62–3
couple therapy 256–7
Court of Protection 228–9
court reports 209
crack (cocaine) 125
crisis houses 165–6
Crossroads 146

day care 166–7
debriefing, PTSD 75
debt, mania 37
deliberate self-harm, useful organisations
    287–8
delusions 30, 41
dementia
  causes 144–5
  defined 143–4
  driving 222–3
  families and friends
    effect on 146
    support from 146–9
  numbers diagnosed 144
  outlook 149–50
  treatment 145
dependence see drinking problems; drug
    misuse
dependent personality disorder 135t
depression 31
  anorexia nervosa 103
  case story 39–41
  causes 42–3
  defined 41–2
  driving 221
  elderly people 143
  ethnic minorities 246, 248
  families and friends
    effect on 46
    support from 47, 95
  issues to consider 37
  numbers diagnosed 42
  outlook 48
  primary care 181t, 182
  PTSD 72–3
  treatment 33, 43–6
  useful organisations 288–9
  see also bipolar affective disorder
determination, drinking problems 113
detoxification 128
dexamphetamines (dexies) 125
diagnosis, PTSD 74
diamorphine 126
diazepam 44, 52, 124–5

disability discrimination
  employment 225
  insurance 226
  travel 225–6
Disability Discrimination Act (1995) 200,
    204, 224–5
disability living allowance 198
disabled persons' tax credit 198
discharge guidance 155
disclosure 232, 233, 234
dissocial personality disorder 135t, 136
dopamine 19
dothiepin 33
drinking problems
  case story 108–10
  causes 113
  defined 110–12
  driving 222
  ethnic minorities 248
  families and friends
    effect on 114–16
    support from 117–20
  mental health services 168–9
  numbers diagnosed 112
  outlook 120
  primary care 181t
  PTSD 73
  treatment 113–14
  useful organisations 284–5
Driver and Vehicle Licensing Agency (DVLA)
    220–1, 223
driving
  dementia 222–3
  mania 37
  medication 223
  and mental illness 221–2
  regulation by DVLA 220–1
  substance misuse 222
drop-in centres 166
droperidol 20t
drug misuse
  case story 121–3
  causes 127
  defined 123–6
  driving 222
  families and friends
    effect on 129
    support from 129–30
  mental health services 168–9
  numbers involved 126–7
  outlook 130–1
  primary care 181t
  PTSD 73
  treatment 127–9

useful organisations 289–90
dynamic psychotherapy 75–6

eating disorders
  case story 97–9
  causes 102
  defined 99–102
  families and friends
    effect on 104–5
    support from 105–7
  numbers diagnosed 102
  outlook 107
  treatment 102–4
  useful organisations 290
Eating Disorders Association 105
ecstasy 125
education, and employment 205, 206t
elderly people, mental illness
  case story 141–2
  dementia see dementia
  services for 168
  types of 143
  useful organisations 285–6
electroconvulsive therapy (ECT) 33, 46
EMDR see eye movement desensitisation and
    reprocessing
emergency services
  mental health 165–6
  social services 188
emotional numbness 72
emotional strategies, drinking problems 117
employment
  alternatives and progress to paid 205–7
  disability discrimination 225
  effect on carers 251
  help from carers 207–8
  schemes 166–7, 200
  and unemployment 203–5
  useful organisations 290–1
encouragement
  and reassurance 66–7
  when to give 67
"enduring power of attorney" 228
environment, personality disorders 137
ethnic minorities
  mental health services 169
  mental illness
    reasons for 243–4
    supporting relatives with 244–5
    types of 182, 245–9
  useful organisations 291–2
exercises
  anxiety disorders 54, 55
  medically unexplained symptoms 85

extrapyramidal side effects 20, 21
eye movement desensitisation and
    reprocessing 75

falls, dementia 148
families and friends
  effects of
    anxiety disorders 57
    bipolar affective disorder 36
    dementia 146
    depression 46
    drinking problems 114–16
    drug misuse 129
    eating disorders 104–5
    mental and physical illness 93–4
    OCD 65
    personality disorders 138
    PTSD 76
    schizophrenia 24–5
    violent behaviour 265
  support from
    anxiety disorders 57–8
    bipolar affective disorder 36–8
    dementia 146–9
    depression 47
    drinking problems 117–20
    drug misuse 129–30
    eating disorders 105–7
    mental and physical illness 94–6
    OCD 65–8
    personality disorders 138–9
    PTSD 76–7
    schizophrenia 25–6
family interventions, psychoses 24
family life, carers 252
family therapy 256–7
fear, PTSD 71
finances
  effects of caring 251
  mental capacity 228–9
  risk of debt 37
financial incentives, joint working 155–6
firearm certificates 227
flashbacks 71
flight or fight response 74, 83
fluoxetine 33, 44, 64
flupenthixol 20t, 22t
fluphenazine 20t, 22t
forensic psychiatry 209–12
friends see families and friends
functional somatic syndromes see medically
    unexplained physical symptoms

GAD see generalised anxiety disorder

gay couples, effect on, alcohol dependants 116

General Medical Council (GMC), on confidentiality 232

general practitioners
in primary care 181
primary care groups 183
PTSD 74–5
role 175–6

generalised anxiety disorder 52
treatment 56–7

genes
bipolar affective disorder 31
depression 42–3
eating disorders 102
personality disorders 136, 137
schizophrenia 18

glossary, terminology 268–82

Government's Modernisation Programme (1999) 186t

Government's National Strategy for Carers (1999) 186t

GPs see general practitioners

group therapy 104, 255

guilt, PTSD 73

gun licences 227

hallucinations 31, 41, 148

haloperidol 20t, 22t, 34, 45

hands, compulsive washing 62

health
of carers 253
see also mental health

health anxiety 82

Health of the Nation 155

health and social care
consumerist agenda 155
future policy directions 156–7
initiatives (1989–1996) 154t
joint working 155–6

helpfulness, OCD 67–8

heroin 126, 128

histrionic personality disorder 135t

hoarding, compulsive 62

Home from Home 146

homeless, mental health services 169–70

hospital chaplains 176

hospitals
admissions 35–6, 45, 46
see also mental hospitals; secure hospitals

hostels 192

hostile behaviour 37

housing see accommodation

housing benefit 193, 194, 198, 205

hypochondriasis 82

imipramine 33

impulsive personality disorder 135t

inaction, drinking problems 117

incapacity benefit 198

incontinence, dementia 148

independent living 190–1

individual therapy 255

infections, from injecting drugs 126

injecting drugs 126

inpatient services 163–4

insomnia, dementia 148

insurance 226

invalid care allowance 198

irritable bowel syndrome 81–2

isolation, coping with 241

job creation 206t

key workers 162, 163

lamotrigine 35

legal issues 224–30

legislation 186t, 213–19
see also specific acts

leisure activities, carers 252

lesbian couples, alcohol dependants 116

liaison psychiatry 92

liaison services 167

light treatment 45

lithium 33–4, 45

lofepramine 33

lofexidine 128

loxapine 20t

maintenance, changes, drinking problems 113

maintenance treatment 128

mania 30–1
issues to consider 37
treatment of 33–4

manic depression see bipolar affective disorder

marijuana 124

Maudsley body mass index 100f

media, perceptions of mental illness 237

medically unexplained physical symptoms
case story 79–81
causes 82–4
defined 81–2
families and friends
effect on 86
support from 86–8

numbers diagnosed 82
outlook 88
treatment 85–6
medication
  bipolar affective disorder 33–5
  depression 43–4
  driving 223
  drug misuse 128–9
  OCD 64
  personality disorders 138
  PTSD 75
  schizophrenia 19–21, 22–3t
  stigma 241
mental capacity 228–9
mental health
  confidentiality 231–5
  driving 220–3
  legal issues 224–30
  legislation 213–19
  primary care groups 183–4
  see also mental illness
Mental Health Act (1983) 25, 36, 46, 93,
    103, 155, 164, 185, 188, 210, 214–17,
    218–19, 227
Mental Health Act Review Tribunal 210
mental health professionals
  confidentiality 231–2
  day in life of a CPN 176–9
  primary care 182–3
  roles 172–6
  teams 171
  see also specific professionals
mental health services
  for adults 163–7
  community care 153
  depression 45
  ethnic minorities 246–7
  evolution of 152–3
  government policy 153–7
  for other populations 168–70
  primary care see primary care
  principles of service provision 160–3
  supported employment schemes 200
  types of 160
mental hospitals 152
mental illness
  accommodation 190–6
  alongside physical illness 89–96
  benefits 197–202
  elderly people 141–50
  employment 203–8
  ethnic minorities 243–9
  primary care 181–2
  stigma 236–41

targeting, service provision 161–2
  see also mental health; specific disorders
mental rituals 63
methadone 128
Modernising Mental Health Services. Safe. Sound.
    Supportive 156
mood stabilisers 34–5, 138
motivational work 127–8
multi-infarct dementia 145
multidisciplinary crisis teams 165

National Health Service Plan (2000) 9–10
National Schizophrenia Fellowship 26, 188
National Service Framework for Mental
    Health (1999) 9, 26, 157, 165, 183,
    186t, 235
negative symptoms 17
neuroleptics see antipsychotics
neurotransmitters
  antipsychotics 19
  bipolar affective disorder 32
  depression 42
  PTSD 74
New NHS Modern Dependable, The 156
noradrenalin 32, 42

obsessions 62
obsessive compulsive disorder
  case story 60–2
  causes 63
  defined 62–3
  families and friends
    effect on 65
    support from 65–8
  numbers diagnosed 63
  outlook 68
  primary care 181t
  treatment 64–5
  useful organisations 292
occupational therapists 174–5
occupational therapy 24
OCD see obsessive compulsive disorder
offenders, mental health services 168
olanzapine 22t, 45
open employment 206t
organisations, useful 284–95
outpatient clinics 164–5
outpatient treatment, eating disorders 104
overdoses 260
overseas travel 226

paid employment see employment
panic attacks
  dealing with sufferers 94–5

defined 51
treatment 53–6
paranoia, dementia 149
paranoid personality disorder 135t
paroxetine 33, 44, 64
partners, of alcohol dependants 114–15, 116
past traumas 73–4
Patient's Charter, The 155
PCGs *see* primary care groups
persistent delusional disorder 17
personality disorders
 case story 132–4
 causes 136–7
 classification 135t
 defined 134
 families and friends
  effect on 138
  support from 138–9
 numbers diagnosed 136
 outlook 140
 treatment 137–8
pharmacists 176
phobias
 defined 51
 depression 41
 treatment 54–5
 useful organisations 286–7
physical arousal, PTSD 72
physical and mental illness (combined)
 case story 89–91
 causes 92
 defined 91
 families and friends
  effect on 93–4
  support from 94–6
 numbers diagnosed 91–2
 outlook 96
 treatment 92–3
physical rituals 63
pimozide 20t
pipothiazine palmitate 22t
policy, mental health services 153–7
post-traumatic stress disorder
 case story 69–71
 causes 74
 defined 71–4
 families and friends
  effect on 76
  support from 76–7
 numbers diagnosed 74
 outlook 78
 treatment 74–6
 useful organisations 292–3
Pre-Tenancy Determination 193

precontemplation, drinking problems 113
pregnancies, unwanted 37
primary care
 mental illness 181–2
 organisation of 180–1
primary care groups (PCGs) 183–4
privacy, confidentiality 231
problem solving 56f, 57
procyclidine 34
psychiatrists 172–3
 forensic 209, 210, 211
psychodynamic psychotherapy 255–6
psychoeducation 24
psychologists, clinical 173, 182
psychoses
 defined 16–18
 driving 221
 primary care 181t
 South Asians 247
 see also schizophrenia
psychotherapists 174
psychotherapy 254–8
 anxiety disorders 53–7
 bipolar affective disorder 35
 depression 44–5
 drug misuse 127–8
 eating disorders 104
 medically unexplained symptoms 85–6
 OCD 64–5
 physical and mental illness combined 92–3
 PTSD 75–6
 schizophrenia 22–4
PTST *see* post-traumatic stress disorder
public interest, confidentiality 231–2

quietapine 23t

re-experiencing, of trauma 71
reasonable adjustments, DDA 204, 225
reasonable behaviour, OCD 65–6
reassurance
 medically unexplained symptoms 84, 87
 OCD 66–7
reattribution 85–6
Reed Committee Report on the Mentally Disordered
  Offender 155
referrals, social services 185–7
refugees
 mental health services 169
 mental illness 249
rehabilitation services 129, 166, 169
relapse prevention 114, 128
relationships, mental and physical illness 94

relatives, rights, roles and responsibilities 217–18
relaxation training
  anxiety disorders 56
  medically unexplained symptoms 85
residential care 192–3
residential services 167
responsible medical officers (RMOs) 210
rewards, for carers 253
rights, relatives 217–18
risk assessments 155, 211
risk drinking 110
risperidone 22t, 45
rituals, OCD 62–3
routines, carers 251
Royal College of Psychiatrists 238

SAD see seasonal affective disorder
SANE 26
Saving Lives: Our Healthier Nation 155
schizoaffective disorder 17
schizoid personality disorder 135t
schizophrenia
  case story 15–16
  causes 18–19
  defined 16–18
  ethnic minorities 246
  families and friends
    effect on 24–5
    support from 25–6
  numbers diagnosed 18
  outlook 27
  treatment 19–24
  useful organisations 293
seasonal affective disorder 43
  treatment 45
sectors, service provision 160–1
secure hospitals 210–11
  moving on from 211–12
selective serotonin reuptake inhibitors 33, 43–4, 75, 138
self-blame, PTSD 73
self-cutting 261
self-harm
  bipolar affective disorder 37
  see also suicide
self-help groups 26, 129, 168–9
self-neglect 37
sensible drinking 110
serious mental illness 16
serotonin 32, 42
sertraline 33, 44, 75
severe disablement allowance 198

sexual relationships, mental and physical illness 94
shame
  coping with 238–41
  PTSD 73
side effects
  anticonvulsants 35
  antidepressants 33
  antipsychotics 21, 34
  lithium 34–5
sleep disturbance, PTSD 72
social care see health and social care
social housing 191
social life, carers 252
social phobia 51, 54
social services
  and carers 185
  emergency services 188
  options available 187–8
  referrals and assessment 185–7
  support, psychoses 24
social therapies, schizophrenia 22–4
social workers
  help from 188–9
  role 175
society, fear of psychoses 17–18
sodium valproate 35
somatoform disorders see medically unexplained physical symptoms
South Asians
  drinking problems 248
  mental illness 247, 248
  suicide 248
special carer status 235
specific phobia 51, 54, 57
stages of change model 113
stigma
  campaigns to reduce 238
  coping strategies 238–41
  defined 236
  effects of 237
  getting treatment 241
  reasons for 236–7
Stigma Watch 238
stimulants (drugs) 125
subjective awareness, compulsion to drink 112
substitute prescribing 128
suicide
  coping with 261–2
  depression 42
  ethnic minorities 248
  living with long-term risk of 262
  repeated self-cutting 261

useful organisations 287–8
when someone has harmed themselves 260
when someone has thoughts of 259–60
sulpiride 20t
Supervised Discharge Orders 234
support
social services 24
see also carers; families and friends; self-help groups
support groups, carers 188
supported employment schemes 200
supported housing 191–2
symptom focusing 83, 87
symptom misinterpretation 83–4
symptoms see medically unexplained physical symptoms
systemic therapy 256–7

talking therapy 35, 93, 127–8
temazepam 124–5
therapeutic relationships 85
thioridazine 20t
thyroxine 45
tolerance
drinking problems 117
to alcohol 111
training, useful organisations 290–1
tranquillisers 44, 52, 124–5
trauma
personality disorders 137
see also post-traumatic stress disorder
travel 225–6
treatment
consent to 217
see also medication; psychotherapy
tricyclic antidepressants 33, 44
trifluperazine 20t
triggers
bipolar affective disorder 32
OCD 65
trusts, local NHS 161
typical antipsychotics 20, 22t

unemployment 203–5

Valium see diazepam
violence 263
causes of 264–5
dealing with 265–6
effect on families 265
help for carers 266–7
preventing 266
PTSD 77
vomiting, bulimia nervosa 101

voting rights 227

wandering, dementia 147–8
washing, compulsive 62
websites 296
welfare advice 24
wills 229–30
withdrawal symptoms
alcohol 111–12
drugs 124, 128
women
borderline personality disorder 137
partners of alcoholic 116
work see employment
Working for Patients and Caring for People 153
worry postponement 57

zotepine 23t
zuclopenthixol 20t